Investment Management

Investment Management

Edited by
Henry Stamp

Larsen & Keller
www.larsen-keller.com

Investment Management
Edited by Henry Stamp
ISBN: 978-1-63549-668-0 (Hardback)

Larsen & Keller

Published by Larsen and Keller Education,
5 Penn Plaza,
19th Floor,
New York, NY 10001, USA

Cataloging-in-Publication Data

Investment management / edited by Henry Stamp.
p. cm.
Includes bibliographical references and index.
ISBN 978-1-63549-668-0
1. Portfolio management. 2. Investments. I. Stamp, Henry.
HG4529.5 .I58 2018
332.6--dc23

Printed and bound in China.

For more information regarding Larsen and Keller Education and its products, please visit the publisher's website www.larsen-keller.com

Table of Contents

Preface

The art of managing investments and allocation of assets of individuals or companies is referred to as investment management. Some of these assets include bonds, real estate, shares and other securities. Financial analysis, stock selection, investment monitoring, risk analysis, asset selection, etc. are some key aspects of this field. For someone with an interest and eye for detail, this book covers the most significant topics in the field of investment management. It is an essential guide for both academicians and those who wish to pursue this discipline further. Coherent flow of topics, student-friendly language and extensive use of examples make this textbook an invaluable source of knowledge.

Given below is the chapter wise description of the book:

Chapter 1- Investment management is the management of securities, like bonds and shares. It is done with a view to profit in the future. The important features of investment management are dealing, settlement, internal auditing, research, etc. The chapter on investment management offers an insightful focus, keeping in mind the complex subject matter.

Chapter 2- Returns in investment management can be classified into prospective or historical. Usually investment returns contain high amounts of risks. The different types of risks discussed are business risk, liquidity risk, country risk, market risk, exchange and financial risk. This chapter is an overview of the subject matter incorporating all the major aspects of risk and return in investment management.

Chapter 3- The efficiency of the market can be recognized on the basis of its informational efficiency. The different types of efficient market hypotheses are weak form of market efficiency, semi-strong form of market efficiency and strong form of market efficiency. This chapter provides a plethora of interdisciplinary topics for better comprehension of market efficiency.

Chapter 4- Modern portfolio theory is a theory used for creating a portfolio of assets. This is done with the intention of increasing the expected returns. The aspects elucidated in this chapter are of vital importance, and provide a better understanding of portfolio management.

Indeed, my job was extremely crucial and challenging as I had to ensure that every chapter is informative and structured in a student-friendly manner. I am thankful for the support provided by my family and colleagues during the completion of this book.

Editor

1

Fundamentals of Investment Management

Investment management is the management of securities, like bonds and shares. It is done with a view to profit in the future. The important features of investment management are dealing, settlement, internal auditing, research, etc. The chapter on investment management offers an insightful focus, keeping in mind the complex subject matter.

Investment Management

Investment is employing money in different instruments or assets in the present, with the expectation of a positive rate of return in the future. In other words investment is the sacrifice in the present in the expectation of a future gain. The future returns are expected to compensate the time the investors hold the asset, expected rate of inflation and uncertainty of the future. The emphasis has been given mostly on the financial assets and it is also extended to physical and real assets. Investment management is the process of administering the employment of money in financial and other instruments in the present, with the expectation of a positive rate of return in the future.

Investment management is the professional asset management of various securities (shares, bonds and other securities) and other assets (e.g., real estate) in order to meet specified investment goals for the benefit of the investors. Investors may be institutions (insurance companies, pension funds, corporations, charities, educational establishments etc.) or private investors (both directly via investment contracts and more commonly via collective investment schemes e.g. mutual funds or exchange-traded funds).

The term asset management is often used to refer to the investment management of collective investments, while the more generic fund management may refer to all forms of institutional investment as well as investment management for private investors. Investment managers who specialize in *advisory* or *discretionary* management on behalf of (normally wealthy) private investors may often refer to their services as money management or portfolio management often within the context of so-called "private banking".

The provision of investment management services includes elements of financial statement analysis, asset selection, stock selection, plan implementation and ongoing monitoring of investments. Coming under the remit of financial services many of the world's largest companies are at least in part investment managers and employ millions of staff.

The term fund manager (or investment advisor in the United States) refers to both a firm that provides investment management services and an individual who directs fund management decisions.

According to a Boston Consulting Group study, the assets managed professionally for fees reached an all-time high of US$62.4 trillion in 2012, after remaining flat-lined since 2007. Furthermore, these industry assets under management were expected to reach US$70.2 trillion at the end of 2013 as per a Cerulli Associates estimate.

The global investment management industry is highly concentrated in nature, in a universe of about 70,000 funds roughly 99.7% of the US fund flows in 2012 went into just 185 funds. Additionally, a majority of fund managers report that more than 50% of their inflows go to only three funds.

Industry Scope

The business of investment has several facets, the employment of professional fund managers, research (of individual assets and asset classes), dealing, settlement, marketing, internal auditing, and the preparation of reports for clients. The largest financial fund managers are firms that exhibit all the complexity their size demands. Apart from the people who bring in the money (marketers) and the people who direct investment (the fund managers), there are compliance staff (to ensure accord with legislative and regulatory constraints), internal auditors of various kinds (to examine internal systems and controls), financial controllers (to account for the institutions' own money and costs), computer experts, and "back office" employees (to track and record transactions and fund valuations for up to thousands of clients per institution).

Key Problems of Running Such Businesses

Key problems include:

- revenue is directly linked to market valuations, so a major fall in asset prices can cause a precipitous decline in revenues relative to costs;
- above-average fund performance is difficult to sustain, and clients may not be patient during times of poor performance;
- successful fund managers are expensive and may be headhunted by competitors;
- above-average fund performance appears to be dependent on the unique skills of the fund manager; however, clients are loath to stake their investments on the ability of a few individuals- they would rather see firm-wide success, attributable to a single philosophy and internal discipline;

- analysts who generate above-average returns often become sufficiently wealthy that they avoid corporate employment in favor of managing their personal portfolios.

Representing the Owners of Shares

Institutions often control huge shareholdings. In most cases they are acting as fiduciary agents rather than principals (direct owners). The owners of shares theoretically have great power to alter the companies via the voting rights the shares carry and the consequent ability to pressure managements, and if necessary out-vote them at annual and other meetings.

In practice, the ultimate owners of shares often do not exercise the power they collectively hold (because the owners are many, each with small holdings); financial institutions (as agents) sometimes do. There is a general belief that shareholders – in this case, the institutions acting as agents—could and should exercise more active influence over the companies in which they hold shares (e.g., to hold managers to account, to ensure Board's effective functioning). Such action would add a pressure group to those (the regulators and the Board) overseeing management.

However, there is the problem of how the institution should exercise this power. One way is for the institution to decide, the other is for the institution to poll its beneficiaries. Assuming that the institution polls, should it then: (i) Vote the entire holding as directed by the majority of votes cast? (ii) Split the vote (where this is allowed) according to the proportions of the vote? (iii) Or respect the abstainers and only vote the respondents' holdings?

The price signals generated by large active managers holding or not holding the stock may contribute to management change. For example, this is the case when a large active manager sells his position in a company, leading to (possibly) a decline in the stock price, but more importantly a loss of confidence by the markets in the management of the company, thus precipitating changes in the management team.

Some institutions have been more vocal and active in pursuing such matters; for instance, some firms believe that there are investment advantages to accumulating substantial minority shareholdings (i.e. 10% or more) and putting pressure on management to implement significant changes in the business. In some cases, institutions with minority holdings work together to force management change. Perhaps more frequent is the sustained pressure that large institutions bring to bear on management teams through persuasive discourse and PR. On the other hand, some of the largest investment managers—such as BlackRock and Vanguard—advocate simply owning every company, reducing the incentive to influence management teams. A reason for this last strategy is that the investment manager prefers a closer, more open and honest relationship with a company's management team than would exist if they exercised control; allowing them to make a better investment decision.

The national context in which shareholder representation considerations are set is variable and important. The USA is a litigious society and shareholders use the law as a lever to pressure management teams. In Japan it is traditional for shareholders to be low in the 'pecking order,' which often allows management and labor to ignore the rights of the ultimate owners. Whereas US firms generally cater to shareholders, Japanese businesses generally exhibit a *stakeholder* mentality, in which they seek consensus amongst all interested parties (against a background of strong unions and labour legislation).

Size of the Global Fund Management Industry

Conventional assets under management of the global fund management industry increased by 10% in 2010, to $79.3 trillion. Pension assets accounted for $29.9 trillion of the total, with $24.7 trillion invested in mutual funds and $24.6 trillion in insurance funds. Together with alternative assets (sovereign wealth funds, hedge funds, private equity funds and exchange traded funds) and funds of wealthy individuals, assets of the global fund management industry totalled around $117 trillion. Growth in 2010 followed a 14% increase in the previous year and was due both to the recovery in equity markets during the year and an inflow of new funds.

The US remained by far the biggest source of funds, accounting for around a half of conventional assets under management or some $36 trillion. The UK was the second largest centre in the world and by far the largest in Europe with around 8% of the global total.

Philosophy, Process and People

The 3-P's (Philosophy, Process and People) are often used to describe the reasons why the manager is able to produce above average results.

- Philosophy refers to the overarching beliefs of the investment organization. For example: (i) Does the manager buy growth or value shares, or a combination of the two (and why)? (ii) Do they believe in market timing (and on what evidence)? (iii) Do they rely on external research or do they employ a team of researchers? It is helpful if any and all of such fundamental beliefs are supported by proof-statements.

- Process refers to the way in which the overall philosophy is implemented. For example: (i) Which universe of assets is explored before particular assets are chosen as suitable investments? (ii) How does the manager decide what to buy and when? (iii) How does the manager decide what to sell and when? (iv) Who takes the decisions and are they taken by committee? (v) What controls are in place to ensure that a rogue fund (one very different from others and from what is intended) cannot arise?

- People refers to the staff, especially the fund managers. The questions are, Who are they? How are they selected? How old are they? Who reports to whom? How deep is the team (and do all the members understand the philosophy and process they are supposed to be using)? And most important of all, How long has the team been working together? This last question is vital because whatever performance record was presented at the outset of the relationship with the client may or may not relate to (have been produced by) a team that is still in place. If the team has changed greatly (high staff turnover or changes to the team), then arguably the performance record is completely unrelated to the existing team (of fund managers).

Investment Managers and Portfolio Structures

At the heart of the investment management industry are the managers who invest and divest client investments.

A certified company investment advisor should conduct an assessment of each client's individual needs and risk profile. The advisor then recommends appropriate investments.

Asset Allocation

The different asset class definitions are widely debated, but four common divisions are stocks, bonds, real estate and commodities. The exercise of allocating funds among these assets (and among individual securities within each asset class) is what investment management firms are paid for. Asset classes exhibit different market dynamics, and different interaction effects; thus, the allocation of money among asset classes will have a significant effect on the performance of the fund. Some research suggests that allocation among asset classes has more predictive power than the choice of individual holdings in determining portfolio return. Arguably, the skill of a successful investment manager resides in constructing the asset allocation, and separate individual holdings, so as to outperform certain benchmarks (e.g., the peer group of competing funds, bond and stock indices).

Long-term Returns

It is important to look at the evidence on the long-term returns to different assets, and to holding period returns (the returns that accrue on average over different lengths of investment). For example, over very long holding periods (e.g. 10+ years) in most countries, equities have generated higher returns than bonds, and bonds have generated higher returns than cash. According to financial theory, this is because equities are riskier (more volatile) than bonds which are themselves more risky than cash.

Diversification

Against the background of the asset allocation, fund managers consider the degree of diversification that makes sense for a given client (given its risk preferences) and construct a list of planned holdings accordingly. The list will indicate what percentage of the fund should be invested in each particular stock or bond. The theory of portfolio diversification was originated by Markowitz (and many others). Effective diversification requires management of the correlation between the asset returns and the liability returns, issues internal to the portfolio (individual holdings volatility), and cross-correlations between the returns.

Investment Styles

There are a range of different styles of fund management that the institution can implement. For example, growth, value, growth at a reasonable price (GARP), market neutral, small capitalisation, indexed, etc. Each of these approaches has its distinctive features, adherents and, in any particular financial environment, distinctive risk characteristics. For example, there is evidence that growth styles (buying rapidly growing earnings) are especially effective when the companies able to generate such growth are scarce; conversely, when such growth is plentiful, then there is evidence that value styles tend to outperform the indices particularly successfully.

Large asset managers are increasingly profiling their equity portfolio managers to trade their orders more effectively. While this strategy is less effective with small-cap trades, it has been effective for portfolios with large-cap companies.

Performance Measurement

Fund performance is often thought to be the acid test of fund management, and in the institutional context, accurate measurement is a necessity. For that purpose, institutions measure the performance of each fund (and usually for internal purposes components of each fund) under their management, and performance is also measured by external firms that specialize in performance measurement. The leading performance measurement firms (e.g. Frank Russell in the US or BI-SAM in Europe) compile aggregate industry data, e.g., showing how funds in general performed against given indices and peer groups over various time periods.

In a typical case (let us say an equity fund), then the calculation would be made (as far as the client is concerned) every quarter and would show a percentage change compared with the prior quarter (e.g., +4.6% total return in US dollars). This figure would be compared with other similar funds managed within the institution (for purposes of monitoring internal controls), with performance data for peer group funds, and with relevant indices (where available) or tailor-made performance benchmarks where appropriate. The specialist performance measurement firms calculate quartile and decile data and close attention would be paid to the (percentile) ranking of any fund.

Generally speaking, it is probably appropriate for an investment firm to persuade its clients to assess performance over longer periods (e.g., 3 to 5 years) to smooth out very short-term fluctuations in performance and the influence of the business cycle. This can be difficult however and, industry wide, there is a serious preoccupation with short-term numbers and the effect on the relationship with clients (and resultant business risks for the institutions).

An enduring problem is whether to measure before-tax or after-tax performance. After-tax measurement represents the benefit to the investor, but investors' tax positions may vary. Before-tax measurement can be misleading, especially in regimens that tax realised capital gains (and not unrealised). It is thus possible that successful active managers (measured before tax) may produce miserable after-tax results. One possible solution is to report the after-tax position of some standard taxpayer.

Risk-adjusted Performance Measurement

Performance measurement should not be reduced to the evaluation of fund returns alone, but must also integrate other fund elements that would be of interest to investors, such as the measure of risk taken. Several other aspects are also part of performance measurement: evaluating if managers have succeeded in reaching their objective, i.e. if their return was sufficiently high to reward the risks taken; how they compare to their peers; and finally whether the portfolio management results were due to luck or the manager's skill. The need to answer all these questions has led to the development of more sophisticated performance measures, many of which originate in modern portfolio theory. Modern portfolio theory established the quantitative link that exists between portfolio risk and return. The Capital Asset Pricing Model (CAPM) developed by Sharpe (1964) highlighted the notion of rewarding risk and produced the first performance indicators, be they risk-adjusted ratios (Sharpe ratio, information ratio) or differential returns compared to benchmarks (alphas). The Sharpe ratio is the simplest and best known performance measure. It measures the return of a portfolio in excess of the risk-free rate, compared to the total risk of the portfolio. This measure is said to be absolute, as it does not refer to any benchmark, avoiding drawbacks related to a poor choice of benchmark. Meanwhile, it does not allow the separation of the performance of the market in which the portfolio is invested from that of the manager. The information ratio is a more general form of the Sharpe ratio in which the risk-free asset is replaced by a benchmark portfolio. This measure is relative, as it evaluates portfolio performance in reference to a benchmark, making the result strongly dependent on this benchmark choice.

Portfolio alpha is obtained by measuring the difference between the return of the portfolio and that of a benchmark portfolio. This measure appears to be the only reliable performance measure to evaluate active management. In fact, we have to distinguish between normal returns, provided by the fair reward for portfolio exposure to different risks, and obtained through passive management, from abnormal performance (or outperformance) due to the manager's skill (or luck), whether through market timing, stock picking, or good fortune. The first component is related to allocation and style investment choices, which may not be under the sole control of the manager, and depends on the economic context, while the second component is an evaluation of the success of the manager's decisions. Only the latter, measured by alpha, allows the evaluation of the manager's true performance (but then, only if you assume that any outperformance is due to skill and not luck).

Portfolio return may be evaluated using factor models. The first model, proposed by Jensen (1968), relies on the CAPM and explains portfolio returns with the market index as the only factor. It quickly becomes clear, however, that one factor is not enough to explain the returns very well and that other factors have to be considered. Multi-factor models were developed as an alternative to the CAPM, allowing a better description of portfolio risks and a more accurate evaluation of a portfolio's performance. For example, Fama and French (1993) have highlighted two important factors that characterize a company's risk in addition to market risk. These factors are the book-to-market ratio and the company's size as measured by its market capitalization. Fama and French therefore proposed three-factor model to describe portfolio normal returns (Fama–French three-factor model). Carhart (1997) proposed to add momentum as a fourth factor to allow the short-term persistence of returns to be taken into account. Also of interest for performance measurement is Sharpe's (1992) style analysis model, in which factors are style indices. This model allows a custom benchmark for each portfolio to be developed, using the linear combination of style indices that best replicate portfolio style allocation, and leads to an accurate evaluation of portfolio alpha.

Education or Certification

Increasingly, international business schools are incorporating the subject into their course outlines and some have formulated the title of 'Investment Management' or 'Asset Management' conferred as specialist bachelor's degrees (e.g. Cass Business School, London). Due to global cross-recognition agreements with the 2 major accrediting agencies AACSB and ACBSP which accredit over 560 of the best business school programs, the Certification of MFP Master Financial Planner Professional from the American Academy of Financial Management is available to AACSB and ACBSP business school graduates with finance or financial services-related concentrations. For people with aspirations to become an investment manager, further education may be needed beyond a bachelors in business, finance, or economics. Designations, such as the Chartered Investment Manager (CIM) in Canada, are required for practitioners in the investment management industry. A graduate degree or an investment qualification such as the Chartered Financial Analyst designation (CFA) may help in having a career in investment management.

There is no evidence that any particular qualification enhances the most desirable characteristic of an investment manager, that is the ability to select investments that result in an above average (risk weighted) long-term performance. The industry has a tradition of seeking out, employing and generously rewarding such people without reference to any formal qualifications.

Security (Finance)

A security is a tradable financial asset. The term commonly refers to any form of financial instrument, but its legal definition varies by jurisdiction. In some jurisdictions the term specifically excludes financial instruments other than equities and fixed income instruments. In some jurisdictions it includes some instruments that are close to equities and fixed income, e.g. equity warrants. In some countries and/or languages the term "security" is commonly used in day-to-day parlance to mean any form of financial instrument, even though the underlying legal and regulatory regime may not have such a broad definition.

In the United Kingdom, the national competent authority for financial markets regulation is the Financial Conduct Authority; the definition in its Handbook of the term "security" applies only to equities, debentures, alternative debentures, government and public securities, warrants, certificates representing certain securities, units, stakeholder pension schemes, personal pension schemes, rights to or interests in investments, and anything that may be admitted to the Official List.

In the United States, a security is a tradable financial asset of any kind. Securities are broadly categorized into:

- debt securities (e.g., banknotes, bonds and debentures)
- equity securities (e.g., common stocks)
- derivatives (e.g., forwards, futures, options and swaps).

The company or other entity issuing the security is called the issuer. A country's regulatory structure determines what qualifies as a security. For example, private investment pools may have some features of securities, but they may not be registered or regulated as such if they meet various restrictions.

Securities may be represented by a certificate or, more typically, "non-certificated", that is in electronic (dematerialized) or "book entry" only form. Certificates may be bearer, meaning they entitle the holder to rights under the security merely by holding the security, or registered, meaning they entitle the holder to rights only if he or she appears on a security register maintained by the issuer or an intermediary. They include shares of corporate stock or mutual funds, bonds issued by corporations or governmental agencies, stock options or other options, limited partnership units, and various other formal investment instruments that are negotiable and fungible.

Classification

Securities may be classified according to many categories or classification systems:

- Currency of denomination

- Ownership rights
- Terms to maturity
- Degree of liquidity
- Income payments
- Tax treatment
- Credit rating
- Industrial sector or "industry". ("Sector" often refers to a higher level or broader category, such as Consumer Discretionary, whereas "industry" often refers to a lower level classification, such as Consumer Appliances.)
- Region or country (such as country of incorporation, country of principal sales/ market of its products or services, or country in which the principal securities exchange where it trades is located)
- Market capitalization
- State (typically for municipal or "tax-free" bonds in the US)

New Capital

Securities are the traditional way that commercial enterprises raise new capital. These may be an attractive alternative to bank loans depending on their pricing and market demand for particular characteristics. Another disadvantage of bank loans as a source of financing is that the bank may seek a measure of protection against default by the borrower via extensive financial covenants. Through securities, capital is provided by investors who purchase the securities upon their initial issuance. In a similar way, a government may issue securities too when it needs to increase government debt.

Type of Holder

Investors in securities may be retail, i.e. members of the public investing other than by way of business. The greatest part of investment, in terms of volume, is wholesale, i.e. by financial institutions acting on their own account, or on behalf of clients. Important institutional investors include investment banks, insurance companies, pension funds and other managed funds.

Investment

The traditional economic function of the purchase of securities is investment, with the view to receiving income and/or achieving capital gain. Debt securities generally offer a higher rate of interest than bank deposits, and equities may offer the prospect of capital growth. Equity investment may also offer control of the business of the issuer. Debt holdings may also offer some measure of control to the investor if the company is a fledgling start-up or an old giant undergoing 'restructuring'. In these cases, if interest payments are missed, the creditors may take control of the company and liquidate it to recover some of their investment.

Collateral

The last decade has seen an enormous growth in the use of securities as collateral. Purchasing securities with borrowed money secured by other securities or cash itself is called "buying on margin". Where A is owed a debt or other obligation by B, A may require B to deliver property rights in securities to A, either at inception (transfer of title) or only in default (non-transfer-of-title institutional). For institutional loans, property rights are not transferred but nevertheless enable A to satisfy its claims in the event that B fails to make good on its obligations to A or otherwise becomes insolvent. Collateral arrangements are divided into two broad categories, namely security interests and outright collateral transfers. Commonly, commercial banks, investment banks, government agencies and other institutional investors such as mutual funds are significant collateral takers as well as providers. In addition, private parties may utilize stocks or other securities as collateral for portfolio loans in securities lending scenarios.

On the consumer level, loans against securities have grown into three distinct groups over the last decade: 1) Standard Institutional Loans, generally offering low loan-to-value with very strict call and coverage regimens, akin to standard margin loans; 2) Transfer-of-Title (ToT) Loans, typically provided by private parties where borrower ownership is completely extinguished save for the rights provided in the loan contract; and 3) Non-Transfer-of-Title Credit Line facilities where shares are not sold and they serve as assets in a standard lien-type line of cash credit. Of the three, transfer-of-title loans have fallen into the very high-risk category as the number of providers has dwindled as regulators have launched an industry-wide crackdown on transfer-of-title structures where the private lender may sell or sell short the securities to fund the loan. Institutionally managed consumer securities-based loans, on the other hand, draw loan funds from the financial resources of the lending institution, not from the sale of the securities.

Collateral and sources of collateral are changing, in 2012 gold became a more acceptable form of collateral. However more recently Exchange-traded funds (ETFs) seen by many as the ugly ducklings of the collateral world have started to become more readily available and acceptable. But in a world where collateral is becoming scarce and efficiency is everything, many of these mallards are proving themselves to be not so ugly after all—many more are veritable swans. The problem, until now, for collateral managers has been deciphering the bad eggs from the good, which proves to be a time consuming and inefficient task.

Debt and Equity

Securities are traditionally divided into debt securities and equities.

Debt

Debt securities may be called debentures, bonds, deposits, notes or commercial paper depending on their maturity, collateral and other characteristics. The holder of a debt security is typically entitled to the payment of principal and interest, together with other contractual rights under the terms of the issue, such as the right to receive certain information. Debt securities are generally issued for a fixed term and redeemable by the issuer at the end of that term. Debt securities may be protected by collateral or may be unsecured, and, if they are unsecured, may be contractually "senior" to other unsecured debt meaning their holders would have a priority in a bankruptcy of the issuer. Debt that is not senior is "subordinated".

Corporate bonds represent the debt of commercial or industrial entities. Debentures have a long maturity, typically at least ten years, whereas notes have a shorter maturity. Commercial paper is a simple form of debt security that essentially represents a post-dated cheque with a maturity of not more than 270 days.

Money market instruments are short term debt instruments that may have characteristics of deposit accounts, such as certificates of deposit, Accelerated Return Notes (ARN), and certain bills of exchange. They are highly liquid and are sometimes referred to as "near cash". Commercial paper is also often highly liquid.

Euro debt securities are securities issued internationally outside their domestic market in a denomination different from that of the issuer's domicile. They include eurobonds and euronotes. Eurobonds are characteristically underwritten, and not secured, and interest is paid gross. A euronote may take the form of euro-commercial paper (ECP) or euro-certificates of deposit.

Government bonds are medium or long term debt securities issued by sovereign governments or their agencies. Typically they carry a lower rate of interest than corporate bonds, and serve as a source of finance for governments. U.S. federal government bonds are called treasuries. Because of their liquidity and perceived low risk, treasuries are used to manage the money supply in the open market operations of non-US central banks.

Sub-sovereign government bonds, known in the U.S. as municipal bonds, represent the debt of state, provincial, territorial, municipal or other governmental units other than sovereign governments.

Supranational bonds represent the debt of international organizations such as the World Bank, the International Monetary Fund, regional multilateral development banks[vague] and others.

Equity

An equity security is a share of equity interest in an entity such as the capital stock of a company, trust or partnership. The most common form of equity interest is common stock, although preferred equity is also a form of capital stock. The holder of an equity is a shareholder, owning a share, or fractional part of the issuer. Unlike debt securities, which typically require regular payments (interest) to the holder, equity securities are not entitled to any payment. In bankruptcy, they share only in the residual interest of the issuer after all obligations have been paid out to creditors. However, equity generally entitles the holder to a pro rata portion of control of the company, meaning that a holder of a majority of the equity is usually entitled to control the issuer. Equity also enjoys the right to profits and capital gain, whereas holders of debt securities receive only interest and repayment of principal regardless of how well the issuer performs financially. Furthermore, debt securities do not have voting rights outside of bankruptcy. In other words, equity holders are entitled to the "upside" of the business and to control the business.

Hybrid

Hybrid securities combine some of the characteristics of both debt and equity securities.

Preference shares form an intermediate class of security between equities and debt. If the issuer is liquidated, they carry the right to receive interest and/or a return of capital in priority to ordinary shareholders. However, from a legal perspective, they are capital stock and therefore may entitle holders to some degree of control depending on whether they contain voting rights.

Convertibles are bonds or preferred stock that can be converted, at the election of the holder of the convertibles, into the common stock of the issuing company. The convertibility, however, may be forced if the convertible is a callable bond, and the issuer calls the bond. The bondholder has about 1 month to convert it, or the company will call the bond by giving the holder the call price, which may be less than the value of the converted stock. This is referred to as a forced conversion.

Equity warrants are options issued by the company that allow the holder of the warrant to purchase a specific number of shares at a specified price within a specified time. They are often issued together with bonds or existing equities, and are, sometimes, detachable from them and separately tradeable. When the holder of the warrant exercises it, he pays the money directly to the company, and the company issues new shares to the holder.

Warrants, like other convertible securities, increases the number of shares outstanding, and are always accounted for in financial reports as fully diluted earnings per share, which assumes that all warrants and convertibles will be exercised.

Markets

Primary and Secondary Market

Public securities markets are either primary or secondary markets. In the primary market, the money for the securities is received by the issuer of the securities from investors, typically in an initial public offering (IPO). In the secondary market, the securities are simply assets held by one investor selling them to another investor, with the money going from one investor to the other.

An initial public offering is when a company issues public stock newly to investors, called an "IPO" for short. A company can later issue more new shares, or issue shares that have been previously registered in a shelf registration. These later new issues are also sold in the primary market, but they are not considered to be an IPO but are often called a "secondary offering". Issuers usually retain investment banks to assist them in administering the IPO, obtaining SEC (or other regulatory body) approval of the offering filing, and selling the new issue. When the investment bank buys the entire new issue from the issuer at a discount to resell it at a markup, it is called a firm commitment underwriting. However, if the investment bank considers the risk too great for an underwriting, it may only assent to a best effort agreement, where the investment bank will simply do its best to sell the new issue.

For the primary market to thrive, there must be a secondary market, or aftermarket that provides liquidity for the investment security—where holders of securities can sell them to other investors for cash. Otherwise, few people would purchase primary issues, and, thus, companies and governments would be restricted in raising equity capital (money) for their operations. Organized exchanges constitute the main secondary markets. Many smaller issues and most debt securities trade in the decentralized, dealer-based over-the-counter markets.

In Europe, the principal trade organization for securities dealers is the International Capital Market Association. In the U.S., the principal trade organization for securities dealers is the Securities Industry and Financial Markets Association, which is the result of the merger of the Securities Industry Association and the Bond Market Association. The Financial Information Services Division of the Software and Information Industry Association (FISD/SIIA) represents a round-table of market data industry firms, referring to them as Consumers, Exchanges, and Vendors. In India the equivalent organisation is the securities exchange board of India (SEBI).

Public Offer and Private Placement

In the primary markets, securities may be offered to the public in a public offer. Alternatively, they may be offered privately to a limited number of qualified persons in a private placement. Sometimes a combination of the two is used. The distinction between the two is important to securities regulation and company law. Privately placed securities are not publicly tradable and may only be bought and sold by sophisticated qualified investors. As a result, the secondary market is not nearly as liquid as it is for public (registered) securities.

Another category, sovereign bonds, is generally sold by auction to a specialized class of dealers.

Listing and Over-the-counter Dealing

Securities are often listed in a stock exchange, an organized and officially recognized market on which securities can be bought and sold. Issuers may seek listings for their securities to attract investors, by ensuring there is a liquid and regulated market that investors can buy and sell securities in.

Growth in informal electronic trading systems has challenged the traditional business of stock exchanges. Large volumes of securities are also bought and sold "over the counter" (OTC). OTC dealing involves buyers and sellers dealing with each other by telephone or electronically on the basis of prices that are displayed electronically, usually by financial data vendors such as SuperDerivatives, Reuters, Investing.com and Bloomberg.

There are also eurosecurities, which are securities that are issued outside their domestic market into more than one jurisdiction. They are generally listed on the Luxembourg Stock Exchange or admitted to listing in London. The reasons for listing eurobonds include regulatory and tax considerations, as well as the investment restrictions.

Market

London is the centre of the eurosecurities markets. There was a huge rise in the eurosecurities market in London in the early 1980s. Settlement of trades in eurosecurities is currently effected through two European computerized clearing/depositories called Euroclear (in Belgium) and Clearstream (formerly Cedelbank) in Luxembourg.

The main market for Eurobonds is the EuroMTS, owned by Borsa Italiana and Euronext. There are ramp up market in Emergent countries, but it is growing slowly.

Physical Nature

Certificated Securities

Securities that are represented in paper (physical) form are called certificated securities. They may be bearer or registered.

DRS Securities

Securities may also be held in the Direct Registration System (DRS), which is a method of recording shares of stock in book-entry form. Book-entry means the company's transfer agent maintains the shares on the owner's behalf without the need for physical share certificates. Shares held in un-certificated book-entry form have the same rights and privileges as shares held in certificated form.

Bearer Securities

1969 $100,000 Treasury Bill

Bearer securities are completely negotiable and entitle the holder to the rights under the security (e.g. to payment if it is a debt security, and voting if it is an equity security). They are transferred by delivering the instrument from person to person. In some cases, transfer is by endorsement, or signing the back of the instrument, and delivery.

Regulatory and fiscal authorities sometimes regard bearer securities negatively, as they may be used to facilitate the evasion of regulatory restrictions and tax. In the United Kingdom, for example, the issue of bearer securities was heavily restricted firstly by the Exchange Control Act 1947 until 1953. Bearer securities are very rare in the United States because of the negative tax implications they may have to the issuer and holder.

In Luxembourg, the law of 28 July 2014 concerning the compulsory deposit and immobilisation of shares and units in bearer form adopts the compulsory deposit and immobilisation of bearer shares and units with a depositary allowing identification of the hoders thereof.

Registered Securities

1981 $10,000 15.875% Registered Note

In the case of registered securities, certificates bearing the name of the holder are issued, but these merely represent the securities. A person does not automatically acquire legal ownership by having possession of the certificate. Instead, the issuer (or its appointed agent) maintains a register in which details of the holder of the securities are entered and updated as appropriate. A transfer of registered securities is effected by amending the register.

Non-certificated Securities and Global Certificates

Modern practice has developed to eliminate both the need for certificates and maintenance of a complete security register by the issuer. There are two general ways this has been accomplished.

Non-certificated Securities

In some jurisdictions, such as France, it is possible for issuers of that jurisdiction to maintain a legal record of their securities electronically.

In the United States, the current "official" version of Article 8 of the Uniform Commercial Code permits non-certificated securities. However, the "official" UCC is a mere draft that must be enacted individually by each U.S. state. Though all 50 states (as well as the District of Columbia and the U.S. Virgin Islands) have enacted some form of Article 8, many of them still appear to use older versions of Article 8, including some that did not permit non-certificated securities.

Global Certificates, Book Entry Interests, Depositories

To facilitate the electronic transfer of interests in securities without dealing with inconsistent versions of Article 8, a system has developed whereby issuers deposit a single global certificate representing all the outstanding securities of a class or series with a universal depository. This depository is called The Depository Trust Company, or DTC. DTC's parent, Depository Trust & Clearing Corporation (DTCC), is a non-profit cooperative owned by approximately thirty of the largest Wall Street players that typically act as brokers or dealers in securities. These thirty banks are called the DTC participants. DTC, through a legal nominee, owns each of the global securities on behalf of all the DTC participants.

All securities traded through DTC are in fact held, in electronic form, on the books of various intermediaries between the ultimate owner, e.g. a retail investor, and the DTC participants. For example, Mr. Smith may hold 100 shares of Coca-Cola, Inc. in his brokerage account at local broker Jones & Co. brokers. In turn, Jones & Co. may hold 1000 shares of Coca-Cola on behalf of Mr. Smith and nine other customers. These 1000 shares are held by Jones & Co. in an account with Goldman Sachs, a DTC participant, or in an account at another DTC participant. Goldman Sachs in turn may hold millions of Coca-Cola shares on its books on behalf of hundreds of brokers similar to Jones & Co. Each day, the DTC participants settle their accounts with the other DTC participants and adjust the number of shares held on their books for the benefit of customers like Jones & Co. Ownership of securities in this fashion is called beneficial ownership. Each intermediary holds on behalf of someone beneath him in the chain. The ultimate owner is called the beneficial owner. This is also referred to as owning in "Street name".

Among brokerages and mutual fund companies, a large amount of mutual fund share transactions take place among intermediaries as opposed to shares being sold and redeemed directly with the transfer agent of the fund. Most of these intermediaries such as brokerage firms clear the shares electronically through the National Securities Clearing Corp. or "NSCC", a subsidiary of DTCC.

Other Depositories

Besides DTC, two other large securities depositories exist, both in Europe: Euroclear and Clearstream.

Divided and Undivided Security

The terms "divided" and "undivided" relate to the proprietary nature of a security.

Each divided security constitutes a separate asset, which is legally distinct from each other security in the same issue. Pre-electronic bearer securities were divided. Each instrument constitutes the separate covenant of the issuer and is a separate debt.

With undivided securities, the entire issue makes up one single asset, with each of the securities being a fractional part of this undivided whole. Shares in the secondary markets are always undivided. The issuer owes only one set of obligations to shareholders under its memorandum, articles of association and company law. A share represents an undivided fractional part of the issuing company. Registered debt securities also have this undivided nature.

Fungible and Non-fungible Security

The terms "fungible" and "non-fungible" are a feature of assets.

If an asset is fungible, this means that if such an asset is lent, or placed with a custodian, it is customary for the borrower or custodian to be obliged at the end of the loan or custody arrangement to return assets equivalent to the original asset, rather than the specific identical asset. In other words, the redelivery of fungibles is equivalent and not in specie. For example, if an owner of 100 shares of IBM transfers custody of those shares to another party to hold for a purpose, at the end of the arrangement, the holder need simply provide the owner with 100 shares of IBM identical to those received. Cash is also an example of a fungible asset. The exact currency notes received need not be segregated and returned to the owner.

Undivided securities are always fungible by logical necessity. Divided securities may or may not be fungible, depending on market practice. The clear trend is towards fungible arrangements.

Regulation

In the US, the public offer and sale of securities must be either registered pursuant to a registration statement that is filed with the U.S. Securities and Exchange Commission (SEC) or are offered and sold pursuant to an exemption therefrom. Dealing in securities is regulated by both federal authorities (SEC) and state securities departments. In addition, the brokerage industry is supposedly self policed by Self Regulatory Organizations (SROs), such as the Financial Industry Regulatory Authority (FINRA), formerly the National Association of Securities Dealers (or NASD) or the MSRB.

With respect to investment schemes that do not fall within the traditional categories of securities listed in the definition of a security (Sec. 2(a)(1) of the 33 act and Sec. 3(a)(10) of the 34 act) the US Courts have developed a broad definition for securities that must then be registered with the SEC. When determining if there is an "investment contract" that must be registered the courts look for an investment of money, a common enterprise and expectation of profits to come primarily from the efforts of others.

Financial Statement Analysis

Financial statement analysis (or financial analysis) is the process of reviewing and analyzing a company's financial statements to make better economic decisions. These statements include the income statement, balance sheet, statement of cash flows, and a statement of changes in equity. Financial statement analysis is a method or process involving specific techniques for evaluating risks, performance, financial health, and future prospects of an organization.

It is used by a variety of stakeholders, such as credit and equity investors, the government, the public, and decision-makers within the organization. These stakeholders have different interests and apply a variety of different techniques to meet their needs. For example, equity investors are interested in the long-term earnings power of the organization and perhaps the sustainability and growth of dividend payments. Creditors want to ensure the interest and principal is paid on the organizations debt securities (e.g., bonds) when due.

Common methods of financial statement analysis include fundamental analysis, DuPont analysis, horizontal and vertical analysis and the use of financial ratios. Historical information combined with a series of assumptions and adjustments to the financial information may be used to project future performance. The Chartered Financial Analyst designation is available for professional financial analysts.

History

Benjamin Graham and David Dodd first published their influential book "Security Analysis" in 1934. A central premise of their book is that the market's pricing mechanism for financial securities such as stocks and bonds is based upon faulty and irrational analytical processes performed by many market participants. This results in the market price of a security only occasionally coinciding with the intrinsic value around which the price tends to fluctuate. Investor Warren Buffett is a well-known supporter of Graham and Dodd's philosophy.

The Graham and Dodd approach is referred to as Fundamental analysis and includes: 1) Economic analysis; 2) Industry analysis; and 3) Company analysis. The latter is the primary realm of financial statement analysis. On the basis of these three analyses the intrinsic value of the security is determined.

Horizontal and Vertical Analysis

Horizontal analysis compares financial information over time, typically from past quarters or years. Horizontal analysis is performed by comparing financial data from a past statement, such as the income statement. When comparing this past information one will want to look for variations such as higher or lower earnings.

Vertical analysis is a percentage analysis of financial statements. Each line item listed in the financial statement is listed as the percentage of another line item. For example, on an income statement each line item will be listed as a percentage of gross sales. This technique is also referred to as normalization or common-sizing.

Financial Ratio Analysis

Financial ratios are very powerful tools to perform some quick analysis of financial statements. There are four main categories of ratios: liquidity ratios, profitability ratios, activity ratios and leverage ratios. These are typically analyzed over time and across competitors in an industry.

- Liquidity ratios are used to determine how quickly a company can turn its assets into cash if it experiences financial difficulties or bankruptcy. It essentially is a measure of a company's ability to remain in business. A few common liquidity ratios are the current ratio and the liquidity index. The current ratio is current assets/current liabilities and measures how much liquidity is available to pay for liabilities. The liquidity index shows how quickly a company can turn assets into cash and is calculated by: (Trade receivables x Days to liquidate) + (Inventory x Days to liquidate)/Trade Receivables + Inventory.

- Profitability ratios are ratios that demonstrate how profitable a company is. A few popular profitability ratios are the breakeven point and gross profit ratio. The breakeven point calculates how much cash a company must generate to break even with their start up costs. The gross profit ratio is equal to (revenue - the cost of goods sold)/revenue. This ratio shows a quick snapshot of expected revenue.
- Activity ratios are meant to show how well management is managing the company's resources. Two common activity ratios are accounts payable turnover and accounts receivable turnover. These ratios demonstrate how long it takes for a company to pay off its accounts payable and how long it takes for a company to receive payments, respectively.
- Leverage ratios depict how much a company relies upon its debt to fund operations. A very common leverage ratio used for financial statement analysis is the debt-to-equity ratio. This ratio shows the extent to which management is willing to use debt in order to fund operations. This ratio is calculated as: (Long-term debt + Short-term debt + Leases)/ Equity.

DuPont analysis uses several financial ratios that multiplied together equal return on equity, a measure of how much income the firm earns divided by the amount of funds invested (equity).

A Dividend discount model (DDM) may also be used to value a company's stock price based on the theory that its stock is worth the sum of all of its future dividend payments, discounted back to their present value. In other words, it is used to value stocks based on the net present value of the future dividends.

Financial statement analyses are typically performed in spreadsheet software and summarized in a variety of formats.

Recasting Financial Statements

Investors typically are attempting to understand how much cash the company will generate in the future and its rate of profit growth, relative to the amount of capital deployed. Analysts may modify ("recast") the financial statements by adjusting the underlying assumptions to aid in this computation. For example, operating leases (treated like a rental transaction) may be recast as capital leases (indicating ownership), adding assets and liabilities to the balance sheet. This affects the financial statement ratios.

Recasting financial statements requires a solid understanding of accounting theory. Once the cash flow in future years is projected, a discount rate or interest rate will be applied to measure the value of the company and its stock or debt.}

Certifications

Financial analysts typically have finance and accounting education at the undergraduate or graduate level. Persons may earn the Chartered Financial Analyst (CFA) designation through a series of challenging examinations.

How the Investments are Done?

Income level of the investor is the most important factor, which affects their investmnets decision. In the process when the current income exceeds the current consumption the remaining amount of savings are generally invested in the market. When the current consumption exceeds the current income also the investors can participate in the investmnet process through borrowings from the banks and other financial institutions. In this case they have to pay back the borrowing amount as well as the interest charged on this borrowed amount.

Types of Investors

Types of investors in the market are classified on the basis of the individuals' objective, investmnet horizon period and risk appetite or risk tolerance limit. Individuals who are just using the market to make money quickly for a short period of time are called a traders. Their risk level has been high and they invest with their own money as well as borrowed money. The market participants who like to stay in the morket for a longer period of time, take moderate risk and usually invest with their own money are called as investors. Other type of investors are referred as gamblers, who invest in a very short period of time and take the highest risk among all the investors.

Investment Constraints

Major constraints of investment include liquidity, time horizon, tax concerns, legal and regulatory concerns and unique circumstances.

Liquidity refers to the need for cash in excess of any savings or new contributions available at a specific point in the future. A Liquidity needs may be planned (child's college funding in 10 years) or unplanned (a medical emergency) but both require ready ability to convert investments into cash. Some assets, such as real estate, may take considerable time to sell. Others, such as certificates of deposit, may impose early withdrawal penalties. Time horizon typically refers to the time at which an investment objective must be met. Some objectives such as saving for a house may have a short time horizon, while retirement or endowment planning can have long horizons. Investors must often plan for several time horizons at once. The time horizon influences the ability to accept risk and could modify asset allocation strategy. Investors with little tolerance for temporary return fluctuations may need a different plan than would be suggested by time horizon alone, and multiple time horizons can further constrain allocation decisions.

Tax concerns include differences between the tax rates for different types of investment return (interest versus capital gains or dividends), estate taxes, differences between current income and retirement income tax rates, and the potential for tax legislation to change. Legal and regulatory factors may include limits on the allocation to specific assets, the ability to access certain funds and even prohibitions on certain investments. Unique circumstances may include social concerns and specific family needs. These include a desire for socially responsible investments, health needs, dependent needs, and the investors experience with certain types of investments. Apart from these the macroeconomic environment has been also an important factor to be considered for the investment.

Investmnet Decision Process

Investment process involves analyzing the basic nature of investmnet decisions and organizing the activities in the decision process. In investments it is critical to distinguish between an expected return i.e. the anticipated return for some future period and a realized return i.e. the actual return over some past period. Investors must always consider the risk involved in investing. Risk is defined as the chance that the actual return on an investmnet will be different from its expected return. In the fianncial market most of the investors are risk averse. A risk averse investor is one who will not assume risk simply for its own sake and will not incur any given level of risk unless there is an expectation of adequate compensation for having done so. In competitive financial markets, the largest risks have the largest payoffs. In financial markets, investors are constantly on the lookout for either the same risk for a larger return, or the same return for lower risk. Investors manage risk at a cost - lower expected returns (ER).

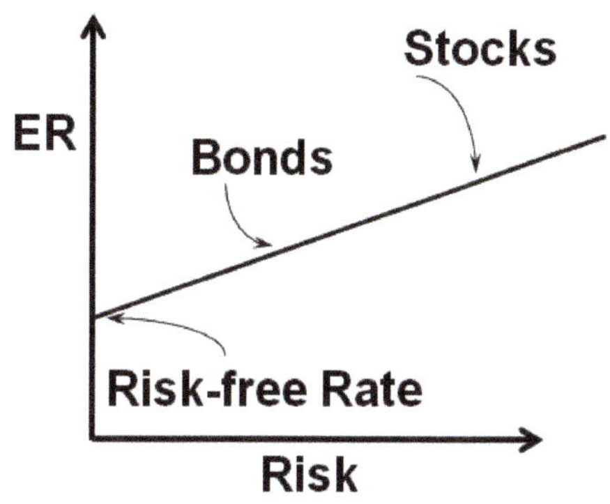

The expected return-risk Trade-off available to investors

Expected risk return trade-off between different financial assets has been shown in the Figure. The risk free rate of return is defined as the return on risk less asset often proxied by the rate of return on treasury bills. From the figure it can be seen that bonds are less risky than stocks and therefore, the expected return on bond is also lower than the expected return on stock. Investors can choose from a wide range of securities in their attempt to maximize the expected return from these opportunities. They face constraints; however, the most important factor has been the risk they face. Traditionally, investors have analyzed and managed securities using a broad two-step process: security analysis and portfolio management. Security analysis is the first part of the investment decision process involving the valuation and analysis of individual securities. Portfolio management is the second step in the investment decision process involving the management of a group of assets (i.e. a portfolio as a unit. The different steps of portfolio management process are as follows:

- Objectives and constraints of the investors
- Choice of the assets mix
- Formulation of investment strategy
- Selection of securities
- Execution of the portfolio
- Portfolio revision
- Portfolio performance evaluation

The factors which affect the portfolio management process are as follows:

- Uncertainty in the ex-post or realized returns
- Availability of investment opportunities
- Types of investors
- Market efficiency

In the investment management process the common errors which take place are as follows:

- Inadequate idea about risk and return
- Biased formulation of investment policy
- Extrapolation of the past data
- Love for cheap stocks
- Over or under diversification of assets
- Wrong attitude towards losses and profits

The major qualities of successful investments are: (i) Creative dynamic thinking, (ii) patience, (iii) flexibility and (iv)decisiveness.

Financial System and Financial Market

Financial system or financial sector of an economy consists of several constituent aspects such as: specialised and non-specialised financial institutions, organised and unorganised financial markets, financial instruments and cervices which facilitate transfer of funds and finally procedures and practices adopted in the market for the overall operation and regulation. 1 Encompassing the major parts of the above mentioned definition, the following diagram will give a broad representation of the financial system. A well- developed financial sector performs the following functions: 2 (i) it promotes overall savings of the economy by providing alternative instruments; (2) it allocates resources efficiently among the sectors; and it provides an effective channel for the transmission of policy impulses provided the financial markets are competitive, efficient & integrated.

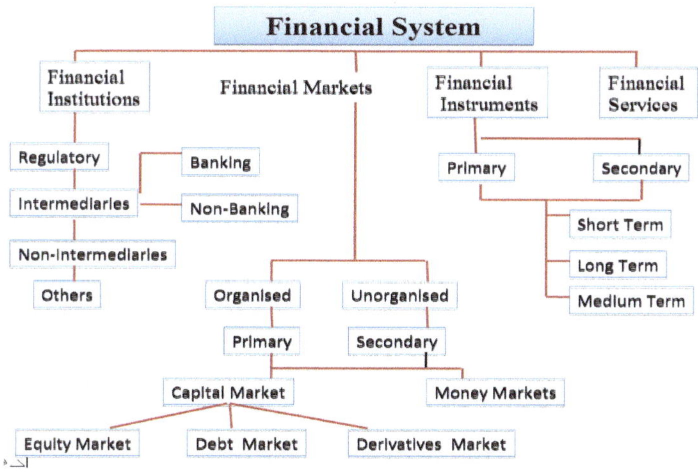

In a more theoretical sense financial markets can be defined as the centers or arrangements that provide facilities for demand and supply side of financial claims and services. The primary role of financial markets, broadly interpreted, is to intermediate resources from savers to investors, and allocates them in an efficient manner among competing uses in the economy, thereby contributing to growth both through increased investment and through enhanced efficiency in resource use.

Classification of financial markets can be made on the basis of several aspects such as: (i) Nature of Claims (e.g., debt market, equity market); (2) Maturity of Claims (e.g., money market, capital market); (3) Seasoning of Claims (e.g., primary market, secondary market); (4) Timing of Delivery (e.g., cash or spot market, forward or futures market); (5) Organizational Structure (e.g., exchange traded market, over the counter market). The important characteristics of a good market for goods and services are as follows:

1. Timely and accurate information: timely and accurate information is available on the price and volume of past transactions and the prevailing bid and ask prices.

2. Liquidity: an asset can be bought or sold quickly at a price close to the prices for previous transactions (has price continuity), assuming no new information has been received. In turn, price continuity requires depth.

3. Price continuity: prices do not change much from one transaction to the next unless substantial new information becomes available.

4. Depth: Presence of numerous potential buyers and sellers who are willing to trade at prices above and below the current market price. These buyers and sellers enter the market in response to changes in supply and demand or both and thereby prevent drastic price changes.

5. Low transaction cost: as transactions entail low costs, including the cost of reaching the market, the actual brokerage costs, and the cost of transferring the asset.

6. Informational efficiency: prices rapidly adjust to new information; thus, the prevailing price is fair because it reflects all available information regarding the asset.

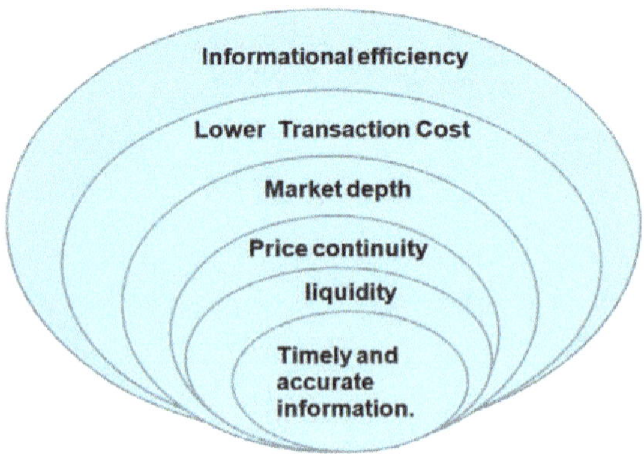

Financial markets are said to be perfect when, (i) a large number of savers and investors operate in markets, (ii) the savers and investors are rational, (iii) all operations in the markets are well informed and information is freely available to all of them, (iv) there are no transaction costs, (v) the financial assets are infinitely divisible, (vi) the participants in markets have homogeneous expectations, and (vii) there are no taxes. The equilibrium in financial markets is usually determined by assuming that there would be perfect competition, and by using the well known tool of supply and demand. Following the above mentioned ideal conditions, the financial market equilibrium position when the expected demand for funds (credit) for short-term and long-term investments matcheswith the planned supply of funds generated out of savings and credit creation. 5Equilibrium is established when the expected demand for funds (credit) for short-term & long-term investment matches with the planned supply of funds generated out of savings and credit creation (Figure A,B &C). Interest rate can also be fixed irrespective of the equilibrium rate of interest i.e. Administered Interest rate (Figure D) in order to match/adjust supply and demand for funds as per economic policy requirement.

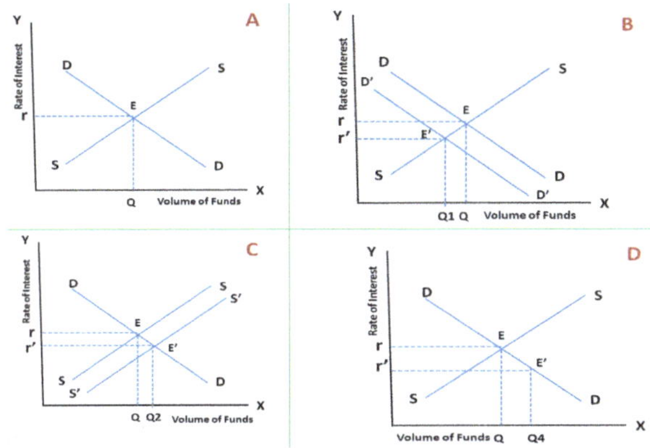

Investment Decision, Alternative Markets and Asset Allocation

An investment is the current commitment of dollars for a period of time in order to derive future payments that will compensate the investor for (1) the time the funds are committed, (2) the expected rate of inflation, and (3) the uncertainty of the future payments. In all cases, the investor is trading a known dollar amount today for some expected future stream of payments that will be greater than the current outlay. They invest to earn a return from savings due to their deferred consumption. The major investment characteristics of financial assets are, liquidity, marketability, reversibility, transferability, transaction costs, default risk, maturity period, tax status, buy-back options, price volatility and finally, the rate of return. Asset allocation is the process of deciding how to distribute an investor's wealth among different countries and asset classes for investment purposes. An asset class is comprised of securities that have similar characteristics, attributes, and risk/return relationships.

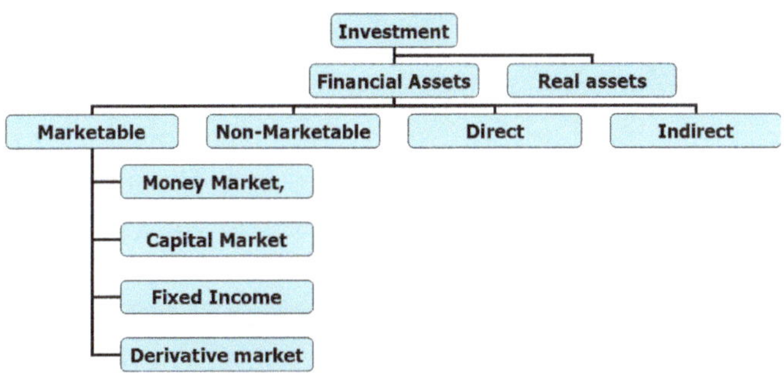

The alternative financial assets under consideration for investment can be marketable and non-marketable assets. In case of marketable assets investor can manage and-control the investment and subsequent liquidation process by his/her own decision.

However these are less liquid in nature (e.g., all the market traded securities). In case of non-marketable assets although investor looses the day to day management but these are highly liquid (e.g., bank deposits, post office deposits etc.). The selected investment asset class may also be direct or indirect in terms of the ownership of the portfolio by the investor. In case of the direct financial assets investor owns the desired portfolio, whereas in case of indirect investor owns a portion of investment companies fund.

The broad range of financial markets that offer such financial assets can be categorised under the following four categories:

In order to have a risk return trade-off Investors follow calculate the expected rate of return and evaluate the uncertainty, or risk, of an investment by identifying the range of possible returns from that investment and assigning each possible return a weight based on the probability that it will occur. Most investors demand a higher rate of return on investments if they perceive that there is any uncertainty about the expected rate of return. The increase in the required rate of return over the zero risk return is called as the risk premium. Investors want a rate of return "investor's required or expected rate of return" that compensates them for the time, the expected rate of inflation, and the uncertainty of the return. In a more formal way this risk is the uncertainty that an investment will earn its expected rate of return. Although the required risk premium for investing in a asset class represents a composite of all uncertainty, it is possible to consider several fundamental sources of uncertainty including: (a) business risk, (b) liquidity risk, (c) financial risk or leverage risk, (d) exchange rate risk, and (e) country (political) risk.

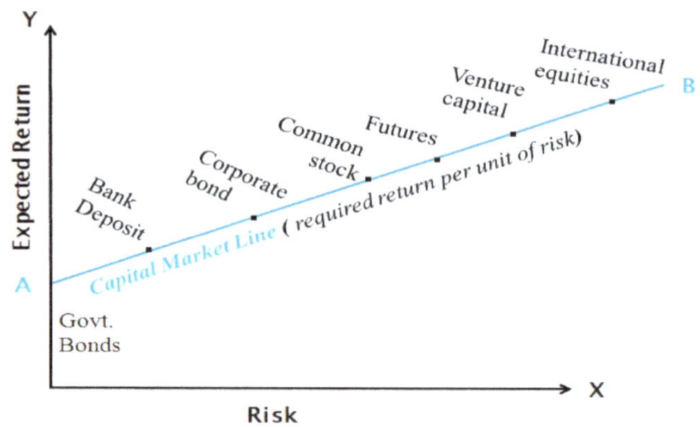

The objective of maximising return can be pursued only at the cost of incurring higher risk. The financial markets offer a wide range of assets from very safe to very risky, with corresponding low to high returns. The above figure shows the risk return trade-off in a capital market line example. It shows the expected return risk spectrum such that the representative asset classes are arrayed over a range of risk on it. The figure shows a positive linear relationship between expected return and risk for different set of asset classes. The rational risk averse investor will chose the appropriate investment opportunity by considering the desired level of risk.

Important Concepts Related to Capital Market

1. Margin Trading: This is the part of a transaction value that a customer has equity in the transaction. Use of Margin: to buy more, to borrow money. Concepts associated with margin: Initial margin: Amount Investor Puts up / value of transaction or It is the part of transaction's value the customer must pay to initiate the transaction with other part being borrowed from the broker. Maintenance Margin: The percentage of a security's value that must be on hand as equity. Margin Call: Demand from the broker for additional cash or securities as a result of the actual margin declining below the maintenance margin

2. Private Placement Vs. Preferential AllotmentPrivate placements refer to sale of equity or equity related instruments of an unlisted company or sale of debentures of a listed or unlisted company. Preferential allotments refer to sale of equity or equity related instruments of an listed company.

3. Open Outcry Trading System: Under this system traders shout and resort to signals on the trading floor of the exchange which consists of several trading posts for different securities. Buyers make their bids and sellers make their offers and bargains are closed at mutually agreed-upon prices.

4 Screen-based Trading System: Started in November 4,1994 in India. The important features are: buyers and sellers place their orders on the computer. They can be limit order or best market price order. The computer constantly tries to match mutually compatible orders on price and time priority. The limit order book or the list of unmatched limit orders is displayed on the screen. Increases efficiency, confidence and transparency in the market

5. Settling: Electronic Delivery system and it is facilitated by depositories which is an institution which dematerializes physical certificates and effects transfer of ownership by electronic book entries. Example: National Securities Depository Limited (NSDL), Central Securities Depositories Limited (CSDL)

6. Settlement Procedure: Weekly Settlement, Carry forward system (badla and undha badla), Rolling Settlement (T+1).

7. Badla and Undha badla: When a bull buys in the anticipation of an immediate rise in price, but finds at the end of the accounting period that the price has not risen, he may either pay for the shares and take delivery, or he may carry over his transaction to the next accounting period by paying carry over charges or Seedha badla to the seller. When a bear sells in anticipation of a fall in prices in the immediate future (so that he can pick up shares later for delivery and make a profit), but the fall does not happen within the accounting period, he has the option to borrow or buy the shares for delivery, or have his sales carried over to the next accounting period on payment of Undha badla or backwardation charges to the buyer.

8. Short Selling: In a normal transaction a security is bought and owned because the investor believes the price is likely to rise. Eventually the security is sold and the position is closed out. First you buy then you sell. A short-sell involves selling a security because of belief that the price will decline and buying back the security later to close the position. First you sell and then buy.

9. Actual selling and buying procedure: Procedure for Buying - Locating the broker----- Placement of order (De-mat account in a depository) then -→ execution of order (Contract note for tax and other legal purposes). Order may be Limit Order (upper limit of the price has been given by the investor) or Market Order (to prevail the best market price).Procedure for selling- Placement of order--→ sale order-----→ execution of order (same as buying)

10. Important abbreviations used in stock exchange quotations: Con-Convertible, Xd- ex (excluding) dividend, Cd- cum (with) dividend, Xr- ex(excluding) right.

Stock Market Index

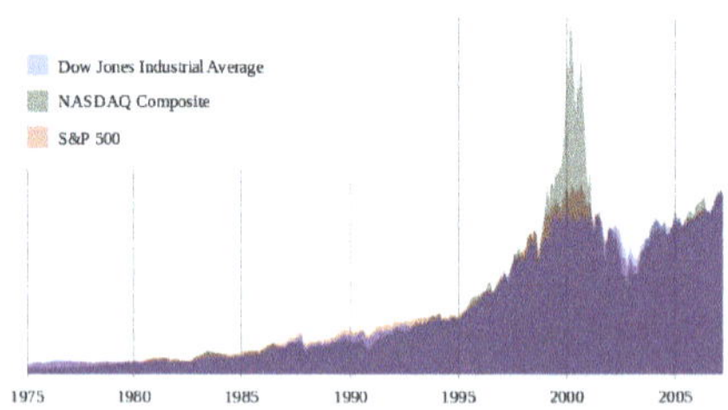

A comparison of three major U.S. stock indices: the NASDAQ Composite, Dow Jones Industrial Average, and S&P 500. All three have the same height at March 2007. Notice the large dot-com spike on the NASDAQ, a result of the large number of technology companies on that index.

A stock index or stock market index is a measurement of the value of a section of the stock market. It is computed from the prices of selected stocks (typically a weighted average). It is a tool used by investors and financial managers to describe the market, and to compare the return on specific investments.

An index is a mathematical construct, so it may not be invested in directly. But many mutual funds and exchange-traded funds attempt to "track" an index, and those funds that do not may be judged against those that do.

Types of Indices

Stock market indices may be classified in many ways. A 'world' or 'global' stock market index — such as the MSCI World or the S&P Global 100 — includes stocks from multiple regions. Regions may be defined geographically (e.g., Europe, Asia) or by levels of industrialization or income (e.g., Developed Markets, Frontier Markets).

A 'national' index represents the performance of the stock market of a given nation—and by proxy, reflects investor sentiment on the state of its economy. The most regularly quoted market indices are national indices composed of the stocks of large companies listed on a nation's largest stock exchanges, such as the American S&P 500, the Japanese Nikkei 225, and the British FTSE 100.

Other indices may be regional, such as the FTSE Developed Europe Index or the FTSE Developed Asia Pacific Index. Indexes may be based on exchange, such as the NASDAQ-100 or NYSE US 100, or groups of exchanges, such as the Euronext 100 or OMX Nordic 40.

The concept may be extended well beyond an exchange. The Wilshire 5000 Index, the original total market index, represents the stocks of nearly every publicly traded company in the United States, including all U.S. stocks traded on the New York Stock Exchange (but not ADRs or limited partnerships), NASDAQ and American Stock Exchange. Russell Investment Group added to the family of indices by launching the Russel Global Index.

More specialized indices exist tracking the performance of specific sectors of the market. Some examples include the Wilshire US REIT which tracks more than 80 American real estate investment trusts and the Morgan Stanley Biotech Index which consists of 36 American firms in the biotechnology industry. Other indices may track companies of a certain size, a certain type of management, or even more specialized criteria – one index published by Linux Weekly News tracks stocks of companies that sell products and services based on the Linux operating environment.

Index Versions

Some indices, such as the S&P 500, have multiple versions. These versions can differ based on how the index components are weighted and on how dividends are accounted for. For example, there are three versions of the S&P 500 index: price return, which only considers the price of the components, total return, which accounts for dividend reinvestment, and net total return, which accounts for dividend reinvestment after the deduction of a withholding tax. As another example, the Wilshire 4500 and Wilshire 5000 indices have five versions each: full capitalization total return, full capitalization price, float-adjusted total return, float-adjusted price, and equal weight. The difference between the full capitalization, float-adjusted, and equal weight versions is in how index components are weighted.

Weighting

An index may also be classified according to the method used to determine its price. In a *price-weighted index* such as the Dow Jones Industrial Average, NYSE Arca Major Market Index, and the NYSE ARCA Tech 100 Index, the price of each component stock is the only consideration when determining the value of the index. Thus, price movement of even a single security will heavily influence the value of the index even though the dollar shift is less significant in a relatively highly valued issue, and moreover ignoring the relative size of the company as a whole. In contrast, a *capitalization-weighted* (also called market-value-weighted) index such as the Hang Seng Index factors in the size of the company. Thus, a relatively small shift in the price of a large company will heavily influence the value of the index.

Traditionally, capitalization- or share-weighted indices all had a *full* weighting, i.e. all outstanding shares were included. Recently, many of them have changed to a *float-adjusted* weighting which helps indexing.

An *equal-weighted index* is one in which all components are assigned the same value. For example, the Barron's 400 Index assigns an equal value of 0.25% to each of the 400 stocks included in the index, which together add up to the 100% whole.

A *modified capitalization-weighted index* is a hybrid between capitalization weighting and equal weighting. It is similar to a capitalization weighting with one main difference: the largest stocks are capped to a percent of the weight of the total stock index and the excess weight will be redistributed equally amongst the stocks under that cap. Moreover, in 2005, Standard & Poor's introduced the S&P Pure Growth Style Index and S&P Pure Value Style Index which was attribute-weighted. That is, a stock's weight in the index is decided by the score it gets relative to the value attributes that define the criteria of a specific index, the same measure used to select the stocks in the first place. For these two indexes, a score is calculated for every stock, be it their growth score or the value score (a stock cannot be both) and accordingly they are weighted for the index.

Criticism of Capitalization-weighting

One argument for capitalization weighting is that investors must, in aggregate, hold a capitalization-weighted portfolio anyway. This then gives the average return for all investors; if some investors do worse, other investors must do better (excluding costs).

Investors use theories such as modern portfolio theory to determine allocations. This considers risk and return and does not consider weights relative to the entire market. This may result in overweighting assets such as value or small-cap stocks, if they are believed to have a better return for risk profile. These investors believe that they can get a better result because other investors are not very good. The capital asset pricing model says that *all* investors are highly intelligent, and it is impossible to do better than the market portfolio, the capitalization-weighted portfolio of all assets. However, empirical tests conclude that market indices are not efficient. This can be explained by the fact that these indices do not include all assets or by the fact that the theory does not hold. The practical conclusion is that using capitalization-weighted portfolios is not necessarily the optimal method.

As a consequence, capitalization-weighting has been subject to severe criticism, pointing out that the mechanics of capitalization-weighting lead to trend-following strategies that provide an inefficient risk-return trade-off.

Also, while capitalization-weighting is the standard in equity index construction, different weighting schemes exist. First, while most indices use capitalization-weighting, additional criteria are often taken into account, such as sales/revenue and net income. Second, as an answer to the critiques of capitalization-weighting, equity indices with different weighting schemes have emerged, such as "wealth"-weighted (Morris, 1996), "fundamental"-weighted (Arnott, Hsu and Moore 2005), "diversity"-weighted (Fernholz, Garvy, and Hannon 1998) or equal-weighted indices.

Indices and Passive Investment Management

There has been an accelerating trend in recent decades to create passively managed mutual funds that are based on market indices, known as index funds. Advocates claim that index funds routinely beat a large majority of actively managed mutual funds; one study claimed that over time, the average actively managed fund has returned 1.8% less than the S&P 500 index - a result nearly equal to the average expense ratio of mutual funds (fund expenses are a drag on the funds' return by exactly that ratio). Since index funds attempt to replicate the holdings of an index, they eliminate the need for — and thus many costs of — the research entailed in active management, and have a lower churn rate (the turnover of securities which lose fund managers' favor and are sold, with the attendant cost of commissions and capital gains taxes).

Indices are also a common basis for a related type of investment, the exchange-traded fund or ETF. Unlike an index fund, which is priced daily, an ETF is priced continuously, is optionable, and can be sold short.

Ethical Stock Market Indices

A notable specialized index type is those for ethical investing indices that include only those companies satisfying ecological or social criteria, e.g. those of The Calvert Group, KLD, FTSE4Good Index, Dow Jones Sustainability Index, STOXX Global ESG Leaders Index, Standard Ethics Italian Index and Wilderhill Clean Energy Index.

In 2010, the OIC announced the initiation of a stock index that complies with Islamic law's ban on alcohol, tobacco and gambling. Other such equities, such as the Dow Jones Islamic Market World Index, already exist.

Another important trend is strict mechanical criteria for inclusion and exclusion to prevent market manipulation, e.g. in Canada when Nortel was permitted to rise to over 30% of the TSE 300 index value. Ethical indices have a particular interest in mechanical criteria, seeking to avoid accusations of ideological bias in selection, and have pioneered techniques for inclusion and exclusion of stocks based on complex criteria. Another means of mechanical selection is mark-to-future methods that exploit scenarios produced by multiple analysts weighted according to probability, to determine which stocks have become too risky to hold in the index of concern.

Critics of such initiatives argue that many firms satisfy mechanical "ethical criteria", e.g. regarding board composition or hiring practices, but fail to perform ethically with respect to shareholders, e.g. Enron. Indeed, the seeming "seal of approval" of an ethical index may put investors more at ease, enabling scams. One response to these criticisms is that trust in the corporate management, index criteria, fund or index manager, and securities regulator, can never be replaced by mechanical means, so "market transparency" and "disclosure" are the only long-term-effective paths to fair markets. From a financial perspective, it is not obvious whether ethical indices or ethical funds will out-perform their more conventional counterparts. Theory might suggest that returns would be lower since the investible universe is artificially reduced and with it portfolio efficiency. On the other hand, companies with good social performances might be better run, have more committed workers and customers, and be less likely to suffer reputational damage from incidents (oil spillages, industrial tribunals, etc.) and this might result in lower share price volatility. The empirical evidence on the performance of ethical funds and of ethical firms versus their mainstream comparators is very mixed for both stock and debt markets.

Innovations Awards to Stock Indices

Your stock index chart makes me feel much better.

The William F. Sharpe Indexing Achievement Awards are presented annually in order to recognize the most important contributions to the indexing industry over the preceding year.

- Most Innovative Benchmark Index
  - 2004 — CBOE S&P 500 BuyWrite Index (BXM)
  - 2005 — FTSE/RAFI Fundamental Index Series
  - 2006 — Standard and Poor's Case-Shiller House Prices Indices
  - 2007 - CBOE S&P 500 PutWrite Index (PUT)
  - 2011 - S&P GSCI Dynamic Roll Index
- Most Innovative ETF
  - 2004 — iShares MSCI EAFE (EFA) and Emerging Markets
  - 2005 — EasyETF GSCI Commodities ETF
  - 2006 — PowerShares DB Commodity Index Tracking Fund (DBC) and PowerShares G10 Currency Harvest Fund (DBV)
  - 2007 - SPDR DJ Wilshire International Real Estate ETF
  - 2011 - ProShares VIX Short-term Futures ETF (VIXY)
- Most Innovative Index Product
  - 2004 — CBOE Volatility Index (VIX) Futures
  - 2005 — Options on Vanguard VIPERS at the CBOE
  - 2006 — Chicago Board Options Exchange Options on the CBOE Volatility Index (VIX)
  - 2007 - iPath ETNs
  - 2009 - Thomson Reuters Realized Volatility Index
- Best Index-related Research Paper
  - 2004 — Steven Schoenfeld
  - 2005 — Rob Arnott
  - 2006 — Eugene F. Fama and Kenneth R. French
  - 2007 - Benchmarking Benchmarks: Measuring Characteristic Selectivity, By Kingsley Fong, David R. Gallagher, Adrian Lee, University of New South Wales
  - 2011 - Index Volatility in Perspective, by Joanne Hill
- Lifetime Achievement Award
  - 2004 — Tim Harbert

- 2005 — William Sharpe and Nathan Most
- 2006 — Burton G. Malkiel and Ronald J. Ryan
- 2007 - John C. Bogle, Paul A. Samuelson, Patricia C. Dunn, William L. Fouse and John A. Prestbo
- 2008 - Leo Melamed, Joanne Hill, Joe Levin, and Kelly Haughton
- 2009 - William J. Brodsky and Gus Sauter
- 2011 - Lee Kranefuss

Importance of Stock Market Index

Three major advantage: to judge the performance of individual investor, to measure the market rates of return, to predict the market movements. Factors affecting the construction of stock market index: sample, it should be representative of total population, base year, it should be a normal year, weighting criteria, equally weighted series, price weighted series, market value weighted series.

Example:

Stock	Quantity	Beta	Price
A	60,000	30	45
B	20,000	25	80
C	90,000	65	85

Solution:

Equally weighted series---

1/3 (45/30 + 80/ 25 + 85 / 65) = 2.0033

Price weighted series---

(45 + 80 + 85)/)(30 + 25 + 65) = 1.75

Market value weighted series = (60 000*45 + 20 000*80 + 90 000* 85) / (60 000*30 + 20 000*25 + 90 000* 65) = 1.46

Interest Rate

Interest rate is the price that the borrowers must pay to lenders to obtain the use of money for a period of time. As we know market interest rate plays a significant role for pricing of the bond and there is an inverse relationship between bond prices and interest ratesi.e. when interest rates decline, the prices of bonds increase; when interest rates rise, there is a decline in bond prices. Understanding interest rates and what makes them change is necessary for an investor who hopes to maximize returns from investing in bonds. Therefore, in this session we have made the discussion on the following topics: what determines the market interest rate and why alternative bonds have different interest rates?

An interest rate, is the amount of interest due per period, as a proportion of the amount lent, deposited or borrowed (called the principal sum). The total interest on an amount lent or borrowed depends on the principal sum, the interest rate, the compounding frequency, and the length of time over which it is lent, deposited or borrowed.

It is defined as the proportion of an amount loaned which a lender charges as interest to the borrower, normally expressed as an annual percentage. It is the rate a bank or other lender charges to borrow its money, or the rate a bank pays its savers for keeping money in an account.

Annual interest rate is the rate over a period of one year. Other interest rates apply over different periods, such as a month or a day, but they are usually annualised.

Factors Influencing Interest Rates

Interest rates vary according to:

- the government's directives to the central bank to accomplish the government's goals
- the currency of the principal sum lent or borrowed
- the term to maturity of the investment
- the perceived default probability of the borrower
- supply and demand in the market

as well as other factors.

Example

A company borrows capital from a bank to buy assets for its business. In return, the bank charges the company interest. (The lender might also require rights over the new assets as collateral.)

Related Terms

Base rate usually refers to the annualized rate offered on overnight deposits by the central bank or other monetary authority.

Annual percentage rate (APR) and *effective annual rate* or *annual equivalent rate* (AER) are used to help consumers compare products with different payment structures on a common basis.

A *discount rate* is applied to calculate present value.

For an interest-bearing security, *coupon rate* is the ratio of the annual coupon amount (the coupon paid per year) per unit of par value, whereas *current yield* is the ratio of the annual coupon divided by its current market price. *Yield to maturity* is a bond's expected internal rate of return, assuming it will be held to maturity, that is, the discount rate which equates all remaining cash flows to the investor (all remaining coupons and repayment of the par value at maturity) with the current market price.

Monetary Policy

Interest rate targets are a vital tool of monetary policy and are taken into account when dealing with variables like investment, inflation, and unemployment. The central banks of countries generally tend to reduce interest rates when they wish to increase investment and consumption in the country's economy. However, a low interest rate as a macro-economic policy can be risky and may lead to the creation of an economic bubble, in which large amounts of investments are poured into the real-estate market and stock market. In developed economies, interest-rate adjustments are thus made to keep inflation within a target range for the health of economic activities or cap the interest rate concurrently with economic growth to safeguard economic momentum.

Historical Interest Rates

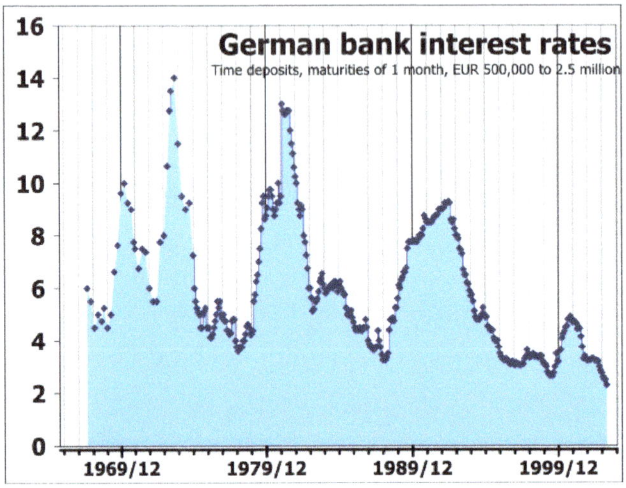

Germany experienced deposit interest rates from 14% in 1969 down to almost 2% in 2003

In the past two centuries, interest rates have been variously set either by national governments or central banks. For example, the Federal Reserve federal funds rate in the

United States has varied between about 0.25% to 19% from 1954 to 2008, while the Bank of England base rate varied between 0.5% and 15% from 1989 to 2009, and Germany experienced rates close to 90% in the 1920s down to about 2% in the 2000s. During an attempt to tackle spiraling hyperinflation in 2007, the Central Bank of Zimbabwe increased interest rates for borrowing to 800%.

The interest rates on prime credits in the late 1970s and early 1980s were far higher than had been recorded – higher than previous US peaks since 1800, than British peaks since 1700, or than Dutch peaks since 1600; "since modern capital markets came into existence, there have never been such high long-term rates" as in this period.

Possibly before modern capital markets, there have been some accounts that savings deposits could achieve an annual return of at least 25% and up to as high as 50%.

Reasons for Interest Rate Changes

- Political short-term gain: Lowering interest rates can give the economy a short-run boost. Under normal conditions, most economists think a cut in interest rates will only give a short term gain in economic activity that will soon be offset by inflation. The quick boost can influence elections. Most economists advocate independent central banks to limit the influence of politics on interest rates.
- Deferred consumption: When money is loaned the lender delays spending the money on consumption goods. Since according to time preference theory people prefer goods now to goods later, in a free market there will be a positive interest rate.
- Inflationary expectations: Most economies generally exhibit inflation, meaning a given amount of money buys fewer goods in the future than it will now. The borrower needs to compensate the lender for this.
- Alternative investments: The lender has a choice between using his money in different investments. If he chooses one, he forgoes the returns from all the others. Different investments effectively compete for funds.
- Risks of investment: There is always a risk that the borrower will go bankrupt, abscond, die, or otherwise default on the loan. This means that a lender generally charges a risk premium to ensure that, across his investments, he is compensated for those that fail.
- Liquidity preference: People prefer to have their resources available in a form that can immediately be exchanged, rather than a form that takes time to realize.

- Taxes: Because some of the gains from interest may be subject to taxes, the lender may insist on a higher rate to make up for this loss.
- Banks: Banks can tend to change the interest rate to either slow down or speed up economy growth. This involves either raising interest rates to slow the economy down, or lowering interest rates to promote economic growth.
- Economy: Interest rates can fluctuate according to the status of the economy. It will generally be found that if the economy is strong then the interest rates will be high, if the economy is weak the interest rates will be low.

Real vs Nominal Interest Rates

The nominal interest rate is the rate of interest with no adjustment for inflation.

For example, suppose someone deposits $100 with a bank for 1 year, and they receive interest of $10 (before tax), so at the end of the year, their balance is $110 (before tax). In this case, regardless of the rate of inflation, the nominal interest rate is 10% *per annum* (before tax).

The real interest rate measures the growth in real value of the loan plus interest, taking inflation into account. The repayment of principal plus interest is measured in real terms compared against the buying power of the amount at the time it was borrowed, lent, deposited or invested.

If inflation is 10%, then the $110 in the account at the end of the year has the same purchasing power (that is, buys the same amount) as the $100 had a year ago. The real interest rate is zero in this case.

The real interest rate is given by the Fisher equation:

$$r = \frac{1+i}{1+p} - 1$$

where p is the inflation rate. For low rates and short periods, the linear approximation applies:

$$r \approx i - p$$

The Fisher equation applies both *ex ante* and *ex post*. *Ex ante*, the rates are projected rates, whereas *ex post*, the rates are historical.

Market Interest Rates

There is a market for investments, including the money market, bond market, stock market, and currency market as well as retail banking.

Interest rates reflect:

- The risk-free cost of capital
- Expected inflation
- Risk premium
- Transaction costs

Inflationary Expectations

According to the theory of rational expectations, borrowers and lenders form an expectation of inflation in the future. The acceptable nominal interest rate at which they are willing and able to borrow or lend includes the real interest rate they require to receive, or are willing and able to pay, plus the rate of inflation they expect.

Risk

The level of risk in investments is taken into consideration. Riskier investments such as shares and junk bonds are normally expected to deliver higher returns than safer ones like government bonds.

The additional return above the risk-free nominal interest rate which is expected from a risky investment is the risk premium. The risk premium an investor requires on an investment depends on the risk preferences of the investor. Evidence suggests that most lenders are risk-averse.

A maturity risk premium applied to a longer-term investment reflects a higher perceived risk of default.

Liquidity Preference

Most investors prefer their money to be in cash than in less fungible investments. Cash is on hand to be spent immediately if the need arises, but some investments require time or effort to transfer into spendable form. This is known as liquidity preference. A 1-year loan, for instance, is very liquid compared to a 10-year loan. A 10-year US Treasury bond, however, is liquid because it can easily be sold on the market.

A Market Interest-rate Model

A basic interest rate pricing model for an asset

$$i_n = i_r + p_e + rp + lp$$

Assuming perfect information, p_e is the same for all participants in the market, and this is identical to:

$$i_n = i_n^* + rp + lp$$

where

i_n is the nominal interest rate on a given investment

i_r is the risk-free return to capital

i^*_n = the nominal interest rate on a short-term risk-free liquid bond (such as U.S. Treasury Bills).

rp = a risk premium reflecting the length of the investment and the likelihood the borrower will default

lp = liquidity premium (reflecting the perceived difficulty of converting the asset into money and thus into goods).

Spread

The *spread* of interest rates is the lending rate minus the deposit rate. This spread covers operating costs for banks providing loans and deposits. A *negative spread* is where a deposit rate is higher than the lending rate.

Interest Rates in Macroeconomics

Elasticity of Substitution

The elasticity of substitution (full name is the marginal rate of substitution of the relative allocation) affects the real interest rate. The larger the magnitude of the elasticity of substitution, the more the exchange, and the lower the real interest rate.

Output and Unemployment

Higher interest rates increase the cost of borrowing which can reduce investment and output and increase unemployment. Expanding businesses, especially entrepreneurs tend to be net debtors. However, the Austrian School of Economics sees higher rates as leading to greater investment in order to earn the interest to pay its creditors. Higher rates encourage more saving and reduce inflation.

Open Market Operations in the United States

The Federal Reserve (often referred to as 'The Fed') implements monetary policy largely by targeting the federal funds rate. This is the rate that banks charge each other for overnight loans of federal funds, which are the reserves held by banks at the Fed. Open market operations are one tool within monetary policy implemented by the Federal Reserve to steer short-term interest rates using the power to buy and sell treasury securities.

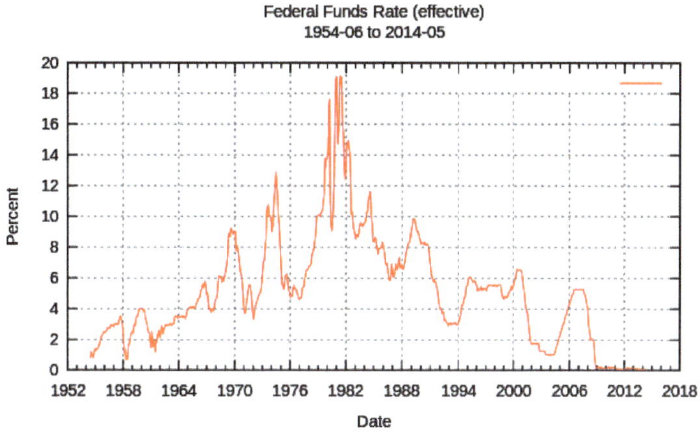

The effective federal funds rate in the US charted over more than half a century

Money and Inflation

Loans, bonds, and shares have some of the characteristics of money and are included in the broad money supply.

By setting i^*_n, the government institution can affect the markets to alter the total of loans, bonds and shares issued. Generally speaking, a higher real interest rate reduces the broad money supply.

Through the quantity theory of money, increases in the money supply lead to inflation.

Impact on Savings and Pensions

Financial economists such as World Pensions Council (WPC) researchers have argued that durably low interest rates in most G20 countries will have an adverse impact on the funding positions of pension funds as "without returns that outstrip inflation, pension investors face the real value of their savings declining rather than ratcheting up over the next few years"

From 1982 until 2012, most Western economies experienced a period of low inflation combined with relatively high returns on investments across all asset classes including government bonds. This brought a certain sense of complacency amongst some pension actuarial consultants and regulators, making it seem reasonable to use optimistic economic assumptions to calculate the present value of future pension liabilities.

This potentially long-lasting collapse in returns on government bonds is taking place against the backdrop of a protracted fall in returns for other core-assets such as blue chip stocks, and, more importantly, a silent demographic shock. Factoring in the corresponding "longevity risk", pension premiums could be raised significantly while disposable incomes stagnate and employees work longer years before retiring.

Mathematical Note

Because interest and inflation are generally given as percentage increases, the formulae above are (linear) approximations.

For instance,

$$i_n = i_r + p_e$$

is only approximate. In reality, the relationship is

$$(1 + i_n) = (1 + i_r)(1 + p_e)$$

so

$$i_r = \frac{1 + i_n}{1 + p_e} - 1$$

The two approximations, eliminating higher order terms, are:

$$(1 + x)(1 + y) = 1 + x + y + xy \qquad \approx 1 + x + y$$

$$\frac{1}{1 + x} = 1 - x + x^2 - x^3 + \cdots \qquad \approx 1 - x$$

The formulae in this article are exact if logarithmic units are used for relative changes, or equivalently if logarithms of indices are used in place of rates, and hold even for large relative changes. Most elegantly, if the natural logarithm is used, yielding the neper as logarithmic units, scaling by 100 to obtain the centineper yields units that are infinitesimally equal to percentage change (hence approximately equal for small values), and for which the linear equations hold for all values.

Zero Interest Rate Policy

A so-called "zero interest rate policy" (ZIRP) is a very low—near-zero—central bank target interest rate. At this zero lower bound the central bank faces difficulties with conventional monetary policy, because it is generally believed that market interest rates cannot realistically be pushed down into negative territory.

Negative Nominal Interest Rates

Nominal interest rates are normally positive, but not always. In contrast, *real* interest rates can be negative, when nominal interest rates are below inflation. When this is done via government policy (for example, via reserve requirements), this is deemed financial repression, and was practiced by countries such as the United States and United Kingdom following World War II (from 1945) until the late 1970s or early 1980s (during and following the Post–World War II economic expansion). In the late 1970s, United States Treasury securities with negative real interest rates were deemed *certificates of confiscation*.

On Central Bank Reserves

A so-called "negative interest rate policy" (NIRP) is a negative (below zero) central bank target interest rate.

Theory

Given the alternative of holding cash, and thus earning 0%, rather than lending it out, profit-seeking lenders will not lend below 0%, as that will guarantee a loss, and a bank offering a negative deposit rate will find few takers, as savers will instead hold cash.

Negative interest rates have been proposed in the past, notably in the late 19th century by Silvio Gesell. A negative interest rate can be described (as by Gesell) as a "tax on holding money"; he proposed it as the *Freigeld* (free money) component of his *Freiwirtschaft* (free economy) system. To prevent people from holding cash (and thus earning 0%), Gesell suggested issuing money for a limited duration, after which it must be exchanged for new bills; attempts to hold money thus result in it expiring and becoming worthless. Along similar lines, John Maynard Keynes approvingly cited the idea of a carrying tax on money, (1936, *The General Theory of Employment, Interest and Money*) but dismissed it due to administrative difficulties. More recently, a carry tax on currency was proposed by a Federal Reserve employee (Marvin Goodfriend) in 1999, to be implemented via magnetic strips on bills, deducting the carry tax upon deposit, the tax being based on how long the bill had been held.

It has been proposed that a negative interest rate can in principle be levied on existing paper currency via a serial number lottery, such as randomly choosing a number 0 through 9 and declaring that notes whose serial number end in that digit are worthless, yielding an average 10% loss of paper cash holdings to hoarders; a drawn two-digit number could match the last two digits on the note for a 1% loss. This was proposed by an anonymous student of Greg Mankiw, though more as a thought experiment than a genuine proposal.

A much simpler method to achieve negative real interest rates and provide a disincentive to holding cash, is for governments to encourage mildly inflationary monetary policy; indeed, this is what Keynes recommended back in 1936.

Practice

Both the European Central Bank starting in 2014 and the Bank of Japan starting in early 2016 pursued the policy on top of their earlier and continuing quantitative easing policies. The latter's policy was said at its inception to be trying to 'change Japan's "deflationary mindset."' In 2016 Sweden, Denmark and Switzerland—not directly participants in the Euro currency zone—also had NIRPs in place.

Countries such as Sweden and Denmark have set negative interest on reserves—that is to say, they have charged interest on reserves.

In July 2009, Sweden's central bank, the Riksbank, set its policy repo rate, the interest rate on its one-week deposit facility, at 0.25%, at the same time as setting its overnight deposit rate at -0.25%. The existence of the negative overnight deposit rate was a technical consequence of the fact that overnight deposit rates are generally set at 0.5% below or 0.75% below the policy rate. This is not technically an example of "negative interest on excess reserves," because Sweden does not have a reserve requirement, but imposing a reserve interest rate without reserve requirements imposes an implied reserve requirement of zero. The Riksbank studied the impact of these changes and stated in a commentary report that they led to no disruptions in Swedish financial markets.

On Bond Yields

During the European debt crisis, government bonds of some countries (Switzerland, Denmark, Germany, Finland, the Netherlands and Austria) have been sold at negative yields. Suggested explanations include desire for safety and protection against the eurozone breaking up (in which case some eurozone countries might redenominate their debt into a stronger currency).

Theories of Interest Rate Determination

Generally speaking interest rate is determined by the forces of demand and supply in the financial markets. Here the question is: supply of and demand for what determine the market interest rate? Different people have answered this question differently which has given rise to different theories about the determination of the rate of interest. A brief discussion on such three different theories like (i) Classical Theory, (ii) Loanable Funds Theory and (iii) Keynesian Theory is given below.

Classical Theory of Interest Rate

It is a static theory and according to this theory rate of interest is a real phenomenon and therefore, it is determined by the real factors. Basically, the theory holds the proposition that the rate of interest is determined by the intersection of the demand for and supply of capital. Thus, an equilibrium rate of interest is determined at a point at which the demand for capital equals its supply. Demand for capital stems from investment decisions of the entrepreneur class. Investment demand schedule, thus, reflects the demand for capital, while the supply of capital results from savings in the community.

The aggregate saving is the difference between the total income and total consumption expenditure. The savings may be affected by individuals, households, business and the government. On the demand side, firms and other economic units demand capital to make profits by producing goods. The investment takes place because by investing in roundabout or indirect methods or processes of production, economic units expect to obtain more consumption in future by sacrificing present consumption. The opportunities to produce more effectively by using roundabout methods of production determine the investment demand.

Loanable Funds Theory

It is a dynamic theory as opposed to the static nature of the classical theory. It also combines the real and monetary factors as determinants of the rate of interest. According to this theory the real supply and demand curves determining interest rates should have added to them a component of the supply of saving which is associated with the creation of new money or credit. The supply of credit may be from banks and other financial institutions in the economy. The demand for credit would be for financing investment plus holding of idle cash i.e. for increasing the cash ratio by different economic units. The rate of interest clears the market for savings plus credit.

Keynesian Theory

According to Keynes, interest rate is a purely monetary phenomenon. This means that the rate of interest is determined by the monetary factors i.e. it depends on the actions of the monetary authorities and on the attitude of economic units towards holding money as an alternative to holding bonds. In other words, interest rate is determined by the interaction between the supply of money and demand for it in the economic system. The supply of money is said to be under ultimate control of the monetary authorities. The demand to hold money is called the "liquidity preference". There are three motives or reasons behind the demand for liquidity and liquidity preference of individuals, firms and institutions. They are (a) transaction motive, (b) precautionary motive, and (c) speculative motive.

The major economic factors like expected inflation rate, growth rate of money supply, growth rate of bank credit, output of the economy which affect the demand and supply forces of the money and loanable funds are responsible for the fluctuations in the rate of interest in the economy.

Theories of Term Structure Interest Rates

The term structure of interest rates refers to the relationship between bonds of different terms. In another way we can state that the term structure of interest rates refers to the relationship between time to maturity and yields for a particular category of bonds at a particular point of time. Ideally, other factors are held constant, particularly the risk of default. The term structure is generally plotted by the yield curve, which is the graphical depiction of the relationship between yields and time for bonds that are identical except for maturity.

Yield Curve

Yield curves plot the interest rates of same bond with the same characteristics (except maturity) against their corresponding different maturity terms. As can be seen, the yield curve is a chart which illustrates the relationship among yields on bonds that differ only in their term to maturity. Generally, there are different types of yield curves: upward sloping, downward sloping, flat and humped. We would like to give different representation of these three curves. Firstly, upward sloping curve can be defined as ascending sloping or normal curve. Secondly, downward sloping can be defined as descending. If a yield curve is upward sloped, short term interest rates are below long term interest rates. In other words, longer term interest rates are usually higher than shorter term interest rates that why we are saying normal yield curve. It is thought to reflect the higher inflation-risk premium that investors demand for longer term bonds. Downward sloping is sometimes called inverted yield curve assuming the normal yield curve has the positive slope. If a yield curve is downward sloped, long run interest rates are below short term interest rates. This shape is often seen when the market expects interest rates to fall. Under this abnormal and contradictory situation, long-term investors will settle for lower yields now if they think the economy will slow or even decline in the future. An inverted curve may indicate a worsening economic situation in the future. If a yield curve is flat, short term interest rates are equal to long term interest rates. A small or negligible difference between short and long term interest rates occurs later in the economic cycle when interest rates increase due to higher inflation expectations and tighter monetary policy. This is called a shallow or flat yield curve and higher short term rates reflect less available money, as monetary policy is tightened and higher inflation later in the economic cycle. A humped yield curve is formed when yields on intermediate-term issues are above those on short-term issues and the rates on long-term issues decline to levels below those for the short term and then level out. The different types of yield curves are explained in Figure.

A theory of the term structure of interest rates is needed to explain the shape and slope of the yield curve and why it shifts over time. Theories traditionally advanced are the expectations theory, the liquidity premium theory, the preferred habitant theory, and the market segmentation theory. Before we discuss these three alternative hypotheses, we must first discuss two rates i.e. spot rate and forward rate that not only are an integral part of the term structure but also are important in the valuation of bonds. Specifically, the spot rate is defined as the discount rate for a cash flow at a specific maturity. Forward rate is calculated on the basis of markets' expectation of future short-term rates.

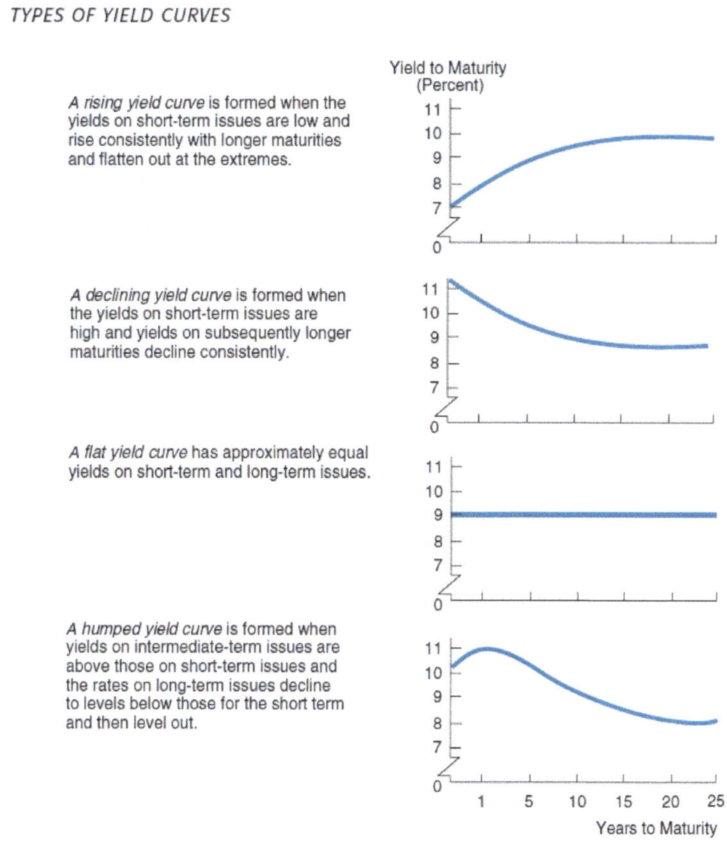

Types of Yield Curve

Expectation Theory: This theory has taken two forms: restrictive and broad. In the restrictive form, it is known as the unbiased or pure expectations theory, and it is based on the following assumptions:

(a) There is a perfect competition in financial markets.

(b) The investors are rational, i.e. they wish to maximise the yield of their holding period.

(c) Investors have perfect foresight, and a large enough body of investors hold uniform expectations about the future level and changes of short-term interest rates and security prices.

(d) There are no transaction costs.

(e) Securities of different maturities are perfect substitutes for each other. i.e. They are homogeneous.

With the help of these assumptions, it is posited that the pure or "unbiased" expectations theory of the term structure of interest rates asserts that financial market participants determine security yields such that the return from holding an n-period security equals the average returns expected from holding a securities of one-year securities over the same n periods. In other words long term rate of interest is equal to an average of the present yield on short term securities plus the expected future yields on short term securities that are expected to prevail over the long period of time. For, each period, the total rate of return is expected to be the same on all securities regardless of time to maturity. In effect, the term structure consists of set of forward rates and a current known rate. Forward rates are rates that are expected to prevail in the future; that is they are un- observable but anticipated future rates.

Under the expectations theory, long rates must be an average of the present and future short-term rates.

Generally, this relationship can be formalized as follows

$$(1+{}_tR_n)=[(1+{}_tR_1)(1+{}_{t+1}r_1)\ldots\ldots\ldots\ldots\ldots\ldots(1+{}_{t+n-1}r_1)]^{1/N}$$

R_n = the actual long-term rate

N = the term to maturity (in years) of long issue

R = the current one-year rate

$t+i\ r1$ = the expected one-year yield during some future period, t + i (these future one-year rates are referred to as forward rates)

Given the relationship set forth in this equation, the formula for computing the one-period forward rate beginning at time t + n and implied in the term structure at time t is

$$1+{}_{t+n}R_{1t}=\frac{(1+{}_tR_{1t})(1+{}_{t+1}r_{1t})(1+{}_{t+2}r_{1t})\ldots(1+{}_{t+n-1}r_{1t})(1+{}_{t+n}r_{1t})}{(1+{}_tR_{1t})(1+{}_{t+1}r_{1t})\ldots(1+{}_{t+n-1}r_{1t})}$$

$$=\frac{(1+{}_tR_{n+1})^{n+1}}{(1+{}_tR_n)^n}$$

$${}_{t+n}r_{1t}=\frac{(1+{}_1R_{n+1})^{n+1}}{(1+{}_tR_n)^n}-1$$

Where,

${}_{t+n}r_{1t}$ is the one-year forward rate prevailing at $t + n$, using the term structure at time t.

For example, a three-year bond would carry an interest rate that is an average of the current rate for one year and the expected forward rates for the next two years. The same principle holds for any number of periods; therefore, the market rate for any period to maturity can be expressed as an average of the current rate and the applicable forward rates. Technically, the average involved is a geometric rather than an arithmetic average.

The rate for the three- year bond referred to earlier must be a geometric average of the current one year rate ($_tR_1$) and the expected forward rates for the subsequent two years.

Therefore, in equation form

$$(1+{}_tR_3)=\left[(1+{}_tR_1)(1+{}_{t+1}r_1)(1+{}_{t+2}r_1)\right]^{1/3}$$

Where

($_tR_3$) = the rate on a three year bond

($_tR_1$) = the current known rate on a one-year bond

($_{t+1}r_1$) = the expected rate on a bond with one year to maturity beginning one year from now

($_{t+2}r_1$) = the expected rate one bond with one year to maturity beginning two years from now

Liquidity Preference theory: The main proponent of this theory is J.R.Hicks. Some people view it as an extension or modification of the pure expectation theory and, therefore sometimes called a biased expectations theory. The liquidity theory states that the interest rates reflect the sum of current and expected short rates, as in the expectations theory, plus liquidity (risk) premiums. Because uncertainty increases with time, investors prefer to lend for the short run. Borrowers, however, prefer to borrow for the long run in order to be assuredof funds. Investors receive a liquidity premium to include them to lend long term, while paying a price premium (in the form of yields) for investing short terms. The implication of this theory is that longer-term bonds should offer higher yields. The difference between expectations theory and the liquidity theory is the recognition that interest rate expectations are uncertain. Risk- averse investors seek to be compensated for this uncertainty. Forward rates and estimated future rates are not the same; they differ by the amount of liquidity premiums.

Market Segmentation Theory: The third major theory of term structure of interest rates is the market segmentation theory propounded by Culbertson. Lutz has called it the theory of risk avoidance. This theory states that various institutional investors, having different maturity needs dictated by the nature of their liabilities, confine themselves to specific maturity segments. Investors are not willing to shift from one maturity sectors to another to take advantage of any opportunities that may arise. Under the market segmentation theory, the shape of yield curve is determined by the supply-and-demand conditions for securities within each of the multiple maturity sectors.

Preferred Habitant Theory: The preferred habitant theory is similar to, but not identical with, the market segmentation theory. Under this hypothesis, investors have preferred maturity sectors, or habitants. For example, a thrift institution with many five year CDs to pay off will not wish to take the reinvestment rate risk that would result from investing in one year Treasury bills. What if imbalances arise in a given maturity range between the demand and supply of funds? The preferred habitat theory states that borrowers and lenders can be induced to shift maturities if they are adequately compensated by an appropriate risk premium, which distinguished this theory from the market segmentation theory. The implications of this theory for the term structure is that both expectations concerning future interest rates and risk premiums play a role, and yield curve can take any shape.

Determinants of General Structure of Interest Rates

- Default Risk
- Call Risk
- Liquidity or Marketability
- Tax Status

Theory of Fructification

In economics, the theory of fructification is a theory of the interest rate which was proposed by French economist and finance minister Anne Robert Jacques Turgot. The term theory of fructification is due to Eugen von Böhm-Bawerk who considered Turgot as the first economist who tried to develop a scientific explanation of the interest rate.

According to Turgot, a capitalist can either lend his money, or employ it in the purchase of a plot of land. Because fruitful land yields an annual rent forever, its price is given by the formula of a perpetual annuity: If A denotes the land's annual rent and r denotes the interest rate, the land price is simply A/r. From this formula, Turgot concluded that "the lower the interest rate, the more valuable is the land." Specifically, if the interest rate approached zero, the land price would become infinite. Because land prices must be finite, it follows that the interest rate is strictly positive. Turgot argued also that the mechanism which keeps interest rates above zero crowds out inefficient capital formation.

Böhm-Bawerk, who sponsored a different interest theory, considered Turgot's approach as circular. However, according to Joseph Schumpeter, the eminent economic historian, "Turgot's contribution is not only by far the greatest performance in the field of interest theory the eighteenth century produced but it clearly foreshadowed much of the best thought of the last decades of the nineteenth."

Much later, economists demonstrated that the theory of fructification can be stated rigorously in a general equilibrium model. They also generalized Turgot's proposition in two respects. First, land which is useful for residential or industrial purposes can be substituted for agricultural land. Second, in a growing economy, the existence of land implies that the interest rate exceeds the growth rate if the land's income share is bounded away from zero. The latter result is notable because it states that land ensures dynamic efficiency.

Yield Curve

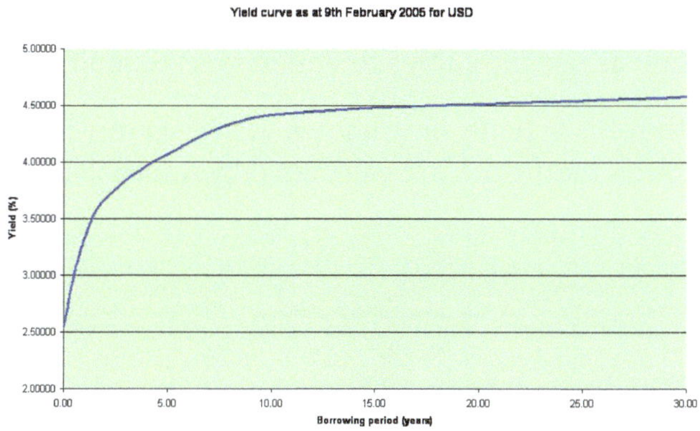

The US dollar yield curve as of February 9, 2005. The curve has a typical upward sloping shape.

In finance, the yield curve is a curve showing several yields or interest rates across different contract lengths (2 month, 2 year, 20 year, etc. ...) for a similar debt contract. The curve shows the relation between the (level of the) interest rate (or cost of borrowing) and the time to maturity, known as the "term", of the debt for a given borrower in a given currency. For example, the U.S. dollar interest rates paid on U.S. Treasury securities for various maturities are closely watched by many traders, and are commonly plotted on a graph such as the one on the right which is informally called "the yield curve". More formal mathematical descriptions of this relation are often called the term structure of interest rates.

The shape of the yield curve indicates the cumulative priorities of all lenders relative to a particular borrower (such as the US Treasury or the Treasury of Japan), or the priorities of a single lender relative to all possible borrowers. With other factors held equal, lenders will prefer to have funds at their disposal, rather than at the disposal of a third party. The interest rate is the "price" paid to convince them to lend. As the term of the loan increases, lenders demand an increase in the interest received. In addition, lenders may be concerned about future circumstances, e.g. a potential default (or rising rates of inflation), so they demand higher interest rates on long-term loans than they demand on shorter-term loans to compensate for the increased risk. Occasionally, when lenders are seeking long-term debt contracts more aggressively than short-term debt contracts, the yield curve "inverts", with interest rates (yields) being lower for the longer periods of repayment so that lenders can attract long-term borrowing.

The yield of a debt instrument is the overall rate of return available on the investment. In general the percentage per year that can be earned is dependent on the length of time that the money is invested. For example, a bank may offer a "savings rate" higher than the normal checking account rate if the customer is prepared to leave money untouched for five years. Investing for a period of time t gives a yield $Y(t)$.

This function Y is called the *yield curve*, and it is often, but not always, an increasing function of t. Yield curves are used by fixed income analysts, who analyze bonds and related securities, to understand conditions in financial markets and to seek trading opportunities. Economists use the curves to understand economic conditions.

The yield curve function Y is actually only known with certainty for a few specific maturity dates, while the other maturities are calculated by interpolation.

Typical Shape

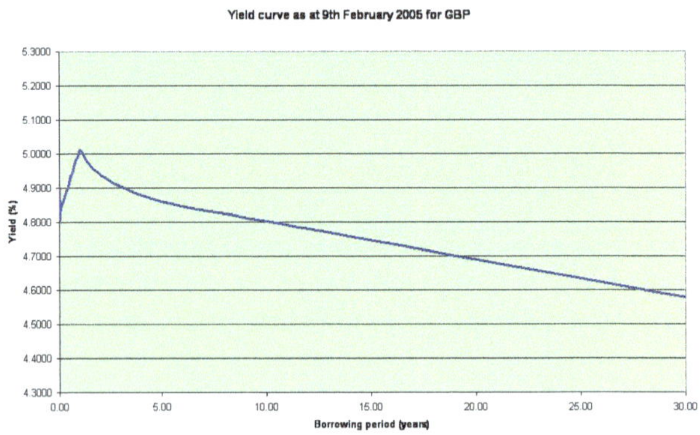

The British pound yield curve on February 9, 2005. This curve is unusual (inverted) in that long-term rates are lower than short-term ones.

Yield curves are usually upward sloping asymptotically: the longer the maturity, the higher the yield, with diminishing marginal increases (that is, as one moves to the right, the curve flattens out). There are two common explanations for upward sloping yield curves. First, it may be that the market is anticipating a rise in the risk-free rate. If investors hold off investing now, they may receive a better rate in the future. Therefore, under the arbitrage pricing theory, investors who are willing to lock their money in now need to be compensated for the anticipated rise in rates—thus the higher interest rate on long-term investments.

Another explanation is that longer maturities entail greater risks for the investor (i.e. the lender). A risk premium is needed by the market, since at longer durations there is more uncertainty and a greater chance of catastrophic events that impact the investment. This explanation depends on the notion that the economy faces more uncertainties in the distant future than in the near term. This effect is referred to as the liquidity spread. If the market expects more volatility in the future, even if interest rates are anticipated to decline, the increase in the risk premium can influence the spread and cause an increasing yield.

The opposite position (short-term interest rates higher than long-term) can also occur. For instance, in November 2004, the yield curve for UK Government bonds was partially *inverted*. The yield for the 10-year bond stood at 4.68%, but was only 4.45% for the 30-year bond. The market's anticipation of falling interest rates causes such incidents. Negative liquidity premiums can also exist if long-term investors dominate the market, but the prevailing view is that a positive liquidity premium dominates, so only the anticipation of falling interest rates will cause an inverted yield curve. Strongly inverted yield curves have historically preceded economic depressions.

The shape of the yield curve is influenced by supply and demand: for instance, if there is a large demand for long bonds, for instance from pension funds to match their fixed liabilities to pensioners, and not enough bonds in existence to meet this demand, then the yields on long bonds can be expected to be low, irrespective of market participants' views about future events.

The yield curve may also be flat or hump-shaped, due to anticipated interest rates being steady, or short-term volatility outweighing long-term volatility.

Yield curves continually move all the time that the markets are open, reflecting the market's reaction to news. A further "stylized fact" is that yield curves tend to move in parallel (i.e., the yield curve shifts up and down as interest rate levels rise and fall).

Types of Yield Curve

There is no single yield curve describing the cost of money for everybody. The most important factor in determining a yield curve is the currency in which the securities are denominated. The economic position of the countries and companies using each currency is a primary factor in determining the yield curve. Different institutions borrow money at different rates, depending on their creditworthiness. The yield curves corresponding to the bonds issued by governments in their own currency are called the government bond yield curve (government curve). Banks with high credit ratings (Aa/AA or above) borrow money from each other at the LIBOR rates. These yield curves are typically a little higher than government curves. They are the most important and widely used in the financial markets, and are known variously as the LIBOR curve or the swap curve. The construction of the swap curve is described below.

Besides the government curve and the LIBOR curve, there are corporate (company) curves. These are constructed from the yields of bonds issued by corporations. Since corporations have less creditworthiness than most governments and most large banks, these yields are typically higher. Corporate yield curves are often quoted in terms of a "credit spread" over the relevant swap curve. For instance the five-year yield curve point for Vodafone might be quoted as LIBOR +0.25%, where 0.25% (often written as 25 basis points or 25bps) is the credit spread.

Normal Yield Curve

From the post-Great Depression era to the present, the yield curve has usually been "normal" meaning that yields rise as maturity lengthens (i.e., the slope of the yield curve is positive). This positive slope reflects investor expectations for the economy to grow in the future and, importantly, for this growth to be associated with a greater expectation that inflation will rise in the future rather than fall. This expectation of higher inflation leads to expectations that the central bank will tighten monetary policy by raising short-term interest rates in the future to slow economic growth and dampen inflationary pressure. It also creates a need for a risk premium associated with the uncertainty about the future rate of inflation and the risk this poses to the future value of cash flows. Investors price these risks into the yield curve by demanding higher yields for maturities further into the future. In a positively sloped yield curve, lenders profit from the passage of time since yields decrease as bonds get closer to maturity (as yield decreases, price *increases*); this is known as rolldown and is a significant component of profit in fixed-income investing (i.e., buying and selling, not necessarily holding to maturity), particularly if the investing is leveraged.

However, a positively sloped yield curve has not always been the norm. Through much of the 19th century and early 20th century the US economy experienced trend growth with persistent deflation, not inflation. During this period the yield curve was typically inverted, reflecting the fact that deflation made current cash flows less valuable than future cash flows. During this period of persistent deflation, a 'normal' yield curve was negatively sloped.

Steep Yield Curve

Historically, the 20-year Treasury bond yield has averaged approximately two percentage points above that of three-month Treasury bills. In situations when this gap increases (e.g. 20-year Treasury yield rises higher than the three-month Treasury yield), the economy is expected to improve quickly in the future. This type of curve can be seen at the beginning of an economic expansion (or after the end of a recession). Here, economic stagnation will have depressed short-term interest rates; however, rates begin to rise once the demand for capital is re-established by growing economic activity.

In January 2010, the gap between yields on two-year Treasury notes and 10-year notes widened to 2.92 percentage points, its highest ever.

Flat or Humped Yield Curve

A flat yield curve is observed when all maturities have similar yields, whereas a humped curve results when short-term and long-term yields are equal and medium-term yields are higher than those of the short-term and long-term. A flat curve sends signals of uncertainty in the economy. This mixed signal can revert to a normal curve or could later result into an inverted curve. It cannot be explained by the Segmented Market theory discussed below.

Inverted Yield Curve

An inverted yield curve occurs when long-term yields fall below short-term yields.

Under unusual circumstances, long-term investors will settle for lower yields now if they think the economy will slow or even decline in the future. Campbell R. Harvey's 1986 dissertation showed that an inverted yield curve accurately forecasts U.S. recessions. An inverted curve has indicated a worsening economic situation in the future 7 times since 1970. The New York Federal Reserve regards it as a valuable forecasting tool in predicting recessions two to six quarters ahead. In addition to potentially signaling an economic decline, inverted yield curves also imply that the market believes inflation will remain low. This is because, even if there is a recession, a low bond yield will still be offset by low inflation. However, technical factors, such as a flight to quality or global economic or currency situations, may cause an increase in demand for bonds on the long end of the yield curve, causing long-term rates to fall. Falling long-term rates in the presence of rising short-term rates is known as "Greenspan's Conundrum".

Relationship to the Business Cycle

The slope of the yield curve is one of the most powerful predictors of future economic growth, inflation, and recessions. One measure of the yield curve slope (i.e. the difference between 10-year Treasury bond rate and the 3-month Treasury bond rate) is included in the Financial Stress Index published by the St. Louis Fed. A different measure of the slope (i.e. the difference between 10-year Treasury bond rates and the federal funds rate) is incorporated into the Index of Leading Economic Indicators published by The Conference Board.

An inverted yield curve is often a harbinger of recession. A positively sloped yield curve is often a harbinger of inflationary growth. Work by Arturo Estrella and Tobias Adrian has established the predictive power of an inverted yield curve to signal a recession. Their models show that when the difference between short-term interest rates (they use 3-month T-bills) and long-term interest rates (10-year Treasury bonds) at the end of a federal reserve tightening cycle is negative or less than 93 basis points positive that a rise in unemployment usually occurs. The New York Fed publishes a monthly recession probability prediction derived from the yield curve and based on Estrella's work.

All the recessions in the US since 1970 (up through 2016) have been preceded by an inverted yield curve (10-year vs 3-month). Over the same time frame, every occurrence of an inverted yield curve has been followed by recession as declared by the NBER business cycle dating committee.

Event	Date of Inversion Start	Date of the Recession Start	Time from Inversion to Recession Start	Duration of Inversion	Time from Recession Start to NBER Announcement	Time from Disinversion to Recession End	Duration of Recession	Time from Recession End to NBER Announcement	Max Inversion
			Months	Months	Months	Months	Months	Months	Basis Points
1970 Recession	Dec-68	Jan-70	13	15	NA	8	11	NA	−52
1974 Recession	Jun-73	Dec-73	6	18	NA	3	16	NA	−159
1980 Recession	Nov-78	Feb-80	15	18	4	2	6	12	−328
1981–1982 Recession	Oct-80	Aug-81	10	12	5	13	16	8	−351
1990 Recession	Jun-89	Aug-90	14	7	8	14	8	21	−16
2001 Recession	Jul-00	Apr-01	9	7	7	9	8	20	−70
2008–2009 Recession	Aug-06	Jan-08	17	10	11	24	18	15	−51
Average since 1969			12	12	7	10	12	15	−147
Std Dev since 1969			3.83	4.72	2.74	7.50	4.78	5.45	138.96

Estrella and others have postulated that the yield curve affects the business cycle via the balance sheet of banks (or bank-like financial institutions). When the yield curve is inverted banks are often caught paying more on short-term deposits than they are making on long-term loans leading to a loss of profitability and reluctance to lend resulting in a credit crunch. When the yield curve is upward sloping, banks can profitably take-in short term deposits and make long-term loans so they are eager to supply credit to borrowers. This eventually leads to a credit bubble.

Theory

There are three main economic theories attempting to explain how yields vary with maturity. Two of the theories are extreme positions, while the third attempts to find a middle ground between the former two.

Market Expectations (Pure Expectations) Hypothesis

This hypothesis assumes that the various maturities are perfect substitutes and suggests that the shape of the yield curve depends on market participants' expectations of future interest rates. It assumes that market forces will cause the interest rates on various terms of bonds to be such that the expected final value of a sequence of short-term investments will equal the known final value of a single long-term investment. If this did not hold, the theory assumes that investors would quickly demand more of the current short-term or long-term bonds (whichever gives the higher expected long-term yield), and this would drive down the return on current bonds of that term and drive up the yield on current bomds of the other term, so as to quickly make the assumed equality of expected returns of the two investment approaches hold.

Using this, futures rates, along with the assumption that arbitrage opportunities will be minimal in future markets, and that futures rates are unbiased estimates of forthcoming spot rates, provide enough information to construct a complete expected yield curve. For example, if investors have an expectation of what 1-year interest rates will be next year, the current 2-year interest rate can be calculated as the compounding of this year's 1-year interest rate by next year's expected 1-year interest rate. More generally, returns (1+ yield) on a long-term instrument are assumed to equal the geometric mean of the expected returns on a series of short-term instruments:

$$(1+i_{lt})^n = (1+i_{st}^{\text{year 1}})(1+i_{st}^{\text{year 2}})\cdots(1+i_{st}^{\text{year } n}),$$

where i_{st} and i_{lt} are the expected short-term and actual long-term interest rates (but i_{st}^{year1} is the actual observed short-term rate for the first year).

This theory is consistent with the observation that yields usually move together. However, it fails to explain the persistence in the shape of the yield curve.

Shortcomings of expectations theory include that it neglects the interest rate risk inherent in investing in bonds.

Liquidity Premium Theory

The liquidity premium theory is an offshoot of the pure expectations theory. The liquidity premium theory asserts that long-term interest rates not only reflect investors' assumptions about future interest rates but also include a premium for holding long-term bonds (investors prefer short term bonds to long term bonds), called the term premium or the liquidity premium. This premium compensates investors for the added risk of having their money tied up for a longer period, including the greater price uncertainty. Because of the term premium, long-term bond yields tend to be higher than short-term yields and the yield curve slopes upward. Long term yields are also higher not just because of the liquidity premium, but also because of the risk premium added by the risk of default from holding a security over the long term. The market expectations hypothesis is combined with the liquidity premium theory:

$$(1+i_{lt})^n = rp_n + ((1+i_{st}^{\text{year1}})(1+i_{st}^{\text{year2}})\cdots(1+i_{st}^{\text{year}n}))$$

Where rp_n is the risk premium associated with an n year bond.

Preferred Habitat Theory

The preferred habitat theory is a variant of the liquidity premium theory, and states that in addition to interest rate expectations, investors have distinct investment horizons and require a meaningful premium to buy bonds with maturities outside their "preferred" maturity, or habitat. Proponents of this theory believe that short-term investors are more prevalent in the fixed-income market, and therefore longer-term rates tend to be higher than short-term rates, for the most part, but short-term rates can be higher than long-term rates occasionally. This theory is consistent with both the persistence of the normal yield curve shape and the tendency of the yield curve to shift up and down while retaining its shape.

Market Segmentation Theory

This theory is also called the segmented market hypothesis. In this theory, financial instruments of different terms are not substitutable. As a result, the supply and demand in the markets for short-term and long-term instruments is determined largely independently. Prospective investors decide in advance whether they need short-term or long-term instruments. If investors prefer their portfolio to be liquid, they will prefer short-term instruments to long-term instruments. Therefore, the market for short-term instruments will receive a higher demand. Higher demand for the instrument implies higher prices and lower yield. This explains the stylized fact that short-term yields are usually lower than long-term yields. This theory explains the predominance of the normal yield curve shape. However, because the supply and demand of the two markets are independent, this theory fails to explain the observed fact that yields tend to move together (i.e., upward and downward shifts in the curve).

Historical Development of Yield Curve Theory

On 15 August 1971, U.S. President Richard Nixon announced that the U.S. dollar would no longer be based on the gold standard, thereby ending the Bretton Woods system and initiating the era of floating exchange rates.

Floating exchange rates made life more complicated for bond traders, including those at Salomon Brothers in New York City. By the middle of the 1970s, encouraged by the head of bond research at Salomon, Marty Liebowitz, traders began thinking about bond yields in new ways. Rather than think of each maturity (a ten-year bond, a five-year, etc.) as a separate marketplace, they began drawing a curve through all their yields. The bit nearest the present time became known as the *short end*—yields of bonds further out became, naturally, the *long end.*

Academics had to play catch up with practitioners in this matter. One important theoretic development came from a Czech mathematician, Oldrich Vasicek, who argued in a 1977 paper that bond prices all along the curve are driven by the short end (under risk neutral equivalent martingale measure) and accordingly by short-term interest rates. The mathematical model for Vasicek's work was given by an Ornstein–Uhlenbeck process, but has since been discredited because the model predicts a positive probability that the short rate becomes negative and is inflexible in creating yield curves of different shapes. Vasicek's model has been superseded by many different models including the Hull–White model (which allows for time varying parameters in the Ornstein–Uhlenbeck process), the Cox–Ingersoll–Ross model, which is a modified Bessel process, and the Heath–Jarrow–Morton framework. There are also many modifications to each of these models, but see the article on short rate model. Another modern approach is the LIBOR market model, introduced by Brace, Gatarek and Musiela in 1997 and advanced by others later. In 1996 a group of derivatives traders led by Olivier Doria (then head of swaps at Deutsche Bank) and Michele Faissola, contributed to an extension of the swap yield curves in all the major European currencies. Until then the market would give prices until 15 years maturities. The team extended the maturity of European yield curves up to 50 years (for the lira, French franc, Deutsche mark, Danish krone and many other currencies including the ecu). This innovation was a major contribution towards the issuance of long dated zero coupon bonds and the creation of long dated mortgages.

Construction of the Full Yield Curve From Market Data

Typical inputs to the money market curve		
Type	**Settlement date**	**Rate (%)**
Cash	Overnight rate	5.58675
Cash	Tomorrow next rate	5.59375
Cash	1m	5.625
Cash	3m	5.71875
Future	Dec-97	5.76
Future	Mar-98	5.77

Future	Jun-98	5.82
Future	Sep-98	5.88
Future	Dec-98	6.00
Swap	2y	6.01253
Swap	3y	6.10823
Swap	4y	6.16
Swap	5y	6.22
Swap	7y	6.32
Swap	10y	6.42
Swap	15y	6.56
Swap	20y	6.56
Swap	30y	6.56
A list of standard instruments used to build a money market yield curve.		
The data is for lending in US dollar, taken from October 6, 1997		

The usual representation of the yield curve is a function P, defined on all future times t, such that P(t) represents the value today of receiving one unit of currency t years in the future. If P is defined for all future t then we can easily recover the yield (i.e. the annualized interest rate) for borrowing money for that period of time via the formula

$$Y(t) = P(t)^{-1/t} - 1.$$

The significant difficulty in defining a yield curve therefore is to determine the function P(t). P is called the discount factor function or the zero coupon bond.

Yield curves are built from either prices available in the *bond market* or the *money market*. Whilst the yield curves built from the bond market use prices only from a specific class of bonds (for instance bonds issued by the UK government) yield curves built from the money market use prices of "cash" from today's LIBOR rates, which determine the "short end" of the curve i.e. for $t \leq$ 3m, interest rate futures which determine the midsection of the curve (3m $\leq t \leq$ 15m) and interest rate swaps which determine the "long end" (1y $\leq t \leq$ 60y).

The example given in the table at the right is known as a LIBOR curve because it is constructed using either LIBOR rates or swap rates. A LIBOR curve is the most widely used interest rate curve as it represents the credit worth of private entities at about A+ rating, roughly the equivalent of commercial banks. If one substitutes the LIBOR and swap rates with government bond yields, one arrives at what is known as a government curve, usually considered the risk free interest rate curve for the underlying currency. The spread between the LIBOR or swap rate and the government bond yield, usually positive, meaning private borrowing is at a premium above government borrowing, of similar maturity is a measure of risk tolerance of the lenders. For the U. S. market, a common benchmark for such a spread is given by the so-called TED spread.

In either case the available market data provides a matrix A of cash flows, each row representing a particular financial instrument and each column representing a point in time. The (i,j)-th element of the matrix represents the amount that instrument i will pay out on day j. Let the vector F represent today's prices of the instrument (so that the i-th instrument has value $F(i)$), then by definition of our discount factor function P we should have that $F = AP$ (this is a matrix multiplication). Actually, noise in the financial markets means it is not possible to find a P that solves this equation exactly, and our goal becomes to find a vector P such that

$$AP = F + \varepsilon$$

where ε is as small a vector as possible (where the size of a vector might be measured by taking its norm, for example).

Note that even if we can solve this equation, we will only have determined $P(t)$ for those t which have a cash flow from one or more of the original instruments we are creating the curve from. Values for other t are typically determined using some sort of interpolation scheme.

Practitioners and researchers have suggested many ways of solving the A*P = F equation. It transpires that the most natural method – that of minimizing ϵ by least squares regression – leads to unsatisfactory results. The large number of zeroes in the matrix A mean that function P turns out to be "bumpy".

In their comprehensive book on interest rate modelling James and Webber note that the following techniques have been suggested to solve the problem of finding P:

1. Approximation using Lagrange polynomials
2. Fitting using parameterised curves (such as splines, the Nelson-Siegel family, the Svensson family, or the Cairns restricted-exponential family of curves). Van Deventer, Imai and Mesler summarize three different techniques for curve fitting that satisfy the maximum smoothness of either forward interest rates, zero coupon bond prices, or zero coupon bond yields
3. Local regression using kernels
4. Linear programming

In the money market practitioners might use different techniques to solve for different areas of the curve. For example, at the short end of the curve, where there are few cashflows, the first few elements of P may be found by bootstrapping from one to the next. At the long end, a regression technique with a cost function that values smoothness might be used.

How the Yield Curve Affects Bond Prices

There is a time dimension to the analysis of bond values. A 10-year bond at purchase becomes a 9-year bond a year later, and the year after it becomes an 8-year bond, etc. Each year the bond moves incrementally closer to maturity, resulting in lower volatility and shorter duration and demanding a lower interest rate when the yield curve is rising. Since falling rates create increasing prices, the value of a bond initially will rise as the lower rates of the shorter maturity become its new market rate. Because a bond is always anchored by its final maturity, the price at some point must change direction and fall to par value at redemption.

A bond's market value at different times in its life can be calculated. When the yield curve is steep, the bond is predicted to have a large capital gain in the first years before falling in price later. When the yield curve is flat, the capital gain is predicted to be much less, and there is little variability in the bond's total returns over time.

Rising (or falling) interest rates rarely rise by the same amount all along the yield curve—the curve rarely moves up in parallel. Because longer-term bonds have a larger duration, a rise in rates will cause a larger capital loss for them, than for short-term bonds. But almost always, the long maturity's rate will change much less, flattening the yield curve. The greater change in rates at the short end will offset to some extent the advantage provided by the shorter bond's lower duration.

Long duration bonds tend to be mean reverting, meaning that they readily gravitate to a long-run average. The middle of the curve (5–10 years) will see the greatest percentage gain in yields if there is anticipated inflation even if interest rates have not changed. The long-end does not move quite as much percentage-wise because of the mean reverting properties.

The yearly 'total return' from the bond is a) the sum of the coupon's yield plus b) the capital gain from the changing valuation as it slides down the yield curve and c) any capital gain or loss from changing interest rates at that point in the yield curve.

Determinants of General Structure of Interest Rates

- Default Risk
- Call Risk
- Liquidity or Marketability
- Tax Status

Yield Spread

It shows the relationship between bond yields and particular features on various bonds such as quality, callability and tax. These are often calculated among different bonds holding maturity constant.

Why Yield Spread?

- Difference in quality of risk of default
- Callable bonds have high yield to maturity (YTM)
- Lesser liquid bonds have high YTM
- Different Tax treatment

References

- Arnott, R. D.; Hsu, J.; Moore, P. (2005). "Fundamental Indexation". Financial Analysts Journal. 60 (2): 83–99. JSTOR 4480658
- N. Anderson, F. Breedon, M. Deacon, A. Derry and M. Murphy (1996). Estimating and Interpreting the Yield Curve. John Wiley & Sons. ISBN 0-471-96207-4
- Fernholz, R.; Garvy, R.; Hannon, J. (1998). "Diversity-Weighted Indexing". Journal of Portfolio Management. 24 (2): 74–82. doi:10.3905/jpm.24.2.74
- *Homer, Sidney; Sylla, Richard Eugene; Sylla, Richard (1996).* A History of Interest Rates. Rutgers University Press. ISBN 978-0-8135-2288-3. Retrieved 2008-10-27
- Haugen, R. A.; Baker, N. L. (1991). "The Efficient Market Inefficiency of Capitalization-Weighted Stock Portfolios". Journal of Portfolio Management. 17 (3): 35–40. doi:10.3905/jpm.1991.409335
- White, Gerald I.; Sondhi, Ashwinpaul; Fried, Dov (1998). The Analysis and Use of Financial Statements. John Wiley & Sons, Inc. ISBN 0-471-11186-4
- Hsu, Jason (2006). "Cap-Weighted Portfolios are Sub-optimal Portfolios". Journal of Investment Management. 4 (3): 1–10
- Donald R. van Deventer; Kenji Imai; Mark Mesler (2004). Advanced Financial Risk Management, An Integrated Approach to Credit Risk and Interest Rate Risk Management. John Wiley & Sons. ISBN 978-0-470-82126-8

2

Understanding Risk and Return in Investment Management

Returns in investment management can be classified into prospective or historical. Usually investment returns contain high amounts of risks. The different types of risks discussed are business risk, liquidity risk, country risk, market risk, exchange and financial risk. This chapter is an overview of the subject matter incorporating all the major aspects of risk and return in investment management.

Basics of Return

The investors invest in any asset in anticipation of return on the same. In case of financial assets, this can also be termed as the financial results of the investment or financial asset. As one of the foremost criteria, an investor can distinguish different financial assets based on return on such financial assets. Returns can be classified as historical or expected i.e. prospective. Returns can be in absolute value i.e. in terms of currency and in relative terms i.e. in terms of %. For example, if an investment purchased one year back at Rs.120 is sold for Rs.132, the absolute return is Rs.12 and the relative return is 10% (i.e.12 / 120). Return in a way represents total gain or loss on investment. The total gain/ loss can comprise of periodic return and change in the value of investment at the end of the holding period.

Hence a basic formula used for calculation of return can be as below:

$$r_t = \frac{P_t - \mathrm{P}_{t-1} + C_t}{P_t - 1}$$

Where r_t is the actual, required or expected return during period t, P_t is the current price, P_{t-1} is the price during the previous time period, and C_t is any cash flow accruing from the investment.

Suppose one has bought a share of ABC Limited at Rs.300 one year back. Over the last year ABC has distributed dividend of Rs.5 per share. If the share of ABC sells at Rs.340 today, what is the return?

The total return is Rs.45 that comprises of Rs.5 of dividend and Rs.40 (Rs.340 – Rs.300) in terms of appreciation in the market price of the share. Hence the % return is Rs.45/Rs.300 i.e. 15%.

In case the share of ABC sells at Rs.280 today what is the return?

The absolute return (-ve)Rs.15 (i.e. Rs.5 dividend and loss of Rs.20 in terms of fall in price), which is

-5% on origninal ivestment of Rs.300.

Holding Period Returns

The holding period return is the return that an investor would get when holding an investment over a period of n years, when the return during year i is given as r_i:

holding period return $= (1+r_1)\times(1+r_2)\times\ldots\times(1+r_n)-1$

Suppose an investment provides the following periodic return over last five years:

Year	1	2	3	4	5
Return (%)	12	15	-8	14	16

The holding period return on the investment is computed as below:

$$(1+r_1)\times(1+r_2)\times(1+r_3)\times(1+r_4)\times(1+r_5)-1$$
$$=(1.12)\times(1.15)\times(0.92)\times(1.14)\times(1.16)-1$$
$$=.5670=56.70\%$$

This can be interpreted as 56.70% return over five year holding period. In case an asset does not provide any periodic return – like annual return in the previous example – the holding period return (HPR) can be calculated as below:

$$HPR=\frac{Ending\ Value\ of\ Investment}{Beginning\ Value\ of\ Investment}-1$$

Example: A financial asset was purchased at Rs.300 and it grew to Rs.370 over five year period. The HPR over three year period is

$$\frac{400}{300}-1=0.3333=33.33\%$$

This return can be converted to effective annual return which can also be termed as annual holding period return or yield as below:

Annual HPR = $(1+HPR)1^{/n}-1$

Where, n is the number of years the investment is held. In the previous example, the annual HPR is: $(1.3333)^{1/3}-1=0.1006=10.06\%$

Expected Return

Unlike historical return, in case of expected returns are predicted for the future with relevant values being predicted. The prediction can be for different expected outcomes. In such case probability is associated with possible outcomes and expected return from an investment is estimated.

$$E(r) = \sum_{i=1}^{n} P_i r_i$$

Suppose there are two shares A and B and rate of returns in different conditions are expected to be as below:

State of the Economy	Probability of occurrence	Rate of Return (%)	
		A	B
Boom	0.50	22	24
Normal	0.30	18	18
Recession	0.20	14	12

The expected return on Share A = 0.50 x 22 + 0.30 x 18 + 0.20 x 14 = 19.2%. Similarly return from Share B = 0.50 x 24 + 0.30 x 18 + 0.20 x 12 = 19.8%.

Rate of Return

In finance, return is a profit on an investment. It comprises any change in value and interest or dividends or other such cash flows which the investor receives from the investment. It may be measured either in absolute terms (e.g., dollars) or as a percentage of the amount invested. The latter is also called the holding period return.

A loss instead of a profit is described as a *negative return.*

Rate of return is a profit on an investment over a period of time, expressed as a proportion of the original investment. The time period is typically a year, in which case the rate of return is referred to as *annual return.*

To compare returns over time periods of different lengths on an equal basis, it is useful to convert each return into an annual equivalent rate of return, or *annualised return.* This conversion process is called *annualisation*, described below.

Return on investment (ROI) is return per dollar invested. It is a measure of investment performance, as opposed to size (c.f. return on equity, return on assets, return on capital employed).

Calculation

The return, or rate of return, can be calculated over a single period, or where there is more than one time period, the return and rate of return over the overall period can be calculated, based upon the return within each sub-period.

Single-period

Return

The return over a single period is:

$$r = \frac{V_f - V_i}{V_i}$$

where:

V_f = final value, including dividends and interest

V_i = initial value

For example, if you hold 100 shares, with a starting price of 10, then the starting value is 100 x 10 = 1,000. If you then collect 0.50 per share in cash dividends, and the ending share price is 9.80, then at the end you have 100 x 0.50 = 50 in cash, plus 100 x 9.80 = 980 in shares, totalling a final value of 1,030. The change in value is 1,030 - 1,000 = 30, so the return is 30 / 1,000 = 3%.

Currency of Measurement

The return, or rate of return, depends on the currency of measurement. For example, suppose a 10,000 USD (US dollar) cash deposit earns 2% interest over a year, so its value at the end of the year is 10,200 USD including interest. The return over the year is 2%, measured in USD. Let us suppose also that the exchange rate to Japanese yen at the start of the year is 120 yen per USD, and 132 yen per USD at the end of the year. The value in yen of one USD has increased by 10% over the period. The deposit is worth 1.2 million yen at the start of the year, and 10,200 x 132 = 1,346,400 yen at the end of the year. The return on the deposit over the year in yen terms is therefore:

$$\frac{1,346,400 - 1,200,000}{1,200,000} = 12.2\%$$

This is the rate of return experienced either by an investor who starts with yen, converts to dollars, invests in the USD deposit, and converts the eventual proceeds back to yen; or for any investor, who wishes to measure the return in Japanese yen terms, for comparison purposes.

Annualisation

Without any reinvestment, a return R over a period of length t is equivalent to a rate of return:

$$\frac{R}{t}$$

For example, 20,000 USD returned on an initial investment of 100,000 USD is a return of 20%. If the 20,000 USD is paid in 5 installments of 4,000 USD, with no reinvestment, and no information about the timing of the installments, the rate of return is 4,000 / 100,000 = 20% / 5 = 4% per year.

Assuming returns are reinvested however, due to the effect of compounding, the relationship between a rate of return r, and a return R over a period of length t is:

$$1+R=(1+r)^t$$

which can be used to convert the return R to a compound rate of return r:

$$r=(1+R)^{\frac{1}{t}}-1=\sqrt[t]{1+R}-1$$

For example, a 33.1% return over 3 months is equivalent to a rate of:

$$\sqrt[3]{1.331}-1=10\%$$

per month with reinvestment.

Annualisation is the process described above, of converting a return R to an annual rate of return r, where the length of the period t is measured in years and the rate of return r is per year.

According to the CFA Institute's Global Investment Performance Standards (GIPS),

> *"Returns for periods of less than one year must not be annualized."*

This is because an annualised rate of return over a period of less than one year is statistically unlikely to be indicative of the annualised rate of return over the long run, where there is risk involved. Annualizing a return over a period of less than one year might be interpreted as suggesting that the rest of the year is most likely to have the same rate of return, effectively projecting that rate of return over the whole year.

Note that this does not to apply to interest rates or yields where there is no significant risk involved. It is common practice to quote an annualised rate of return for borrowing or lending money for periods shorter than a year, such as overnight interbank rates.

Logarithmic or Continuously Compounded Return

The logarithmic return or continuously compounded return, also known as force of interest, is:

$$R = \ln\left(\frac{V_f}{V_i}\right)$$

and the logarithmic rate of return is:

$$r_{\log} = \frac{\ln\left(\frac{V_f}{V_i}\right)}{t}$$

or equivalently it is the solution r to the equation:

$$V_f = V_i e^{rt}$$

where:

r = logarithmic rate of return

t = length of time period

For example, if a stock is priced at 3.570 USD per share at the close on one day, and at 3.575 USD per share at the close the next day, then the logarithmic return is: ln(3.575/3.570) = 0.0014, or 0.14%.

Annualisation of Logarithmic Return

Under an assumption of reinvestment, the relationship between a logarithmic return and a R logarithmic rate of return r over a period of time of length t is:

$$R = rt$$

so trivially $r = \frac{R}{t}$ is the annualised logarithmic rate of return for a return R, where t is measured in years.

For example, if the logarithmic return of a security per trading day is 0.14%, assuming 250 trading days in a year, then the annualised logarithmic rate of return is 0.14%/(1/250) = 0.14% x 250 = 35%

Returns over Multiple Periods

When returns are calculated over more than one time period, they are based on the investment value at the beginning of each period.

If the returns over n successive time sub-periods are $r_1, r_2, r_3, \cdots, r_n$, then the cumulative return or overall return over the overall time period is:

$$(1+r_1)(1+r_2)\cdots(1+r_n)-1$$

If the returns are logarithmic returns however, the logarithmic return over the overall time period is:

$$\sum_{i=1}^{n} r_i = r_1 + r_2 + r_3 + \cdots + r_n$$

Arithmetic Average Rate of Return

The arithmetic average rate of return over n time periods of equal length is defined as:

$$\overline{r} = \frac{1}{n}\sum_{i=1}^{n} r_i = \frac{1}{n}(r_1 + \cdots + r_n)$$

If you have a sequence of logarithmic rates of return over equal successive periods, the appropriate method of finding their average is the arithmetic average rate of return.

Geometric Average Rate of Return

For ordinary returns, if there is no reinvestment, and losses are made good by topping up the capital invested, so that the value is brought back to its starting-point at the beginning of each new sub-period, use the arithmetic average return.

With reinvestment of all gains and losses however, the appropriate average rate of return is the geometric average rate of return over n periods, which is:

$$\overline{r}_{\text{geometric}} = \left(\prod_{i=1}^{n}(1+r_i)\right)^{-} - 1 = \sqrt{\prod_{i=1}^{n}(1+r_i)} - 1$$

Note that the geometric average return is equivalent to the cumulative return over the whole n periods, converted into a rate of return per period.

In the case where the periods are each a year long, and there is no reinvestment of returns, the annualized cumulative return is the arithmetic average return. Where the individual sub-periods are each a year, and there is reinvestment of returns, the annualized cumulative return is the geometric average rate of return.

For example, assuming reinvestment, the cumulative return for annual returns: 50%, -20%, 30% and -40% is:

$$(1+0.50)(1-0.20)(1+0.30)(1-0.40)-1=-0.0640=-6.40\%$$

and the geometric average is:

$$\sqrt[4]{(1+0.50)(1-0.20)(1+0.30)(1-0.40)}-1=-0.0164=-1.64\%$$

which is equal to the annualized cumulative return:

$$\sqrt[4]{1-0.0640}-1=-0.0164$$

Comparisons between Various Rates of Return

External Flows

In the presence of external flows, such as cash or securities moving into or out of the portfolio, the return should be calculated by compensating for these movements. This is achieved using methods such as the *time-weighted return*. Time-weighted returns compensate for the impact of cash flows. This is useful to assess the performance of a money manager on behalf of his/her clients, where typically the clients control these cash flows.

Fees

To measure returns net of fees, allow the value of the portfolio to be reduced by the amount of the fees. To calculate returns gross of fees, compensate for them by treating them as an external flow, and exclude accrued fees from valuations.

Money-weighted Rate of Return

Like the time-weighted return, the money-weighted rate of return (MWRR) or dollar-weighted rate of return also takes cash flows into consideration. They are useful evaluating and comparing cases where the money manager controls cash flows, for example private equity. (Contrast with the true time-weighted rate of return, which is most applicable to measure the performance of a money manager who does not have control over external flows.)

Internal Rate of Return

The internal rate of return (IRR) (which is a variety of money-weighted rate of return) is the rate of return which makes the net present value of cash flows zero. It is a solution *r* satisfying the following equation:

$$\mathrm{NPV}=\sum_{t=0}^{n}\frac{C_t}{(1+r)^t}=0$$

where:

NPV = net present value

and

C_t = net cash flow at time t, including the initial value C_0 and final value C_n, net of any other flows at the beginning and at the end respectively. (The initial value is treated as an inflow, and the final value as an outflow.)

When the internal rate of return is greater than the cost of capital, (which is also referred to as the required rate of return), the investment adds value, i.e. the net present value of cash flows, discounted at the cost of capital, is greater than zero. Otherwise, the investment does not add value.

Note that there is not always an internal rate of return for a particular set of cash flows (i.e. the existence of a real solution to the equation $NPV = 0$ depends on the pattern of cash flows). There may also be more than one real solution to the equation, requiring some interpretation to determine the most appropriate one.

Comparing Ordinary Return with Logarithmic Return

The value of an investment is doubled if the return r = +100%, that is, if r_{log} = ln($200 / $100) = ln(2) = 69.3%. The value falls to zero when r = -100%. The ordinary return can be calculated for any non-zero initial investment value, and any final value, positive or negative, but the logarithmic return can only be calculated when $V_f / V_i > 0$.

Ordinary returns and logarithmic returns are only equal when they are zero, but they are approximately equal when they are small. The difference between them is large only when percent changes are high. For example, an arithmetic return of +50% is equivalent to a logarithmic return of 40.55%, while an arithmetic return of -50% is equivalent to a logarithmic return of -69.31%.

Comparison of ordinary returns and logarithmic returns
for an initial investment of $100

Initial investment, V_i	$100	$100	$100	$100	$100	$100	$100
Final investment, V_f	$0	$50	$99	$100	$101	$150	$200
Profit/loss, $V_f - V_i$	−$100	−$50	−$1	$0	$1	$50	$100
Ordinary return, r	-100%	-50%	−1%	0%	1%	50%	100%
Logarithmic return, r_{log}	−∞	−69.31%	−1.005%	0%	0.995%	40.55%	69.31%

Symmetry of Logarithmic Returns

Logarithmic returns are useful for mathematical finance. One of the advantages is that the logarithmic returns are symmetric, while ordinary returns are not: positive and negative percent ordinary returns of equal magnitude do not cancel each other out and result in a net change, but logarithmic returns of equal magnitude but opposite signs will cancel each other out. This means that an investment of $100 that yields an arithmetic return of 50% followed by an arithmetic return of -50% will result in $75, while an investment of $100 that yields a logarithmic return of 50% followed by a logarithmic return of -50% will come back to $100.

Comparing Geometric with Arithmetic Average Rates of Return

The geometric average rate of return is in general less than the arithmetic average return. The two averages are equal if (and only if) all the sub-period returns are equal. This is a consequence of the AM–GM inequality. The difference between the annualized return and average annual return increases with the variance of the returns – the more volatile the performance, the greater the difference.

For example, a return of +10%, followed by −10%, gives an arithmetic average return of 0%, but the overall result over the 2 sub-periods is 110% x 90% = 99% for an overall return of −1%. The order in which the loss and gain occurs does not affect the result.

For a return of +20%, followed by −20%, this again has an average return of 0%, but an overall return of −4%.

A return of +100%, followed by −100%, has an average return of 0%, but an overall return of −100%, as the final value is 0.

In cases of leveraged investments, even more extreme results are possible: a return of +200%, followed by −200%, has an average return of 0%, but an overall return of −300%.

This pattern is not followed in the case of logarithmic returns, due to their symmetry, as noted above. A logarithmic return of +10%, followed by −10%, gives an overall return of 10% - 10% = 0%, and an average rate of return of zero also.

Average Returns and Overall Returns

Investment returns are often published as "average returns". In order to translate average returns into overall returns, compound the average returns over the number of periods.

Example #1 Level Rates of Return				
	Year 1	Year 2	Year 3	Year 4
Rate of Return	5%	5%	5%	5%
Geometric Average at End of Year	5%	5%	5%	5%

Capital at End of Year	$105.00	$110.25	$115.76	$121.55
Dollar Profit/(Loss)				$21.55

The geometric average rate of return was 5%. Over 4 years, this translates into an overall return of:

$$1.05^4 - 1 = 21.55\%$$

Example #2 Volatile Rates of Return, including losses				
	Year 1	Year 2	Year 3	Year 4
Rate of Return	50%	-20%	30%	-40%
Geometric Average at End of Year	50%	9.5%	16%	-1.6%
Capital at End of Year	$150.00	$120.00	$156.00	$93.60
Dollar Profit/(Loss)				($6.40)

The geometric average return over the 4-year period was -1.64%. Over 4 years, this translates into an overall return of:

$$(1 - 0.0164)^4 - 1 = -6.4\%$$

Example #3 Highly Volatile Rates of Return, including losses				
	Year 1	Year 2	Year 3	Year 4
Rate of Return	-95%	0%	0%	115%
Geometric Average at End of Year	-95%	-77.6%	-63.2%	-42.7%
Capital at End of Year	$5.00	$5.00	$5.00	$10.75
Dollar Profit/(Loss)				($89.25)

The geometric average return over the 4-year period was -42.74%. Over 4 years, this translates back into an overall return of:

$$(1 - 0.4274)^4 - 1 = -89.25\%$$

Annual Returns and Annualized Returns

Care must be taken not to confuse annual with annualized returns. An annual rate of return is a return over a period of one year, such as January 1 through December 31, or June 3, 2006 through June 2, 2007, whereas an annualized rate of return is a rate of return per year, measured over a period either longer or shorter than one year, such as a month, or two years, annualised for comparison with a one-year return.

The appropriate method of annualization depends on whether returns are reinvested or not.

For example, a return over one month of 1% converts to an annualized rate of return of 12.7% = $((1+0.01)^{12} - 1)$. This means if reinvested, earning 1% return every month, the return over 12 months would compound to give a return of 12.7%.

As another example, a two-year return of 10% converts to an annualized rate of return of 4.88% = $((1+0.1)^{(12/24)} - 1)$, assuming reinvestment at the end of the first year. In other words, the geometric average return per year is 4.88%.

In the cash flow example below, the dollar returns for the four years add up to $265. Assuming no reinvestment, the annualized rate of return for the four years is: $265 ÷ ($1,000 x 4 years) = 6.625% (per year).

Cash Flow Example on $1,000 Investment				
	Year 1	Year 2	Year 3	Year 4
Dollar Return	$100	$55	$60	$50
ROI	10%	5.5%	6%	5%

Uses

- Rates of return are useful for making investment decisions. For nominal risk investments such as savings accounts or Certificates of Deposit, the investor considers the effects of reinvesting/compounding on increasing savings balances over time to project expected gains into the future. For investments in which capital is at risk, such as stock shares, mutual fund shares and home purchases, the investor also takes into consideration the effects of price volatility and risk of loss.
- Ratios typically used by financial analysts to compare a company's performance over time or compare performance between companies include return on investment (ROI), return on equity, and return on assets.
- In the capital budgeting process, companies would traditionally compare the internal rates of return of different projects to decide which projects to pursue in order to maximize returns for the company's stockholders. Other tools employed by companies in capital budgeting include payback period, net present value, and profitability index.
- A return may be adjusted for taxes to give the after-tax rate of return. This is done in geographical areas or historical times in which taxes consumed or consume a significant portion of profits or income. The after-tax rate of return is calculated by multiplying the rate of return by the tax rate, then subtracting that percentage from the rate of return.
- A return of 5% taxed at 15% gives an after-tax return of 4.25%

  0.05 x 0.15 = 0.0075

  0.05 - 0.0075 = 0.0425 = 4.25%

- A return of 10% taxed at 25% gives an after-tax return of 7.5%

  0.10 x 0.25 = 0.025

  0.10 - 0.025 = 0.075 = 7.5%

  Investors usually seek a higher rate of return on taxable investment returns than on non-taxable investment returns, and the proper way to compare returns taxed at different rates of tax is after tax, from the end-investor's perspective.

- A return may be adjusted for inflation. When return is adjusted for inflation, the resulting return in real terms measures the change in purchasing power between the start and the end of the period. Any investment with a nominal annual return (i.e. unadjusted annual return) less than the annual inflation rate represents a loss of value in real terms, even when the nominal annual return is greater than 0%, and the purchasing power at the end of the period is less than the purchasing power at the beginning.

- Many online poker tools include ROI in a player's tracked statistics, assisting users in evaluating an opponent's performance.

Time Value of Money

Investments generate returns to the investor to compensate the investor for the time value of money.

Factors that investors may use to determine the rate of return at which they are willing to invest money include:

- estimates of future inflation rates
- assessment of the risk of the investment, i.e. the uncertainty of returns (including how likely it is that investors will receive interest/dividend payments they expect and the return of their full capital, with or without any possible additional capital gain)
- whether or not the investors want the money available ("liquid") for other uses.

The time value of money is reflected in the interest rate that a bank offers for deposit accounts, and also in the interest rate that a bank charges for a loan such as a home mortgage. The "risk-free" rate on US dollar investments is the rate on U.S. Treasury bills, because this is the highest rate available without risking capital.

The rate of return which an investor requires from a particular investment is called the discount rate, and is also referred to as the (opportunity) cost of capital. Each investment has a different discount rate, based on the cash flow expected in future from the investment. The higher the risk, the higher the discount rate (rate of return) the investor will demand from the investment.

Compounding or Reinvesting

The annualized return of an investment depends on whether or not the return, including interest and dividends, from one period is reinvested in the next period. If the return is reinvested, it contributes to the starting value of capital invested for the next period (or reduces it, in the case of a negative return). Compounding reflects the effect of the return in the next period on the return from the previous period.

For example, if an investor puts $1,000 in a 1-year certificate of deposit (CD) that pays an annual interest rate of 4%, paid quarterly, the CD would earn 1% interest per quarter on the account balance. The account uses compound interest, meaning the account balance is cumulative, including interest previously reinvested and credited to the account. Unless the interest is withdrawn at the end of each quarter, it will earn more interest in the next quarter.

Compound Interest Example				
	1st Quarter	2nd Quarter	3rd Quarter	4th Quarter
Capital at the beginning of the period	$1,000	$1,010	$1,020.10	$1,030.30
Dollar return for the period	$10	$10.10	$10.20	$10.30
Account Balance at end of the period	$1,010.00	$1,020.10	$1,030.30	$1,040.60
Quarterly return	1%	1%	1%	1%

At the beginning of the second quarter, the account balance is $1,010.00, which then earns $10.10 interest altogether during the second quarter. The extra dime was interest on the additional $10 investment from the previous interest accumulated in the account. The annualized return (annual percentage yield, compound interest) is higher than for simple interest, because the interest is reinvested as capital and then itself earns interest. The yield or annualized return on the above investment is $4.06\% = (1.01)^4 - 1$.

Foreign Currency Returns

As explained above, the return, or rate or return, depends on the currency of measurement. In the example given above, a US dollar cash deposit which returns 2% over a year, measured in US dollars, returns 12.2% measured in Japanese yen, over the same period, if the US dollar increases in value by 10% against the Japanese yen over the same period. The return in Japanese yen is the result of compounding the 2% US dollar return on the cash deposit with the 10% return on US dollars against Japanese yen:

$$1.02 \times 1.1 - 1 = 12.2\%$$

In more general terms, the return in a second currency is the result of compounding together the two returns:

$$(1+r_i)(1+r_c)-1$$

where

r_i is the return on the investment in the first currency (US dollars in our example), and

r_c is the return on the first currency against the second currency (which in our example is the return on US dollars against Japanese yen).

This holds true only because there are no flows in or out over the period. If there are flows, it is necessary to recalculate the return in the second currency using one of the methods for compensating for flows.

Foreign Currency Returns over Multiple Periods

It is not meaningful to compound together returns for consecutive periods measured in different currencies. Before compounding together returns over consecutive periods, recalculate or adjust the returns using a single currency of measurement.

Example

A portfolio increases in value in Singapore dollars by 10% over the 2015 calendar year (with no flows in or out of the portfolio over the year). In the first month of 2016, it increases in value by another 7%, in US dollars. (Again, there are no inflows or outflows over the January 2016 period.)

What is the return on the portfolio, from the beginning of 2015, to the end of January 2016?

The answer is that there is insufficient data to compute a return, in any currency, without knowing the return for both periods in the same currency.

If the return in 2015 was 10% in Singapore dollars, and the Singapore dollar rose by 5% against the US dollar over 2015, then so long as there were no flows in 2015, the return over 2015 in US dollars is:

$$1.1 \times 1.05 - 1 = 15.5\%$$

The return between the beginning of 2015 and the end of January 2016 in US dollars is:

$$1.155 \times 1.07 - 1 = 23.585\%$$

Returns when Capital is at Risk

Risk and Volatility

Investments carry varying amounts of risk that the investor will lose some or all of the invested capital. For example, investments in company stock shares put capital at risk. Unlike capital invested in a savings account, the share price, which is the market value of a stock share at a certain point in time, depends on what someone is willing to pay for it, and the price of a stock share tends to change constantly when the market for that share is open. If the price is relatively stable, the stock is said to have "low volatility." If the price often changes a great deal, the stock has "high volatility."

Example: Stock with low volatility and a regular quarterly dividend, reinvested

End of:	1st Quarter	2nd Quarter	3rd Quarter	4th Quarter
Dividend	$1	$1.01	$1.02	$1.03
Stock Price	$98	$101	$102	$99
Shares Purchased	0.010204	0.01	0.01	0.010404
Total Shares Held	1.010204	1.020204	1.030204	1.040608
Investment Value	$99	$103.04	$105.08	**$103.02**
Quarterly ROI	-1%	4.08%	1.98%	-1.96%

US Income Tax on Investment Returns

To the right is an example of a stock investment of one share purchased at the beginning of the year for $100.

- The quarterly dividend is reinvested at the quarter-end stock price.
- The number of shares purchased each quarter = ($ Dividend)/($ Stock Price).
- The final investment value of $103.02 compared with the initial investment of $100 means the return is $3.02 or 3.02%.
- The continuously compounded rate of return in this example is:

$$\ln\left(\frac{103.02}{100}\right) = 2.98\%.$$

To calculate the capital gain for US income tax purposes, include the reinvested dividends in the cost basis. The investor received a total of $4.06 in dividends over the year, all of which were reinvested, so the cost basis increased by $4.06.

- Cost Basis = $100 + $4.06 = $104.06
- Capital gain/loss = $103.02 - $104.06 = -$1.04 (a capital loss)

For U.S. income tax purposes therefore, dividends were $4.06, the cost basis of the investment was $104.06 and if the shares were sold at the end of the year, the sale value would be $103.02, and the capital loss would be $1.04.

Mutual Fund and Investment Company Returns

Mutual funds, exchange-traded funds (ETFs), and other equitized investments (such as unit investment trusts or UITs, insurance separate accounts and related variable products such as variable universal life insurance policies and variable annuity contracts, and bank-sponsored commingled funds, collective benefit funds or common trust funds) are essentially portfolios of various investment securities such as stocks, bonds and money market instruments which are equitized by selling shares or units to investors. Investors and other parties are interested to know how the investment has performed over various periods of time.

Performance is usually quantified by a fund's total return. In the 1990s, many different fund companies were advertising various total returns—some cumulative, some averaged, some with or without deduction of sales loads or commissions, etc. To level the playing field and help investors compare performance returns of one fund to another, the U.S. Securities and Exchange Commission (SEC) began requiring funds to compute and report total returns based upon a standardized formula—so called "SEC Standardized total return" which is the average annual total return assuming reinvestment of dividends and distributions and deduction of sales loads or charges. Funds may compute and advertise returns on other bases (so-called "non-standardized" returns), so long as they also publish no less prominently the "standardized" return data.

Subsequent to this, apparently investors who had sold their fund shares after a large increase in the share price in the late 1990s and early 2000s were ignorant of how significant the impact of income/capital gain taxes was on their fund "gross" returns. That is, they had little idea how significant the difference could be between "gross" returns (returns before federal taxes) and "net" returns (after-tax returns). In reaction to this apparent investor ignorance, and perhaps for other reasons, the SEC made further rule-making to require mutual funds to publish in their annual prospectus, among other things, total returns before and after the impact of U.S federal individual income taxes. And further, the after-tax returns would include 1) returns on a hypothetical taxable account after deducting taxes on dividends and capital gain distributions received during the illustrated periods and 2) the impacts of the items in #1) as well as assuming the entire investment shares were sold at the end of the period (realizing capital gain/loss on liquidation of the shares). These after-tax returns would apply of course only to taxable accounts and not to tax-deferred or retirement accounts such as IRAs.

Lastly, in more recent years, "personalized" brokerage account statements have been demanded by investors. In other words, the investors are saying more or less that the fund returns may not be what their actual account returns are, based upon the actual investment account transaction history. This is because investments may have been made on various dates and additional purchases and withdrawals may have occurred which vary in amount and date and thus are unique to the particular account. More and more funds and brokerage firms are now providing personalized account returns on investor's account statements in response to this need.

With that out of the way, here's how basic earnings and gains/losses work on a mutual fund. The fund records income for dividends and interest earned which typically increases the value of the mutual fund shares, while expenses set aside have an offsetting impact to share value. When the fund's investments increase (decrease) in market value, so too the fund shares value increases (or decreases). When the fund sells investments at a profit, it turns or reclassifies that paper profit or unrealized gain into an actual or realized gain. The sale has no effect on the value of fund shares but it has reclassified a component of its value from one bucket to another on the fund books—which will have future impact to investors. At least annually, a fund usually pays dividends from its net income (income less expenses) and net capital gains realized out to shareholders as an IRS requirement. This way, the fund pays no taxes but rather all the investors in taxable accounts do. Mutual fund share prices are typically valued each day the stock or bond markets are open and typically the value of a share is the net asset value of the fund shares investors own.

Total Returns

Mutual funds report total returns assuming reinvestment of dividend and capital gain distributions. That is, the dollar amounts distributed are used to purchase additional shares of the funds as of the reinvestment/ex-dividend date. Reinvestment rates or factors are based on total distributions (dividends plus capital gains) during each period.

Average Annual Total Return (Geometric)

US mutual funds are to compute average annual total return as prescribed by the U.S. Securities and Exchange Commission (SEC) in instructions to form N-1A (the fund prospectus) as the average annual compounded rates of return for 1-year, 5-year and 10-year periods (or inception of the fund if shorter) as the "average annual total return" for each fund. The following formula is used:

$$P(1+T)^n = ERV$$

Where:

P = a hypothetical initial payment of $1,000.

T = average annual total return.

n = number of years.

ERV = ending redeemable value of a hypothetical \$1,000 payment made at the beginning of the 1-, 5-, or 10-year periods at the end of the 1-, 5-, or 10-year periods (or fractional portion).

Solving for T gives

$$T=\left(\frac{ERV}{P}\right)^{1/n}-1$$

Mutual Fund Capital Gain Distributions

Mutual funds include capital gains as well as dividends in their return calculations. Since the market price of a mutual fund share is based on net asset value, a capital gain distribution is offset by an equal decrease in mutual fund share value/price. From the shareholder's perspective, a capital gain distribution is not a net gain in assets, but it is a realized capital gain (coupled with an equivalent decrease in unrealized capital gain).

Example

Example: Balanced mutual fund during boom times with regular annual dividends, reinvested at time of distribution, initial investment \$1,000 at end of year 0, share price \$14.21

	Year 1	Year 2	Year 3	Year 4	Year 5
Dividend per share	\$0.26	\$0.29	\$0.30	\$0.50	\$0.53
Capital gain distribution per share	\$0.06	\$0.39	\$0.47	\$1.86	\$1.12
Total distribution per share	\$0.32	\$0.68	\$0.77	\$2.36	\$1.65
Share price at end of year	\$17.50	\$19.49	\$20.06	\$20.62	**\$19.90**
Shares owned before distribution	70.373	71.676	74.125	76.859	84.752
Total distribution (distribution per share x shares owned)	\$22.52	\$48.73	\$57.10	\$181.73	\$141.60
Share price at distribution	\$17.28	\$19.90	\$20.88	\$22.98	\$21.31
Shares purchased (total distribution / price)	1.303	2.449	2.734	7.893	6.562
Shares owned after distribution	71.676	74.125	76.859	84.752	**91.314**

- After five years, an investor who reinvested all distributions would own 91.314 shares valued at \$19.90 per share. The return over the five-year period is \$19.90 × 91.314 / \$1,000 - 1 = 81.71%

- Geometric average annual total return with reinvestment = ($19.90 × 91.314 / $1,000) ^ (1 / 5) - 1 = 12.69%
- An investor who did not reinvest would have received total distributions (cash payments) of $5.78 per share. The return over the five-year period for such an investor would be ($19.90 + $5.78) / $14.21 - 1 = 80.72%, and the arithmetic average rate of return would be 80.72%/5 = 16.14% per year.

Abnormal Return

In finance, an abnormal return is the difference between the actual return of a security and the expected return. Abnormal returns are sometimes triggered by "events." Events can include mergers, dividend announcements, company earning announcements, interest rate increases, lawsuits, etc. all of which can contribute to an abnormal return. Events in finance can typically be classified as information or occurrences that have not already been priced by the market.

Stock Market

In stock market trading, abnormal returns are the differences between a single stock or portfolio's performance and the expected return over a set period of time. Usually a broad index, such as the S&P 500 or a national index like the Nikkei 225, is used as a benchmark to determine the expected return. For example, if a stock increased by 5% because of some news that affected the stock price, but the average market only increased by 3% and the stock has a beta of 1, then the abnormal return was 2% (5% - 3% = 2%). If the market average performs better (after adjusting for beta) than the individual stock, then the abnormal return will be negative.

$$\text{Abnormal Return} = \text{Actual Return} - \text{Expected Return}$$

Cumulative Abnormal Return

Cumulative abnormal return, or CAR, is the sum of all abnormal returns. Cumulative Abnormal Returns are usually calculated over small windows, often only days. This is because evidence has shown that compounding daily abnormal returns can create bias in the results.

Return on Investment

Return on Investment (ROI) is the benefit to an investor resulting from an investment of some resource. A high ROI means the investment gains compare favorably to investment cost. As a performance measure, ROI is used to evaluate the efficiency of an investment or to compare the efficiency of a number of different investments. In purely economic terms, it is one way of considering profits in relation to capital invested.

Purpose

In business, the purpose of the "return on investment" (ROI) metric is to measure, per period, rates of return on money invested in an economic entity in order to decide whether or not to undertake an investment. It is also used as indicator to compare different project investments within a project portfolio. The project with best ROI is prioritized. Recently, the concept has also been applied to scientific funding agencies (e.g. National Science Foundation) investments in research of open source hardware and subsequent returns for direct digital replication.

ROI and related metrics provide a snapshot of profitability, adjusted for the size of the investment assets tied up in the enterprise. ROI is often compared to expected (or required) rates of return on money invested. ROI is not net present value-adjusted and most school books describe it with a "Year 0" investment and two to three years income.

Marketing decisions have obvious potential connection to the numerator of ROI (profits), but these same decisions often influence assets usage and capital requirements (for example, receivables and inventories). Marketers should understand the position of their company and the returns expected.

In a survey of nearly 200 senior marketing managers, 77 percent responded that they found the "return on investment" metric very useful.

Return on investment may be calculated in terms other than financial gain. For example, social return on investment (SROI) is a principles-based method for measuring extra-financial value (i.e., environmental and social value not currently reflected in conventional financial accounts) relative to resources invested. It can be used by any entity to evaluate impact on stakeholders, identify ways to improve performance, and enhance the performance of investments.

Risk with ROI Usage

As a decision tool it is simple to understand. The simplicity of the formula allows to freely choose variables e.g., length of the calculation time, if overhead cost should be included, or details such as what variables are used to calculate income or cost components. To use ROI as an indicator for prioritizing investment projects is risky, since usually little is defined together with the ROI figure that explains what is making up the figure.

When long term investments take place, the need for Net Present Value adjustment is high. Similar to Discounted Cash Flow you should use Discounted ROI instead.

Calculation

For a single-period review, divide the return (net profit) by the resources that were committed (investment):

return on investment = Net income / Investment

where:

Net income = gross profit – expenses.

investment = stock + market outstanding + claims.

or

return on investment = (gain from investment – cost of investment) / cost of investment

or

return on investment = (revenue – cost of goods sold) / cost of goods sold

Property

Complications in calculating ROI can occur when real property is refinanced, or a second mortgage is taken out. Interest on a second, or refinanced, loan may increase, and loan fees may be charged, both of which can reduce the ROI, when the new numbers are used in the ROI equation. There may also be an increase in maintenance costs and property taxes, and an increase in utility rates if the owner of a residential rental or commercial property pays these expenses.

Complex calculations may also be required for property bought with an adjustable rate mortgage (ARM) with a variable escalating rate charged annually through the duration of the loan.

Marketing Investment

Marketing not only influences net profits but also can affect investment levels too. New plants and equipment, inventories, and accounts receivable are three of the main categories of investments that can be affected by marketing decisions.

RoA, RoNA, RoC, and RoIC, in particular, are similar measures with variations on how 'investment' is defined.

Risk

Usually, investment returns are not known with certainty. In the context of investment, risk is defined as the chance of suffering a loss. Assets (real or financial) which have a greater chance of loss are considered more risky than those with a lower chance of loss. Risk may be used interchangeably with the term uncertainty to refer to the variability of returns associated with a given asset. The common sources of risk are as below:

- Firm Specific Risks
  - Business Risk: Investors can be subject to bad performance of business or the firm due to several reasons like weak demand for the products/ services, technological changes, supply related problems, mismanagement.
  - Financial Risk: This emanates from the fact that the particular firm has borrowings as its source of finance. Higher the borrowing, higher is the interest outflow. In good condition, borrowing helps better return on shareholders' funds – an implication of financial leverage. However in bad condition, borrowing can harm the firm. Borrowings also invite default risk.
- Investor-Specific Risks
  - Interest rate risk: Change in interest rates can affect the value of interest bearing securities. There is an inverse relationship between interest rate and value of interest bearing securities like bonds, debentures, etc. The equity shares are also affected indirectly by the movement in interest rates.
  - Liquidity risk: The investors can have problem in converting the securities into cash because of inadequate market or for the fact that the securities are not listed. Sometimes, irrespective of listing, the securities are not traded in the market.
  - Market risk: This is not related to the particular firm's performance, but depends upon the overall market condition being pessimistic or optimistic because of several underlying factors. During a bullish period, prices of most of the equity shares move up and vice versa in bearish period. Market also moves in cycles.
- Firm and Investor Risks
  - Event Risk: These are the risks caused due to unforeseen events related to the company or a sector like ad adverse court judgment, regulatory policy change, sudden demise of key people of the organization.
  - Exchange Rate Risk: This risk is caused due to change in currency rates. Companies having exports as major source revenue or imports of supplies are vulnerable to this risk. In the present era of globalization, it is difficult for any company to be immune to this risk.
  - Purchasing-power risk: These are caused by changes in price level in the country. Inflationary conditions can affect the firms adversely because of decrease in demand.

- Tax risk: Change in tax rates for companies and/ or investors can have adverse impact. Sudden change in tax rules may affect the companies favorably or unfavorably. Tax being a major element of expense for any company, adverse change in tax rates can be taxing for the company concerned. Investors' residual income can also be affected by change in personal income tax rules and rates.

Unsystematic vs. Systematic Risk

The risks that can be controlled by diversifying the portfolio of financial assets are known as unsystematic or diversifiable risk. The risks that cannot be controlled by investors are known as systematic risk. Market risks are essentially systematic risk where as investor or firm related risks can be diversified. Systematic risks affect the companies across the system.

Diversification (Finance)

In finance, diversification is the process of allocating capital in a way that reduces the exposure to any one particular asset or risk. A common path towards diversification is to reduce risk or volatility by investing in a variety of assets. If asset prices do not change in perfect synchrony, a diversified portfolio will have less variance than the weighted average variance of its constituent assets, and often less volatility than the least volatile of its constituents.

Diversification is one of two general techniques for reducing investment risk. The other is hedging.

Examples

The simplest example of diversification is provided by the proverb "Don't put all your eggs in one basket". Dropping the basket will break all the eggs. Placing each egg in a different basket is more diversified. There is more risk of losing one egg, but less risk of losing all of them. On the other hand, having a lot of baskets may increase costs.

In finance, an example of an undiversified portfolio is to hold only one stock. This is risky; it is not unusual for a single stock to go down 50% in one year. It is less common for a portfolio of 20 stocks to go down that much, especially if they are selected at random. If the stocks are selected from a variety of industries, company sizes and types it is still less likely.

Since the mid-1970s, it has also been argued that geographic diversification would generate superior risk-adjusted returns for large institutional investors by reducing overall portfolio risk while capturing some of the higher rates of return offered by the emerging markets of Asia and Latin America.

Return Expectations while Diversifying

If the prior expectations of the returns on all assets in the portfolio are identical, the expected return on a diversified portfolio will be identical to that on an undiversified portfolio. Some assets will do better than others; but since one does not know in advance which assets will perform better, this fact cannot be exploited in advance. The return on a diversified portfolio can never exceed that of the top-performing investment, and indeed will always be lower than the highest return (unless all returns are identical). Conversely, the diversified portfolio's return will always be higher than that of the worst-performing investment. So by diversifying, one loses the chance of having invested solely in the single asset that comes out best, but one also avoids having invested solely in the asset that comes out worst. That is the role of diversification: it narrows the range of possible outcomes. Diversification need not either help or hurt expected returns, unless the alternative non-diversified portfolio has a higher expected return.

Amount of Diversification

There is no magic number of stocks that is diversified versus not. Sometimes quoted is 30, although it can be as low as 10, provided they are carefully chosen. This is based on a result from John Evans and Stephen Archer. Similarly, a 1985 book reported that most value from diversification comes from the first 15 or 20 different stocks in a portfolio. More stocks give lower price volatility.

Given the advantages of diversification, many experts recommend maximum diversification, also known as "buying the market portfolio." Unfortunately, identifying that portfolio is not straightforward. The earliest definition comes from the capital asset pricing model which argues the maximum diversification comes from buying a *pro rata* share of all available assets. This is the idea underlying index funds.

Diversification has no maximum so long as more assets are available. Every equally weighted, uncorrelated asset added to a portfolio can add to that portfolio's measured diversification. When assets are not uniformly uncorrelated, a weighting approach that puts assets in proportion to their relative correlation can maximize the available diversification.

"Risk parity" is an alternative idea. This weights assets in inverse proportion to risk, so the portfolio has equal risk in all asset classes. This is justified both on theoretical grounds, and with the pragmatic argument that future risk is much easier to forecast than either future market price or future economic footprint. "Correlation parity" is an extension of risk parity, and is the solution whereby each asset in a portfolio has an equal correlation with the portfolio, and is therefore the "most diversified portfolio". Risk parity is the special case of correlation parity when all pair-wise correlations are equal.

Effect of Diversification on Variance

One simple measure of financial risk is variance of the return on the portfolio. Diversification can lower the variance of a portfolio's return below what it would be if the entire portfolio were invested in the asset with the lowest variance of return, even if the assets' returns are uncorrelated. For example, let asset X have stochastic return x and asset Y have stochastic return y, with respective return variances σ_x^2 and σ_y^2. If the fraction q of a one-unit (e.g. one-million-dollar) portfolio is placed in asset X and the fraction $1-q$ is placed in Y, the stochastic portfolio return is $qx+(1-q)y$. If x and y are uncorrelated, the variance of portfolio return is $\text{var}(qx+(1-q)y)=q^2\sigma_x^2+(1-q)^2\sigma_y^2$. The variance-minimizing value of q is $q=\sigma_y^2/[\sigma_x^2+\sigma_y^2]$, which is strictly between 0 and 1. Using this value of q in the expression for the variance of portfolio return gives the latter as $\sigma_x^2\sigma_y^2/[\sigma_x^2+\sigma_y^2]$, which is less than what it would be at either of the undiversified values $q=1$ and $q=0$ (which respectively give portfolio return variance of σ_x^2 and σ_y^2). Note that the favorable effect of diversification on portfolio variance would be enhanced if x and were negatively correlated but diminished (though not eliminated) if they were positively correlated.

In general, the presence of more assets in a portfolio leads to greater diversification benefits, as can be seen by considering portfolio variance as a function of n, the number of assets. For example, if all assets' returns are mutually uncorrelated and have identical variances σ_x^2, portfolio variance is minimized by holding all assets in the equal proportions $1/n$.. Then the portfolio return's variance equals $\text{var}[(1/n)x_1+(1/n)x_2+...+(1/n)x_n]=n(1/n^2)\sigma_x^2$ $=\sigma_x^2/n$, which is monotonically decreasing in n.

The latter analysis can be adapted to show why *adding* uncorrelated volatile assets to a portfolio, thereby increasing the portfolio's size, is not diversification, which involves subdividing the portfolio among many smaller investments. In the case of adding investments, the portfolio's return is $x_1+x_2+...+x_n$ instead of $(1/n)x_1+(1/n)x_2+...+(1/n)x_n$, and the variance of the portfolio return if the assets are uncorrelated is $\text{var}[x_1+x_2+...+x_n]=\sigma_x^2+\sigma_x^2+...+\sigma_x^2=n\sigma_x^2$, which is *increasing* in n rather than decreasing. Thus, for example, when an insurance company adds more and more uncorrelated policies to its portfolio, this expansion does not itself represent diversification—the diversification occurs in the spreading of the insurance company's risks over a large number of part-owners of the company.

Diversification with Correlated Returns via an Equally Weighted Portfolio

The expected return on a portfolio is a weighted average of the expected returns on each individual asset:

$$\mathbb{E}[R_P]=\sum_{i=1}^{n}x_i\mathbb{E}[R_i]$$

where x_i is the proportion of the investor's total invested wealth in asset .

The variance of the portfolio return is given by:

$$\underbrace{\mathrm{Var}(R_P)}_{\equiv\sigma_P^2} = \mathbb{E}[R_P - \mathbb{E}[R_P]]^2.$$

Inserting in the expression for $\mathbb{E}[R_P]$:

$$\sigma_P^2 = \mathbb{E}\left[\sum_{i=1}^{n} x_i R_i - \sum_{i=1}^{n} x_i \mathbb{E}[R_i]\right]^2.$$

Rearranging:

$$\sigma_P^2 = \mathbb{E}\left[\sum_{i=1}^{n} x_i (R_i - \mathbb{E}[R_i])\right]^2$$

$$\sigma_P^2 = \mathbb{E}\left[\sum_{i=1}^{n}\sum_{j=1}^{n} x_i x_j (R_i - \mathbb{E}[R_i])(R_j - \mathbb{E}[R_j])\right]$$

$$\sigma_P^2 = \mathbb{E}\left[\sum_{i=1}^{n} x_i^2 (R_i - \mathbb{E}[R_i])^2 + \sum_{i=1}^{n}\sum_{j=1,i\neq j}^{n} x_i x_j (R_i - \mathbb{E}[R_i])(R_j - \mathbb{E}[R_j])\right]$$

$$\sigma_P^2 = \sum_{i=1}^{n} x_i^2 \underbrace{\mathbb{E}\left[R_i - \mathbb{E}[R_i]\right]^2}_{\equiv\sigma_i^2} + \sum_{i=1}^{n}\sum_{j=1,i\neq j}^{n} x_i x_j \underbrace{\mathbb{E}\left[(R_i - \mathbb{E}[R_i])(R_j - \mathbb{E}[R_j])\right]}_{\equiv\sigma_{ij}}$$

$$\sigma_P^2 = \sum_{i=1}^{n} x_i^2 \sigma_i^2 + \sum_{i=1}^{n}\sum_{j=1,i\neq j}^{n} x_i x_j \sigma_{ij}$$

where σ_i^2 is the variance on asset i and σ_{ij} is the covariance between assets i and j.

In an equally weighted portfolio, $x_i = x_j = \frac{1}{n}, \forall i, j$. The portfolio variance then becomes:

$$\sigma_P^2 = \frac{1}{n} n\bar{\sigma}_i^2 + n(n-1)\frac{1}{n}\frac{1}{n}\bar{\sigma}_{ij}$$

where $\bar{\sigma}_{ij}$ is the average of the covariances σ_{ij} for $i \neq j$ and $\bar{\sigma}_i^2$ is the average of the variances. Simplifying, we obtain

$$\sigma_P^2 = \frac{1}{n}\bar{\sigma}_i^2 + \frac{n-1}{n}\bar{\sigma}_{ij}.$$

As the number of assets grows we get the asymptotic formula:

$$\lim_{n \to \infty} \sigma_P^2 = \bar{\sigma}_{ij}.$$

Thus, in an equally weighted portfolio, the portfolio variance tends to the average of covariances between securities as the number of securities becomes arbitrarily large.

Diversifiable and Non-diversifiable Risk

The capital asset pricing model introduced the concepts of diversifiable and non-diversifiable risk. Synonyms for diversifiable risk are idiosyncratic risk, unsystematic risk, and security-specific risk. Synonyms for non-diversifiable risk are systematic risk, beta risk and market risk.

If one buys all the stocks in the S&P 500 one is obviously exposed only to movements in that index. If one buys a single stock in the S&P 500, one is exposed both to index movements and movements in the stock based on its underlying company. The first risk is called "non-diversifiable," because it exists however many S&P 500 stocks are bought. The second risk is called "diversifiable," because it can be reduced by diversifying among stocks.

In the presence of per-asset investment fees, there is also the possibility of overdiversifying to the point that the portfolio's performance will suffer because the fees outweigh the gains from diversification.

The capital asset pricing model argues that investors should only be compensated for non-diversifiable risk. Other financial models allow for multiple sources of non-diversifiable risk, but also insist that diversifiable risk should not carry any extra expected return. Still other models do not accept this contention.

An Empirical Example Relating Diversification to Risk Reduction

In 1977 Edwin Elton and Martin Gruber worked out an empirical example of the gains from diversification. Their approach was to consider a population of 3,290 securities available for possible inclusion in a portfolio, and to consider the average risk over all possible randomly chosen n-asset portfolios with equal amounts held in each included asset, for various values of n. Their results are summarized in the following table. The result for n=30 is close to n=1,000, and even four stocks provide most of the reduction in risk compared with one stock.

Number of Stocks in Portfolio	Average Standard Deviation of Annual Portfolio Returns	Ratio of Portfolio Standard Deviation to Standard Deviation of a Single Stock
1	49.24%	1.00
2	37.36	0.76

4	29.69	0.60
6	26.64	0.54
8	24.98	0.51
10	23.93	0.49
20	21.68	0.44
30	20.87	0.42
40	20.46	0.42
50	20.20	0.41
400	19.29	0.39
500	19.27	0.39
1,000	19.21	0.39

Corporate Diversification Strategies

In corporate portfolio models, diversification is thought of as being vertical or horizontal. Horizontal diversification is thought of as expanding a product line or acquiring related companies. Vertical diversification is synonymous with integrating the supply chain or amalgamating distributions channels.

Non-incremental diversification is a strategy followed by conglomerates, where the individual business lines have little to do with one another, yet the company is attaining diversification from exogenous risk factors to stabilize and provide opportunity for active management of diverse resources.

History

Diversification is mentioned in the Bible, in the book of Ecclesiastes which was written in approximately 935 B.C.:

> But divide your investments among many places,
>
> for you do not know what risks might lie ahead.

Diversification is also mentioned in the Talmud. The formula given there is to split one's assets into thirds: one third in business (buying and selling things), one third kept liquid (e.g. gold coins), and one third in land (real estate).

Diversification is mentioned in Shakespeare (*Merchant of Venice*):

> My ventures are not in one bottom trusted,
>
> Nor to one place; nor is my whole estate
>
> Upon the fortune of this present year:
>
> Therefore, my merchandise makes me not sad.

The modern understanding of diversification dates back to the work of Harry Markowitz in the 1950s.

Systemic Risk

In finance, systemic risk is the risk of collapse of an entire financial system or entire market, as opposed to risk associated with any one individual entity, group or component of a system, that can be contained therein without harming the entire system. It can be defined as "financial *system* instability, potentially catastrophic, caused or exacerbated by idiosyncratic events or conditions in financial intermediaries". It refers to the risks imposed by *interlinkages* and *interdependencies* in a system or market, where the failure of a single entity or cluster of entities can cause a cascading failure, which could potentially bankrupt or bring down the entire system or market. It is also sometimes erroneously referred to as "systematic risk".

Explanation

Systemic risk has been associated with a bank run which has a cascading effect on other banks which are owed money by the first bank in trouble, causing a cascading failure. As depositors sense the ripple effects of default, and liquidity concerns cascade through money markets, a panic can spread through a market, with a sudden flight to quality, creating many sellers but few buyers for illiquid assets. These interlinkages and the potential "clustering" of bank runs are the issues which policy makers consider when addressing the issue of protecting a system against systemic risk. Governments and market monitoring institutions (such as the U.S. Securities and Exchange Commission (SEC), and central banks) often try to put policies and rules in place with the justification of safeguarding the interests of the market as a whole, claiming that the trading participants in financial markets are entangled in a web of dependencies arising from their interlinkage. In simple English, this means that some companies are viewed as too big and too interconnected to fail. Policy makers frequently claim that they are concerned about protecting the resiliency of the system, rather than any one individual in that system. Systemic risk arises because of the interaction of market participants, and therefore can be seen as a form of endogenous risk.

Systemic risk should not be confused with market or price risk as the latter is specific to the item being bought or sold and the effects of market risk are isolated to the entities dealing in that specific item. This kind of risk can be mitigated by hedging an investment by entering into a mirror trade.

Insurance is often easy to obtain against "systemic risks" because a party issuing that insurance can pocket the premiums, issue dividends to shareholders, enter insolvency proceedings if a catastrophic event ever takes place, and hide behind limited liability. Such insurance, however, is not effective for the insured entity.

One argument that was used by financial institutions to obtain special advantages in bankruptcy for derivative contracts was a claim that the market is both critical and fragile.

Systemic risk can also be defined as the likelihood and degree of negative consequences to the larger body. With respect to federal financial regulation, the systemic risk of a financial institution is the likelihood and the degree that the institution's activities will negatively affect the larger economy such that unusual and extreme federal intervention would be required to ameliorate the effects.

A general definition of systemic risk which is not limited by its mathematical approaches, model assumptions or focus on one institution, and which is also the first operationalizable definition of systemic risk encompassing the systemic character of financial, political, environmental, and many other risks, was put forth in 2010.

The Systemic Risk Centre at the London School of Economics is focused on the study of systemic risk. It finds that systemic risk is a form of endogenous risk, hence frustrating empirical measurements of systemic risk.

Measurement of Systemic Risk

TBTF/TICTF

According to the Property Casualty Insurers Association of America, there are two key assessments for measuring systemic risk, the "too big to fail" (TBTF) and the "too interconnected to fail" (TICTF) tests. First, the TBTF test is the traditional analysis for assessing the risk of required government intervention. TBTF can be measured in terms of an institution's size relative to the national and international marketplace, market share concentration, and competitive barriers to entry or how easily a product can be substituted. Second, the TICTF test is a measure of the likelihood and amount of medium-term net negative impact to the larger economy of an institution's failure to be able to conduct its ongoing business. The impact is measure beyond the institution's products and activities to include the economic multiplier of all other commercial activities dependent specifically on that institution. The impact is also dependent on how correlated an institution's business is with other systemic risks.

TBTF

Too Big To Fail: The traditional analysis for assessing the risk of required government intervention is the "Too Big to Fail" Test (TBTF). TBTF can be measured in terms of an institution's size relative to the national and international marketplace, market share concentration (using the Herfindahl-Hirschman Index for example), and competitive barriers to entry or how easily a product can be substituted. While there are large companies in most financial marketplace segments, the national insurance marketplace is spread among thousands of companies, and the barriers to entry in a business where capital is the primary input are relatively minor. The policies of one homeowners insurer can be relatively easily substituted for another or picked up by a state residual market provider, with limits on the underwriting fluidity primarily stemming from state-by-state regulatory impediments, such as limits on pricing and capital mobility. During the recent financial crisis, the collapse of the American International Group (AIG) posed a significant systemic risk to the financial system. There are arguably either no or extremely few insurers that are TBTF in the U.S. marketplace.

TICTF

Too Interconnected to Fail: A more useful systemic risk measure than a traditional TBTF test is a "Too Interconnected to Fail" (TICTF) assessment. An intuitive TICTF analysis has been at the heart of most recent federal financial emergency relief decisions. TICTF is a measure of the likelihood and amount of medium-term net negative impact to the larger economy of an institution's failure to be able to conduct its ongoing business. The impact is measured not just on the institution's products and activities, but also the economic multiplier of all other commercial activities dependent specifically on that institution. It is also dependent on how correlated an institution's business is with other systemic risk.

Criticisms of Systemic Risk Measurements

Critisisms of systemic risk measurements: Danielsson et al. express concerns about systemic risk measurements, such as SRISK and CoVaR, because they are based on market outcomes that happen multiple times a year, so that the probability of systemic risk as measured does not correspond to the actual systemic risk in the financial system. Systemic financial crises happen once every 43 years for a typical OECD country and measurements of systemic risk should target that probability.

SRISK

A financial institution represents a systemic risk if it becomes undercapitalized when the financial system as a whole is undercapitalized. In a single risk factor model, Brownlees and Engle, build a systemic risk measure named SRISK. SRISK can be interpreted as the amount of capital that needs to be injected into a financial firm as to restore a certain form of minimal capital requirement. SRISK has several nice properties: SRISK is expressed in monetary terms and is, therefore, easy to interpret. SRISK can be easily aggregated across firms to provide industry and even country specific aggregates. Last, the computation of SRISK involves variables which may be viewed on their own as risk measures, namely the size of the financial firm, the leverage (ratio of assets to market capitalization), and a measure of how the return of the firm evolves with the market (some sort of time varying conditional beta but with emphasis on the tail of the distribution). Because these three dimensions matter simultaneously in the SRISK measure, one may expect to obtain a more balanced indicator than if one had used either one of the three risk variables individually.

Whereas the initial Brownlees and Engle model is tailored to the US market, the extension by Engle, Jondeau, and Rockinger allows for various factors, time varying parameters, and is therefore more adapted to the European market. One factor captures worldwide variations of financial markets, another one the variations of European markets. Then this extension allows for a country specific factor. By taking into account different factors, one captures the notion that shocks to the US or Asian markets may affect Europe but also that bad news within Europe (such as the news about a potential default of one of the countries) matters for Europe. Also, there may be country specific news that do not affect Europe nor the USA but matter for a given country. Empirically the last factor is found to be less relevant than the worldwide or European factor.

Since RISK is measured in terms of currency, the industry aggregates may also be related to Gross Domestic Product. As such one obtains a measure of domestic systemically important banks.

The SRISK Systemic Risk Indicator is computed automatically on a weekly basis and made available to the community. For the US model SRISK and other statistics may be found under the Volatility Lab of NYU Stern School website and for the European model under the Center of Risk Management (CRML) website of HEC Lausanne.

Valuation of Assets and Derivatives Under Systemic Risk

Inadequacy of Classic Valuation Models

One problem when it comes to the valuation of derivatives, debt, or equity under systemic risk is that financial interconnectedness has to be modelled. One particular problem is posed by closed valuations chains, as exemplified here for four firms A, B, C, and D:

> B might hold shares of A, C holds some debt of B, D owns a derivative issued by C, and A owns some debt of D.

For instance, the share price of A could influence all other asset values, including itself.

The Merton (1974) Model

Situations as the one explained earlier, which are present in mature financial markets, cannot be modelled within the single-firm Merton model, but also not by its straightforward extensions to multiple firms with potentially correlated assets. To demonstrate this, consider two financial firms, $i = 1, 2$, with limited liability, which both own system-exogenous assets of a value $a_i \geq 0$ at a maturity $T \geq 0$, and which both owe a single amount of zero coupon debt $d_i \geq 0$, , due at time T. "System-exogenous" here refers to the assumption, that the business asset a_i is not influenced by the firms in the considered financial system. In the classic single firm Merton model, it now holds at maturity for the equity $s_i \geq 0$ and for the recovery value $r_i \geq 0$ of the debt, that

$$r_i = \min\{d_i, a_i\}$$

and

$$s_i = (a_i - d_i)^+.$$

Equity and debt recovery value, s_i and r_i, are thus uniquely and immediately determined by the value a_i of the exogenous business assets. Assuming that the a_i are, for instance, defined by a Black-Scholes dynamic (with or without correlations), risk-neutral no-arbitrage pricing of debt and equity is straightforward.

Non-trivial Asset Value Equations

Consider now again two such firms, but assume that firm 1 owns 5% of firm two's equity and 20% of its debt. Similarly, assume that firm 2 owns 3% of firm one's equity and 10% of its debt. The equilibrium price equations, or liquidation value equations, at maturity are now given by

$$r_1 = \min\{d_1, a_1 + 0.05s_2 + 0.2r_2\}$$

$$r_2 = \min\{d_2, a_2 + 0.03s_1 + 0.1r_1\}$$

$$s_1 = (a_1 + 0.05s_2 + 0.2r_2 - d_1)^+$$

$$s_2 = (a_2 + 0.03s_1 + 0.1r_1 - d_2)^+.$$

This example demonstrates, that systemic risk in the form of financial interconnectedness can already lead to a non-trivial, non-linear equation system for the asset values if only two firms are involved.

Over- and Underestimation of Default Probabilities

It is known that modelling credit risk while ignoring cross-holdings of debt or equity can lead to an under-, but also an over-estimation of default probabilities. The need for proper structural models of financial interconnectedness in quantitative risk management - be it in research or practice - is therefore obvious.

Structural Models Under Financial Interconnectedness

The first authors to consider structural models for financial systems where each firm could own debt of any other firm were Eisenberg and Noe in 2001. In their model, no equity could be cross-owned, and debt had to be of one seniority level, only. In 2002, Suzuki published a model in which equity could be cross-owned as well. His model was developed independently of Eisenberg and Noe's. Elsinger's publication of 2009 was the first in which debt could be of different seniorities, hence allowing to model, for instance, senior and junior debt, while correctly accounting for the order of priority. His model allowed equity cross-ownership, too. With Fischer (2014), the first model which also allowed derivatives was introduced. The fact that Elsinger was unaware of Suzuki's publications, Fischer was unaware of Elsinger's, and the fact that other authors re-discovered parts of Suzuki's and Elsinger's results shows that the research in this field is still somewhat unconsolidated.

Risk-neutral Valuation: Price Indeterminacy and Open Problems

Generally speaking, risk-neutral pricing in structural models of financial interconnectedness requires unique equilibrium prices at maturity in dependence of the exogenous asset price vector, which can be random. While financially interconnected systems with debt and equity cross-ownership without derivatives are fairly well understood in the sense that relatively weak conditions on the ownership structures in the form of ownership matrices are required to warrant uniquely determined price equilibria, the Fischer (2014) model needs very strong conditions on derivatives - which are defined in dependence on any other liability of the considered financial system - to be able to guarantee uniquely determined prices of all system-endogenous liabilities. Furthermore, it is known that there exist examples with no solutions at all, finitely many solutions (more than one), and infinitely many solutions. At present, it is unclear how weak conditions on derivatives can be chosen to still be able to apply risk-neutral pricing in financial networks with systemic risk. It is noteworthy, that the price indeterminacy that evolves from multiple price equilibria is fundamentally different from price indeterminacy that stems from market incompleteness.

Factors

Factors that are found to support systemic risks are:

1. Economic implications of models are not well understood. Though each individual model may be made accurate, the facts that (1) all models across the board use the same theoretical basis, and (2) the relationship between financial markets and the economy is not known lead to aggravation of systemic risks.

2. Liquidity risks are not accounted for in pricing models used in trading on the financial markets. Since all models are not geared towards this scenario, all participants in an illiquid market using such models will face systemic risks.

Diversification

Risks can be reduced in four main ways: avoidance, diversification, hedging and insurance by transferring risk. Systematic risk, also called market risk or un-diversifiable risk, is a risk of a security that cannot be reduced through diversification. Participants in the market, like hedge funds, can be the source of an increase in systemic risk and the transfer of risk to them may, paradoxically, increase the exposure to systemic risk.

Until recently, many theoretical models of finance pointed towards the stabilizing effects of a diversified (i.e., dense) financial system. Nevertheless, some recent work has started to challenge this view, investigating conditions under which diversification may have ambiguous effects on systemic risk. Within a certain range, financial interconnections serve as a shock-absorber (i.e., connectivity engenders robustness and risk-sharing prevails). But beyond the tipping point, interconnections might serve as a shock-amplifier (i.e., connectivity engenders fragility and risk-spreading prevails).

Regulation

One of the main reasons for regulation in the marketplace is to reduce systemic risk. However, regulation arbitrage – the transfer of commerce from a regulated sector to a less regulated or unregulated sector – brings markets a full circle and restores systemic risk. For example, the banking sector was brought under regulations in order to reduce systemic risks. Since the banks themselves could not give credit where the risk (and therefore returns) were high, it was primarily the insurance sector which took over such deals. Thus the systemic risk migrated from one sector to another and proves that regulation of only one industry cannot be the sole protection against systemic risks.

Project Risks

In the fields of project management and cost engineering, systemic risks include those risks that are not unique to a particular project and are not readily manageable by a project team at a given point in time. These risks may be driven by the nature of a company's project system (e.g., funding projects before the scope is defined), capabilities, or culture. They may also be driven by the level of technology in a project or the complexity of a project's scope or execution strategy.

Systemic Risk and Insurance

In February 2010, international insurance economics think tank, The Geneva Association, published a 110-page analysis of the role of insurers in systemic risk.

In the report, the differing roles of insurers and banks in the global financial system and their impact on the crisis are examined. A key conclusion of the analysis is that the core activities of insurers and reinsurers do not pose systemic risks due to the specific features of the industry:

- Insurance is funded by up-front premia, giving insurers strong operating cashflow without the requirement for wholesale funding;

- Insurance policies are generally long-term, with controlled outflows, enabling insurers to act as stabilisers to the financial system;
- During the hard test of the financial crisis, insurers maintained relatively steady capacity, business volumes and prices.

Applying the most commonly cited definition of systemic risk, that of the Financial Stability Board (FSB), to the core activities of insurers and reinsurers, the report concludes that none are systemically relevant for at least one of the following reasons:

- Their limited size means that there would not be disruptive effects on financial markcts;
- An insurance insolvency develops slowly and can often be absorbed by, for example, capital raising, or, in a worst case, an orderly wind down;
- The features of the interrelationships of insurance activities mean that contagion risk would be limited.

The report underlines that supervisors and policymakers should focus on activities rather than financial institutions when introducing new regulation and that upcoming insurance regulatory regimes, such as Solvency II in the European Union, already adequately address insurance activities.

However, during the financial crisis, a small number of quasi-banking activities conducted by insurers either caused failure or triggered significant difficulties. The report therefore identifies two activities which, when conducted on a widespread scale without proper risk control frameworks, have the potential for systemic relevance.

- Derivatives trading on non-insurance balance sheets;
- Mis-management of short-term funding from commercial paper or securities lending.

The industry has put forward five recommendations to address these particular activities and strengthen financial stability:

- The implementation of a comprehensive, integrated and principle-based supervision framework for insurance groups, in order to capture, among other things, any non-insurance activities such as excessive derivative activities.
- Strengthening liquidity risk management, particularly to address potential mis-management issues related to short-term funding.
- Enhancement of the regulation of financial guarantee insurance, which has a very different business model than traditional insurance.
- The establishment of macro-prudential monitoring with appropriate insurance representation.

- The strengthening of industry risk management practices to build on the lessons learned by the industry and the sharing experiences with supervisors on a global scale.

Since the publication of The Geneva Association statement, in June 2010, the International Association of Insurance Supervisors (IAIS) issued its position statement on key financial stability issues. A key conclusion of the statement was that, "The insurance sector is susceptible to systemic risks generated in other parts of the financial sector. For most classes of insurance, however, there is little evidence of insurance either generating or amplifying systemic risk, within the financial system itself or in the real economy."

Other organisations such as the CEA and the Property Casualty Insurers Association of America (PCI) have issued reports on the same subject.

Discussion

Systemic risk evaluates the likelihood and degree of negative consequences to the larger body. The term "systemic risk" is frequently used in recent discussions related to the economic crisis, such as the Subprime mortgage crisis. The systemic risk of a financial institution is the likelihood and the degree that the institution's activities will negatively affect the larger economy such that unusual and extreme federal intervention would be required to ameliorate the effects. The failing of financial firms in 2008 caused systemic risk to the larger economy. Chairman Barney Frank has expressed concerns regarding the vulnerability of highly leveraged financial systems to systemic risk and the US government has debated how to address financial services regulatory reform and systemic risk.

Risk Preferences

By default investors are risk averse, the difference among investors is only with respect to the relative risk averseness. However, based on the preferences for risk, investors can be classified into three categories as below:

- Risk Neutral
- Risk Averse
- Risk Seeking

Risk of a Single Asset: Please refer Figure. Which stock – A or B – is more risky compared to the other? Do note that both the stocks have same average rate of return of 15%. The return distribution of Stock B is more flat than that of Stock A, i.e. the range of possibilities of returns is more compared to Stock A. From this figure one can conclude that Stock B is more risky than Stock A.

Probability Distribution

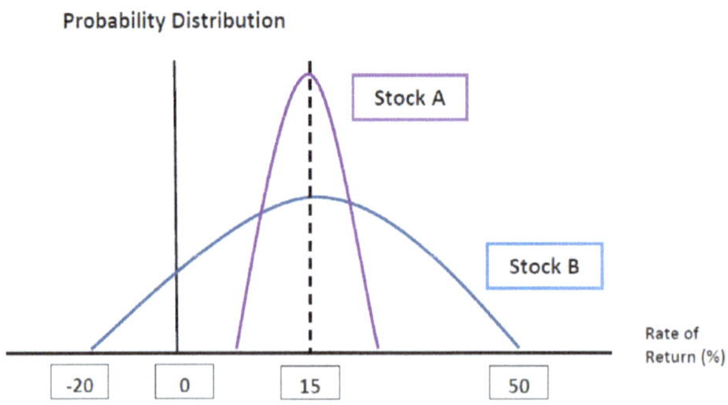

Consider the following Assets for which the returns under various conditions of economy are given.

Economy	Prob.	G-sec	Stock 1	Stock 2	Stock 3	Stock 4
Recession	0.10	8.0%	-22.0%	28.0%	10.0%	-13.0%
Below average	0.20	8.0	-2.0	14.7	-10.0	1.0
Average	0.40	8.0	20.0	0.0	7.0	15.0
Above average	0.20	8.0	35.0	-10.0	45.0	29.0
Boom	0.10	8.0	50.0	-20.0	30.0	43.0
	1.00					
Expected Return		8.0%	17.4%	1.7%	13.8%	15.0%

The G-sec has same return irrespective of the economic outcome. This appears to be risk free.

Stock 1 moves along with the economy (positively correlated) whereas Stock 2 moves in opposite direction of the economy (negatively correlated).

Measuring Risk: the simplest measure of risk is range which is defined as the difference between the highest possible return and lowest possible return. In the above table, the range for Stock 1 is 72.0% whereas for Stock 2 it is 48%. However standard deviation is considered as one of the very well accepted measure of risk. Standard deviation is the square root of variance.

$$\sigma = \sqrt{Variance} = \sqrt{\sigma^2}$$
$$= \sqrt{\sum_{i=1}^{n} (r_i - \hat{r})^2 P_i}$$

For Stock 1:

$\sigma = ((-22 - 17.4)^2 0.10 + (-2 - 17.4)^2 0.20 + (20 - 17.4)^2 0.40 + (35 - 17.4)^2 0.20 + (50 - 17.4)^2 0.10))^{1/2} = 20.0\%$.

Similarly for other investments, the standard deviation is given in the following table.

Investment	G-Sec	Stock 1	Stock 2	Stock 3	Stock 4
σ	0%	20.0%	13.4%	18.8%	15.3%

Risk Neutral

In economics and finance, risk neutral preferences are neither risk averse nor risk seeking. A risk neutral party's decisions are not affected by the degree of uncertainty in a set of outcomes, so a risk neutral party is indifferent between choices with equal expected payoffs even if one choice is riskier. For example, if offered either $50 or a 50% chance each of $100 and $0, a risk neutral person would have no preference. In contrast, a risk averse person would prefer the first offer, while a risk seeking person would prefer the second.

Theory of the Firm

In the context of the theory of the firm, a risk neutral firm facing risk about the market price of its product, and caring only about profit, would maximize the expected value of its profit (with respect to its choices of labor input usage, output produced, etc.). But a risk averse firm in the same environment would typically take a more cautious approach.

Portfolio Theory

In portfolio choice, a risk neutral investor is able to choose any combination of an array of risky assets (various companies' stocks, various companies' bonds, etc.) would invest exclusively in the asset with the highest expected yield, ignoring its risk features relative to those of other assets, and would even sell short the asset with the lowest expected yield as much as is permitted in order to invest the proceeds in the highest expected-yield asset. In contrast, a risk averse investor would diversify among a variety of assets, taking account of their risk features, even though doing so would lower the expected return on the overall portfolio. The risk neutral investor's portfolio would have a higher expected return, but also a greater variance of possible returns.

The Risk Neutral Utility Function

Choice under uncertainty is often characterized as the maximization of expected utility. Utility is often assumed to be a function of profit or final portfolio wealth, with a positive first derivative. The utility function whose expected value is maximized is concave for a risk averse agent, convex for a risk lover, and linear for a risk neutral agent. Thus in the risk neutral case, expected utility of wealth is simply equal to a linear function of expected wealth, and maximizing it is equivalent to maximizing expected wealth itself.

Risk Aversion

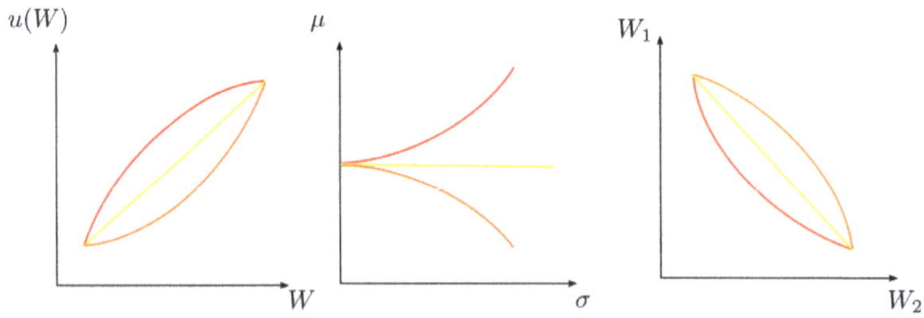

Risk aversion (red) contrasted to risk neutrality (yellow) and risk loving (orange) in different settings. *Left graph*: A risk averse utility function is concave (from below), while a risk loving utility function is convex. *Middle graph*: In standard deviation-expected value space, risk averse indifference curves are upward sloped. *Right graph*: With fixed probabilities of two alternative states 1 and 2, risk averse indifference curves over pairs of state-contingent outcomes are convex.

In economics and finance, risk aversion is the behavior of humans (especially consumers and investors), when exposed to uncertainty, to attempt to reduce that uncertainty. It is the reluctance of a person to accept a bargain with an uncertain payoff rather than another bargain with a more certain, but possibly lower, expected payoff. For example, a risk-averse investor might choose to put his or her money into a bank account with a low but guaranteed interest rate, rather than into a stock that may have high expected returns, but also involves a chance of losing value. Practicality investing in low risk profile commodities.

Example

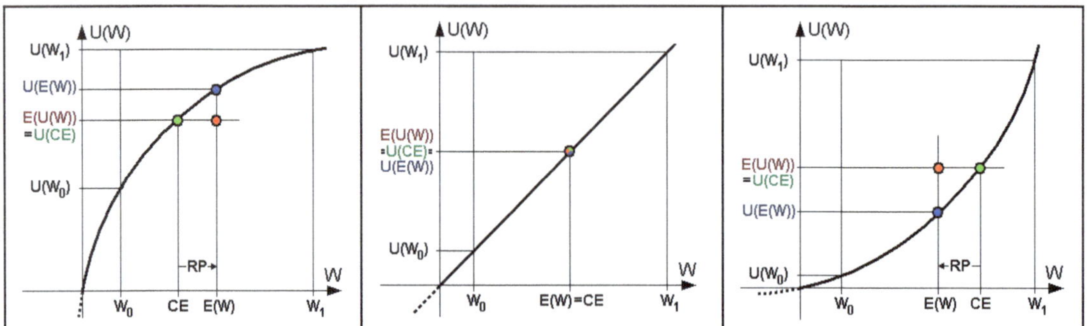

Utility function of a risk-averse (risk-avoiding) individual.	Utility function of a risk-neutral individual.	Utility function of a risk-affine (risk-seeking) individual.

CE - Certainty equivalent; **E(U(W))** - Expected value of the utility (expected utility) of the uncertain payment; **E(W)** - Expected value of the uncertain payment; **U(CE)** - Utility of the certainty equivalent; **U(E(W))** - Utility of the expected value of the uncertain payment; **U(W_0)** - Utility of the minimal payment; **U(W_1)** - Utility of the maximal payment; **W_0** - Minimal payment; **W_1** - Maximal payment; **RP** - Risk premium

A person is given the choice between two scenarios, one with a guaranteed payoff and one without. In the guaranteed scenario, the person receives \$50. In the uncertain scenario, a coin is flipped to decide whether the person receives \$100 or nothing. The expected payoff for both scenarios is \$50, meaning that an individual who was insensitive to risk would not care whether they took the guaranteed payment or the gamble. However, individuals may have different risk attitudes.

A person is said to be:

- risk-averse (or risk-avoiding) - if he or she would accept a certain payment (certainty equivalent) of less than \$50 (for example, \$40), rather than taking the gamble and possibly receiving nothing.
- risk-neutral - if he or she is indifferent between the bet and a certain \$50 payment.
- risk-loving (or risk-seeking) - if he or she would accept the bet even when the guaranteed payment is more than \$50 (for example, \$60).

The average payoff of the gamble, known as its expected value, is \$50. The dollar amount that the individual would accept instead of the bet is called the certainty equivalent, and the difference between the expected value and the certainty equivalent is called the risk premium. For risk-averse individuals, it is positive, for risk-neutral persons it is zero, and for risk-loving individuals their risk premium is negative.

Utility of Money

In expected utility theory, an agent has a utility function $u(x)$ where x represents the value that he might receive in money or goods (in the above example x could be 0 or 100).

Time does not come into this calculation, so inflation does not appear. (The utility function $u(x)$ is defined only up to positive linear affine transformation - in other words a constant offset could be added to the value of $u(x)$ for all x, and/or $u(x)$ could be multiplied by a positive constant factor, without affecting the conclusions).

An agent possesses risk aversion if and only if the utility function is concave. For instance $u(0)$ could be 0, $u(100)$ might be 10, $u(40)$ might be 5, and for comparison $u(50)$ might be 6.

The expected utility of the above bet (with a 50% chance of receiving 100 and a 50% chance of receiving 0) is,

$$E(u) = (u(0) + u(100)) / 2,$$

and if the person has the utility function with $u(0)=0$, $u(40)=5$, and $u(100)=10$ then the expected utility of the bet equals 5, which is the same as the known utility of the amount 40. Hence the certainty equivalent is 40.

The risk premium is ($50 minus $40)=$10, or in proportional terms

$$(\$50 - \$40) / \$40$$

or 25% (where $50 is the expected value of the risky bet: $(\frac{1}{2}0 + \frac{1}{2}100)$. This risk premium means that the person would be willing to sacrifice as much as $10 in expected value in order to achieve perfect certainty about how much money will be received. In other words, the person would be indifferent between the bet and a guarantee of $40, and would prefer anything over $40 to the bet.

In the case of a wealthier individual, the risk of losing $100 would be less significant, and for such small amounts his utility function would be likely to be almost linear, for instance if u(0) = 0 and u(100) = 10, then u(40) might be 4.0001 and u(50) might be 5.0001.

The utility function for perceived gains has two key properties: an upward slope, and concavity. (i) The upward slope implies that the person feels that more is better: a larger amount received yields greater utility, and for risky bets the person would prefer a bet which is first-order stochastically dominant over an alternative bet (that is, if the probability mass of the second bet is pushed to the right to form the first bet, then the first bet is preferred). (ii) The concavity of the utility function implies that the person is risk averse: a sure amount would always be preferred over a risky bet having the same expected value; moreover, for risky bets the person would prefer a bet which is a mean-preserving contraction of an alternative bet (that is, if some of the probability mass of the first bet is spread out without altering the mean to form the second bet, then the first bet is preferred).

Measures of Risk Aversion under Expected Utility Theory

There are multiple measures of the risk aversion expressed by a given utility function. Several functional forms often used for utility functions are expressed in terms of these measures.

Absolute Risk Aversion

The higher the curvature of $u(c)$, the higher the risk aversion. However, since expected utility functions are not uniquely defined (are defined only up to affine transformations), a measure that stays constant with respect to these transformations is needed. One such measure is the Arrow–Pratt measure of absolute risk-aversion (ARA), after the economists Kenneth Arrow and John W. Pratt, also known as the coefficient of absolute risk aversion, defined as

$$A(c) = -\frac{u''(c)}{u'(c)}$$

where $u'(c)$ and $u''(c)$ denote the first and second derivatives with respect to c of $u(c)$.

The following expressions relate to this term:

- Exponential utility of the form $u(c)=1-e^{-\alpha c}$ is unique in exhibiting *constant absolute risk aversion* (CARA): $A(c)=\alpha$ is constant with respect to c.
- Hyperbolic absolute risk aversion (HARA) is the most general class of utility functions that are usually used in practice (specifically, CRRA, CARA (constant absolute risk aversion), and quadratic utility all exhibit HARA and are often used because of their mathematical tractability). A utility function exhibits HARA if its absolute risk aversion is a hyperbolic function, namely

$$A(c)=-\frac{u''(c)}{u'(c)}=\frac{1}{ac+b}$$

The solution to this differential equation (omitting additive and multiplicative constant terms, which do not affect the behavior implied by the utility function) is:

$$u(c)=\frac{(c-c_s)^{1-R}}{1-R}$$

where $R=1/a$ and $c_s=-b/a$. Note that when $a=0$, this is CARA, as $A(c)=1/b=const$, and when $b=0$, this is CRRA, as $cA(c)=1/a=const$.

- *Decreasing/increasing absolute risk aversion* (DARA/IARA) is present if $A(c)$ is decreasing/increasing. Using the above definition of ARA, the following inequality holds for DARA:

$$\frac{\partial A(c)}{\partial c}=-\frac{u'(c)u'''(c)-[u''(c)]^2}{[u'(c)]^2}<0$$

and this can hold only if $u'''(c)>0$. Therefore, DARA implies that the utility function is positively skewed; that is, $u'''(c)>0$. Analogously, IARA can be derived with the opposite directions of inequalities, which permits but does not require a negatively skewed utility function ($u'''(c)<0$). An example of a DARA utility function is $u(c)=\log(c)$, with $A(c)=1/c$, while $u(c)=c-\alpha c^2$, $\alpha>0$, with $A(c)=2\alpha/(1-2\alpha c)$ would represent a quadratic utility function exhibiting IARA.

- Experimental and empirical evidence is mostly consistent with decreasing absolute risk aversion.
- Contrary to what several empirical studies have assumed, wealth is not a good proxy for risk aversion when studying risk sharing in a principal-agent setting.

Although $A(c) = -\frac{u''(c)}{u'(c)}$ is monotonic in wealth under either DARA or IARA and constant in wealth under CARA, tests of contractual risk sharing relying on wealth as a proxy for absolute risk aversion are usually not identified.

Relative Risk Aversion

The Arrow-Pratt measure of relative risk-aversion (RRA) or coefficient of relative risk aversion is defined as

$$R(c) = cA(c) = \frac{-cu''(c)}{u'(c)}.$$

Like for absolute risk aversion, the corresponding terms *constant relative risk aversion* (CRRA) and *decreasing/increasing relative risk aversion* (DRRA/IRRA) are used. This measure has the advantage that it is still a valid measure of risk aversion, even if the utility function changes from risk-averse to risk-loving as c varies, i.e. utility is not strictly convex/concave over all c. A constant RRA implies a decreasing ARA, but the reverse is not always true. As a specific example of constant relative risk aversion, the utility function $u(c) = \log(c)$ implies RRA = 1.

In intertemporal choice problems, the elasticity of intertemporal substitution often cannot be disentangled from the coefficient of relative risk aversion. The isoelastic utility function

$$u(c) = \frac{c^{1-\rho} - 1}{1-\rho}$$

exhibits constant relative risk aversion with $R(c) = \rho$ and the elasticity of intertemporal substitution $\varepsilon_{u(c)} = 1/\rho$. When $\rho = 1$, using l'Hôpital's rule shows that this simplifies to the case of *log utility,* u(c) = log c, and the income effect and substitution effect on saving exactly offset.

A time varying relative risk aversion can be considered.

Implications of Increasing/Decreasing Absolute and Relative Risk Aversion

The most straightforward implications of increasing or decreasing absolute or relative risk aversion, and the ones that motivate a focus on these concepts, occur in the context of forming a portfolio with one risky asset and one risk-free asset. If the person experiences an increase in wealth, he/she will choose to increase (or keep unchanged, or decrease) the *number of dollars* of the risky asset held in the portfolio if *absolute* risk aversion is decreasing (or constant, or increasing). Thus economists avoid using utility functions, such as the quadratic, which exhibit increasing absolute risk aversion, because they have an unrealistic behavioral implication.

Similarly, if the person experiences an increase in wealth, he/she will choose to increase (or keep unchanged, or decrease) the *fraction* of the portfolio held in the risky asset if *relative* risk aversion is decreasing (or constant, or increasing).

In monetary economics, an increase in relative risk aversion increases the impact of households' money holdings on the overall economy. In other words, the more the relative risk aversion increases, the more money demand shocks will impact the economy.

Portfolio Theory

In modern portfolio theory, risk aversion is measured as the additional expected reward an investor requires to accept additional risk. Here risk is measured as the standard deviation of the return on investment, i.e. the square root of its variance. In advanced portfolio theory, different kinds of risk are taken into consideration. They are measured as the n-th root of the n-th central moment. The symbol used for risk aversion is A or A_n.

$$A = \frac{dE(r)}{d\sigma}$$

$$A_n = \frac{dE(r)}{d\sqrt[n]{\mu_n}}$$

Limitations of Expected Utility Treatment of Risk Aversion

The notion of using expected utility theory to analyze risk aversion has come under criticism from behavioral economics. Matthew Rabin has showed that a risk-averse, expected-utility-maximizing individual who,

from any initial wealth level [...] turns down gambles where she loses $100 or gains $110, each with 50% probability [...] will turn down 50-50 bets of losing $1,000 or gaining any sum of money.

Rabin criticizes this implication of expected utility theory on grounds of implausibility. One solution to the problem observed by Rabin is that proposed by prospect theory and cumulative prospect theory, where outcomes are considered relative to a reference point (usually the status quo), rather than to consider only the final wealth.

Another limitation is the reflection effect which demonstrates the reversing of risk aversion. This effect was first presented by Kahneman and Tversky as a part of the prospect theory, in the behavioral economics domain. The reflection effect is an identified pattern of opposite preferences between negative prospects as opposed to positive prospects. According to this effect, people tend to avoid risks under the gain domain, and to seek risks under the loss domain. Meaning, no risk aversion is expected under the loss domain. For example, in the gain domain, most people prefer a certain gain of 3000, than a gain of 4000 with a risk of 80 percent. When posing the same problem under the loss domain - with negative values, most people prefer a loss of 4000 with 80 percent chance, over a certain loss of 3000.

The reflection effect (as well as the certainty effect) is inconsistent with the expected utility hypothesis. It is assumed that the psychological principle which stands behind this kind of behavior is the overweighting of certainty. Meaning, options which are perceived as certain, are over-weighted relative to uncertain options. This pattern is an indication of a risk seeking behavior in negative prospects and eliminates other explanations for the certainty effect such as aversion for uncertainty or variability.

The initial findings regarding the reflection effect faced criticism regarding its validity, as it was claimed that there are insufficient evidence to support the effect on the individual level. Subsequently, an extensive investigation revealed its possible limitations, suggesting that the effect is most prevalent when either small or large amounts and extreme probabilities are involved.

In the Brain

Attitudes towards risk have attracted the interest of the field of neuroeconomics and behavioral economics. A 2009 study by Christopoulos et al. suggested that the activity of a specific brain area (right inferior frontal gyrus) correlates with risk aversion, with more risk averse participants (i.e. those having higher risk premia) also having higher responses to safer options. This result coincides with other studies, that show that neuromodulation of the same area results in participants making more or less risk averse choices, depending on whether the modulation increases or decreases the activity of the target area.

Public Understanding and Risk in Social Activities

In the real world, many government agencies, e.g. Health and Safety Executive, are fundamentally risk-averse in their mandate. This often means that they demand (with the power of legal enforcement) that risks be minimized, even at the cost of losing the utility of the risky activity. It is important to consider the opportunity cost when mitigating a risk; the cost of not taking the risky action. Writing laws focused on the risk without the balance of the utility may misrepresent society's goals. The public understanding of risk, which influences political decisions, is an area which has recently been recognised as deserving focus. David Spiegelhalter is the Winton Professor of the Public Understanding of Risk at Cambridge University, a role he describes as "outreach".

A vaccine to protect children against the three common diseases measles, mumps and rubella was developed and recommended for all children in several countries including the UK. However, a controversy arose around fraudulent allegations that it caused autism. This alleged causal link was thoroughly disproved, and the doctor who made the claims was expelled from the General Medical Council. Even years after the claims were disproved, some parents wanted to avert the risk of causing autism in their own children. They chose to spend significant amounts of their own money on alternatives from private doctors. These alternatives carried their own risks which were not balanced fairly, most often that the children were not properly immunized against the more common diseases of measles, mumps and rubella.

Mobile phones may carry some small health risk. While most people would accept that unproven risk to gain the benefit of improved communication, others remain so risk averse that they do not. (The COSMOS cohort study continues to study the actual risks of mobile phones.)

Risk aversion theory can be applied to many aspects of life and its challenges, for example:

- Bribery and corruption - whether the risk of being implicated or caught outweighs the potential personal or professional rewards
- Drugs - whether the risk of having a bad trip outweighs the benefits of possible transformative one; whether the risk of defying social bans is worth the experience of alteration.
- Sex - judgement whether an experience that goes against social convention, ethical mores or common health prescriptions is worth the risk.
- Extreme sports - weighing the risk of physical injury or death against the adrenaline rush and bragging rights.
- Play by children in playgrounds or beyond the reach of their parents.

A recent experimental study with student-subject playing the game of the TV show Deal or No Deal finds that people are more risk averse in the limelight than in the anonymity of a typical behavioral laboratory. In the laboratory treatments, subjects made decisions in a standard, computerized laboratory setting as typically employed in behavioral experiments. In the limelight treatments, subjects made their choices in a simulated game show environment, which included a live audience, a game show host, and video cameras. In line with this, studies on investor behavior find that investors trade more and more speculatively after switching from phone-based to online trading and that investors tend to keep their core investments with traditional brokers and use a small fraction of their wealth to speculate online.

Influences

Risk aversion has been shown to be influenced by demographic characteristics. For instance, older people tend to be more risk averse than younger, poorer people more risk averse than richer (in financial decisions) and female more risk averse than men.

Risk Assessment

Risk assessment is the determination of quantitative or qualitative estimate of risk related to a well-defined situation and a recognized threat (also called hazard). *Quantitative risk assessment* requires calculations of two components of risk *(R)*: the magnitude of the potential loss *(L)*, and the probability *(p)* that the loss will occur. An acceptable risk is a risk that is understood and tolerated usually because the cost or difficulty of implementing an effective countermeasure for the associated vulnerability exceeds the expectation of loss. "Health risk assessment" includes variations, such as risk as the type and severity of response, with or without a probabilistic context.

In all types of engineering of complex systems sophisticated risk assessments are often made within safety engineering and reliability engineering when it concerns threats to life, environment or machine functioning. The agriculture, nuclear, aerospace, oil, rail and military industries have a long history of dealing with risk assessment. Also, medical, hospital, social service and food industries control risks and perform risk assessments on a continual basis. Methods for assessment of risk may differ between industries and whether it pertains to general financial decisions or environmental, ecological, or public health risk assessment.

Explanation

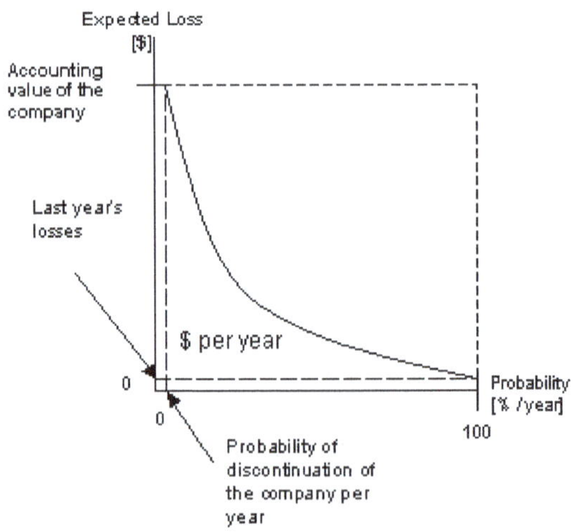

Risk assessment from a financial point of view.

Risk assessment consists of an objective evaluation of risk in which assumptions and uncertainties are clearly considered and presented. Part of the difficulty in risk management is that both the quantities by which risk assessment is concerned – potential loss and probability of occurrence – can be very difficult to measure. The chance of error in measuring these two concepts is high. Risk with a large potential loss and a low probability of occurrence is often treated differently from one with a low potential loss and a high likelihood of occurrence. In theory, both are of near equal priority, but in practice it can be very difficult to manage when faced with the scarcity of resources, especially time, in which to conduct the risk management process. To see this expressed mathematically, one can define total risk as the sum over individual risks, R_i, which can be computed as the product of potential losses, L_i, and their probabilities, $p(L_i)$:

$$R_i = L_i p(L_i)$$

$$R_{total} = \sum_i L_i p(L_i)$$

Even though for some risks R_i, R_j, we might have R_i, R_j, if the probability $p(L_j)$ is small compared to $p(L_i)$, its estimation might be based only on a smaller number of prior events, and hence, more uncertain. On the other hand, since $R_i = R_j L_j$ must be larger than L_i, so decisions based on this uncertainty would be more consequential, and hence, warrant a different approach.

Financial decisions, such as insurance, express loss in terms of dollar amounts. When risk assessment is used for public health or environmental decisions, loss can be quantified in a common metric such as a country's currency or some numerical measure of a location's quality of life. For public health and environmental decisions, loss is simply a verbal description of the outcome, such as increased cancer incidence or incidence of birth defects. In that case, the "risk" is expressed as

$$R_i = p(L_i)$$

If the risk estimate takes into account information on the number of individuals exposed, it is termed a "population risk" and is in units of expected increased cases per a time period. If the risk estimate does not take into account the number of individuals exposed, it is termed an "individual risk" and is in units of incidence rate per a time period. Population risks are of more use for cost/benefit analysis; individual risks are of more use for evaluating whether risks to individuals are "acceptable".

Five-step Process in Risk Assessment and Management

Risk assessment and management process	
Establish the context	understand the operating context and environment
Identify the risks / hazards	identify the internal and external risks / hazards that poses threat
Analyze the risks	systematic analysis of various contributing and leading factors (e.g. extent of the exposure, multiple exposures, vulnerability characteristics of the population or system being assessed)
Evaluate and prioritize the risks	characterize and prioritize the list of risks for further action
Tackle the risks	Identify the range of options to tackle the risk & implement the best choice using available resources

In General Health

There are many resources that provide health risk information.

The National Library of Medicine provides risk assessment and regulation information tools for a varied audience. These include:

- TOXNET (databases on hazardous chemicals, environmental health, and toxic releases),
- the Household Products Database (potential health effects of chemicals in over 10,000 common household products),
- TOXMAP (maps of the U.S. Environmental Protection Agency Superfund and Toxics Release Inventory data).

The United States Environmental Protection Agency provides basic information about environmental health risk assessments for the public for a wide variety of possible environmental exposures.

The Environmental Protection Agency began actively using risk assessment methods to protect drinking water in the United States after passage of the Safe Drinking Water Act of 1974. The law required the National Academy of Sciences to conduct a study on drinking water issues, and in its report the NAS described some methodologies for doing risk assessments for chemicals that were suspected carcinogens, recommendations that top EPA officials have described as perhaps the study's most important part.

Considering the increase in junk food and its toxicity, FDA required in 1973 that cancer-causing compounds must not be present in meat at concentrations that would cause a cancer risk greater than 1 in a million over a lifetime. The US Environmental Protection Agency provides extensive information about ecological and environmental risk assessments for the public via its risk assessment portal. The Stockholm Convention on persistent organic pollutants (POPs) supports a qualitative risk framework for public health protection from chemicals that display environmental and biological persistence, bioaccumulation, toxicity (PBT) and long range transport; most global chemicals that meet this criteria have been previously assessed quantitatively by national and international health agencies.

How Risk is Appraised

In the estimation of risks, three or more steps are involved that require the inputs of different disciplines:

1. *Hazard Identification*, aims to determine the qualitative nature of the potential adverse consequences of the contaminant (chemical, radiation, noise, etc.) and the strength of the evidence it can have that effect. This is done, for chemical hazards, by drawing from the results of the sciences of toxicology and epidemiology. For other kinds of hazard, engineering or other disciplines are involved.

2. *Dose-Response Analysis*, is determining the relationship between dose and the type of adverse response and/or probability or the incidence of effect (dose-response assessment). The complexity of this step in many contexts derives mainly from the need to extrapolate results from experimental animals (e.g. mouse, rat) to humans, and/or from high to lower doses, including from high acute occupational levels to low chronic environmental levels. In addition, the differences between individuals due to genetics or other factors mean that the hazard may be higher for particular groups, called susceptible populations. An alternative to dose-response estimation is to determine a concentration unlikely to yield observable effects, that is, a no effect concentration. In developing such a dose, to account for the largely unknown effects of animal to human extrapolations, increased variability in humans, or missing data, a prudent approach is often adopted by including safety or uncertainty factors in the estimate of the "safe" dose, typically a factor of 10 for each unknown step.

3. *Exposure Quantification*, aims to determine the amount of a contaminant (dose) that individuals and populations will receive, either as a contact level (e.g., concentration in ambient air) or as intake (e.g., daily dose ingested from drinking water). This is done by examining the results of the discipline of exposure assessment. As different location, lifestyles and other factors likely influence the amount of contaminant that is received, a range or distribution of possible values is generated in this step. Particular care is taken to determine the exposure of the susceptible population(s).

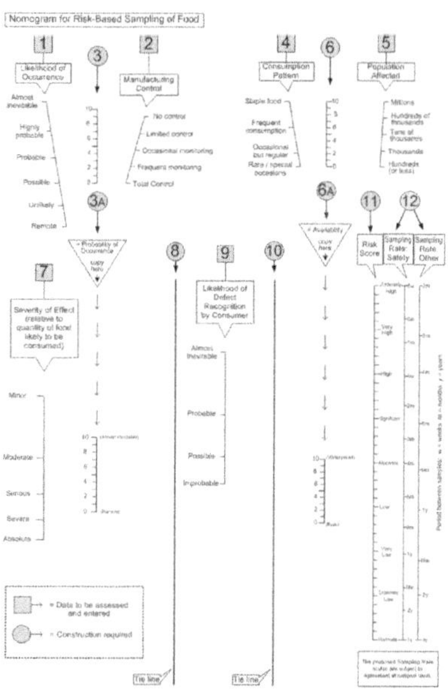

Food risk assessment nomogram

Finally, the results of the three steps above are then combined to produce an estimate of risk. Because of the different susceptibilities and exposures, this risk will vary within a population. An uncertainty analysis is nearly always included in a health risk assessment.

Small Subpopulations

When risks apply mainly to small sub-populations, there is uncertainty at which point intervention is necessary. For example, there may be a risk that is very low for everyone, other than 0.1% of the population. It is necessary to determine whether this 0.1% is represented by:

- all infants younger than *X* days or
- recreational users of a particular product.

If the risk is higher for a particular sub-population because of abnormal exposure rather than susceptibility, strategies to further reduce the exposure of that subgroup are considered. If an identifiable sub-population is more susceptible due to inherent genetic or other factors, public policy choices must be made. The choices are:

- to set policies for protecting the general population that are protective of such groups, e.g. for children when data exists, the Clean Air Act for populations such as asthmatics or
- not to set policies, because the group is too small, or the costs too high.

Acceptable Risk Criteria

The idea of not increasing lifetime risk by more than one in a million has become commonplace in public health discourse and policy. It is a heuristic measure. It provides a numerical basis for establishing a negligible increase in risk.

Environmental decision making allows some discretion for deeming individual risks potentially "acceptable" if less than one in ten thousand chance of increased lifetime risk. Low risk criteria such as these provide some protection for a case where individuals may be exposed to multiple chemicals e.g. pollutants, food additives or other chemicals.

In practice, a true zero-risk is possible only with the suppression of the risk-causing activity.

Stringent requirements of 1 in a million may not be technologically feasible or may be so prohibitively expensive as to render the risk-causing activity unsustainable, resulting in the optimal degree of intervention being a balance between risks vs. benefit. For example, emissions from hospital incinerators result in a certain number of deaths per year. However, this risk must be balanced against the alternatives. There are public health risks, as well as economic costs, associated with all options. The risk associated with no incineration is potential spread of infectious diseases, or even no hospitals. Further investigation identifies options such as separating noninfectious from infectious wastes, or air pollution controls on a medical incinerator.

Intelligent thought about a reasonably full set of options is essential. Thus, it is not unusual for there to be an iterative process between analysis, consideration of options, and follow up analysis.

In Auditing

For audits performed by an outside audit firm, risk assessment is a crucial stage before accepting an audit engagement. According to ISA315 *Understanding the Entity and its Environment and Assessing the Risks of Material Misstatement*, "the auditor should perform risk assessment procedures to obtain an understanding of the entity and its environment, including its internal control."<evidence relating to the auditor's risk assessment of a material misstatement in the client's financial statements. Then, the auditor obtains initial evidence regarding the classes of transactions at the client and the operating effectiveness of the client's internal controls.In auditing, audit risk is defined as the risk that the auditor will issue a clean unmodified opinion regarding the financial statements, when in fact the financial statements are materially misstated, and therefore do not qualify for a clean unmodified opinion. As a formula, audit risk is the product of two other risks: Risk of Material Misstatement and Detection risk. This formula can be further broken down as follows: inherent risk X control risk X detection risk.

In Public Health

In the context of public health, risk assessment is the process of characterizing the nature and likelihood of a harmful effect to individuals or populations from certain human activities. Health risk assessment can be mostly qualitative or can include statistical estimates of probabilities for specific populations. In most countries the use of specific chemicals or the operations of specific facilities (e.g. power plants, manufacturing plants) is not allowed unless it can be shown that they do not increase the risk of death or illness above a specific threshold. For example, the American Food and Drug Administration (FDA) regulates food safety through risk assessment.

In Project Management

In project management, risk assessment is an integral part of the risk management plan, studying the probability, the impact, and the effect of every known risk on the project, as well as the corrective action to take should that risk occur. Of special consideration in this area are the relevant codes of practice that are enforced in the specific jurisdiction. Understanding the regime of regulations that risk management must abide by is integral to formulating safe and compliant risk assessment practices.

In Information Security

IT risk assessment can be performed by a qualitative or quantitative approach, following different methodologies. One important difference in risk assessments in information security is modifying the threat model to account for the fact that any adversarial system connected to the Internet has access to threaten any other connected system. Risk assessments may therefore need to be modified to account for the threats from all adversaries, instead of just those with reasonable access as is done in other fields.

Another notable difference is the strategic nature of IT risk assessments. Unlike tactical vulnerability assessments and penetration testing which aim to identify and close specific gaps in security, IT risk assessments are functional at the executive level to examine the broader picture of IT risk management.

For Megaprojects

Megaprojects (sometimes also called "major programs") are extremely large-scale investment projects, typically costing more than US$1 billion per project. Megaprojects include bridges, tunnels, highways, railways, airports, seaports, power plants, dams, wastewater projects, coastal flood protection, oil and natural gas extraction projects, public buildings, information technology systems, aerospace projects, and defence systems. Megaprojects have been shown to be particularly risky in terms of finance, safety, and social and environmental impacts.

Quantitative Risk Assessment

Quantitative risk assessments include a calculation of the single loss expectancy (SLE) of an asset. The single loss expectancy can be defined as the loss of value to asset based on a single security incident. The team then calculates the Annualized Rate of Occurrence (ARO) of the threat to the asset. The ARO is an estimate based on the data of how often a threat would be successful in exploiting a vulnerability. From this information, the Annualized Loss Expectancy (ALE) can be calculated. The annualized loss expectancy is a calculation of the single loss expectancy multiplied by the annual rate of occurrence, or how much an organization could estimate to lose from an asset based on the risks, threats, and vulnerabilities. It then becomes possible from a financial perspective to justify expenditures to implement countermeasures to protect the asset.

In Software Evolution

Studies have shown that early parts of the system development cycle such as requirements and design specifications are especially prone to error. This effect is particularly notorious in projects involving multiple stakeholders with different points of view. Evolutionary software processes offer an iterative approach to requirement engineering to alleviate the problems of uncertainty, ambiguity and inconsistency inherent in software developments.

Criticisms of Quantitative Risk Assessment

Barry Commoner, Brian Wynne and other critics have expressed concerns that risk assessment tends to be overly quantitative and reductive. For example, they argue that risk assessments ignore qualitative differences among risks. Some charge that assessments may drop out important non-quantifiable or inaccessible information, such as variations among the classes of people exposed to hazards, or social amplification. Furthermore, Commoner and O'Brien claim that quantitative approaches divert attention from precautionary or preventative measures. Others, like Nassim Nicholas Taleb consider risk managers little more than "blind users" of statistical tools and methods.

In shipping Industry

In July 2010, shipping companies agreed to use standardized procedures in order to assess risk in key shipboard operations. These procedures were implemented as part of the amended ISM Code.

In Underwater Diving

Formal risk assessment is a required component of most professional dive planning, but the format and methodology may vary. Consequences of an incident due to an identified hazard are generally chosen from a small number of standardised categories, and probability is estimated based on statistical data on the rare occasions when it is available, and on a best guess estimate based on personal experience and company policy in most cases. A simple matrix is often used to transform these inputs into a level of risk, generally expressed as unacceptable, marginal or acceptable. If unacceptable, measures must be taken to reduce the risk to an acceptablc lcvcl, and the final of the risk assessment must be accepted by the affected parties before a dive commences. Higher levels of risk may be acceptable in special circumstances, such as military or search and rescue operations when there is a chance of recovering a survivor. Diving supervisors are trained in the procedures of hazard identification and risk assessment, and it is part of their planning and operational responsibility. Both health and safety hazards must be considered.

In recreational scuba diving, the extent of risk assessment expected of the diver is relatively basic, and is included in the pre-dive checks. Several mnemonics have been developed by diver certification agencies to remind the diver to pay some attention to risk, but the training is rudimentary. Diving service providers are expected to provide a higher level of care for their customers, and diving instructors and divemasters are expected to assess risk on behalf of their customers and warn them of site-specific hazards and the competence considered appropriate for the planned dive. Technical divers are expected to make a more thorough assessment of risk, but as they will be making an informed choice for a recreational activity, the level of acceptable risk may be considerably higher than that permitted for occupational divers under the direction of an employer.

In Environment: Environmental Risk Assessment

Environmental Risk Assessment (ERA) aim at assessing the effects of stressors, often chemicals, on the local environment. A risk is an integrated assessment of likelihood and severity of an undesired event. In ERA, the undesired event often depends on the chemical of interest and on the risk assessment scenario. This undesired event is usually a detrimental effect on organisms, populations or ecosystems. Current ERAs usually compare an exposure to a no-effect level, such as the Predicted Environmental Concentration/Predicted No-Effect Concentration (PEC/PNEC) ratio in Europe. Although this type of ratio is useful and often used in regulation purposes, it is only an indication of an exceeded apparent threshold. New approaches start to be developed in ERA in order to quantifiy this risk and to communicate effectively on it with both the managers and the general public.

Required Rate of Return and Real Risk Free Rate

Required rate of Return: The investors invest in financial instruments expecting some rate of return. This depends on the return from the next best investment option – known as opportunity cost – and is affected by:

- Time value of money – today's one rupee is better than tomorrow's.
- Expected rate of inflation
- Risk involved because of uncertainty in the cash flows from the investment

Cost of Capital

In economics and accounting, the cost of capital is the cost of a company's funds (both debt and equity), or, from an investor's point of view "the required rate of return on a portfolio company's existing securities". It is used to evaluate new projects of a company. It is the minimum return that investors expect for providing capital to the company, thus setting a benchmark that a new project has to meet.

Basic Concept

For an investment to be worthwhile, the expected return on capital has to be higher than the cost of capital. Given a number of competing investment opportunities, investors are expected to put their capital to work in order to maximize the return. In other words, the cost of capital is the rate of return that capital could be expected to earn in the best alternative investment of equivalent risk; this is the opportunity cost of capital. If a project is of similar risk to a company's average business activities it is reasonable to use the company's average cost of capital as a basis for the evaluation. However, for projects outside the core business of the company, the current cost of capital may not be the appropriate yardstick to use, as the risks of the businesses are not the same.

A company's securities typically include both debt and equity, one must therefore calculate both the cost of debt and the cost of equity to determine a company's cost of capital. Importantly, both cost of debt and equity must be forward looking, and reflect the expectations of risk and return in the future. This means, for instance, that the past cost of debt is not a good indicator of the actual forward looking cost of debt.

Once cost of debt and cost of equity have been determined, their blend, the weighted average cost of capital (WACC), can be calculated. This WACC can then be used as a discount rate for a project's projected free cash flows to firm.

Cost of Debt

When companies borrow funds from outside lenders, the interest paid on these funds is called the cost of debt. The cost of debt is computed by taking the rate on a risk-free bond whose duration matches the term structure of the corporate debt, then adding a default premium. This default premium will rise as the amount of debt increases (since, all other things being equal, the risk rises as the cost of debt rises). Since in most cases debt expense is a deductible expense, the cost of debt is computed on an after-tax basis to make it comparable with the cost of equity (earnings are taxed as well). Thus, for profitable firms, debt is discounted by the tax rate. The formula can be written as

$$K_D = (R_f + \text{credit risk rate})(1 - T),$$

where T is the corporate tax rate and R_f is the risk free rate.

Cost of Equity

The cost of equity is inferred by comparing the investment to other investments (comparable) with similar risk profiles. It is commonly computed using the capital asset pricing model formula:

Cost of equity = Risk free rate of return + Premium expected for risk

Cost of equity = Risk free rate of return + Beta × (market rate of return – risk free rate of return)

where Beta = sensitivity to movements in the relevant market. Thus in symbols we have

$$E_s = R_f + \beta_s(R_m - R_f)$$

where:

E_s is the expected return for a security;

R_f is the expected risk-free return in that market (government bond yield);

β_s is the sensitivity to market risk for the security;

R_m is the historical return of the stock market; and

$(R_m - R_f)$ is the risk premium of market assets over risk free assets.

The risk free rate is the yield on long term bonds in the particular market, such as government bonds.

An alternative to the estimation of the required return by the capital asset pricing model as above, is the use of the Fama–French three-factor model.

Expected Return

The expected return (or required rate of return for investors) can be calculated with the "dividend capitalization model", which is

$$K_{cs} = \frac{\text{Dividend}_{\text{Payment/Share}}(1+\text{Growth})}{\text{Price}_{\text{Market}}} + \text{Growth}_{\text{rate}}.$$

Comments

The models state that investors will expect a return that is the risk-free return plus the security's sensitivity to market risk (β) times the market risk premium.

The risk premium varies over time and place, but in some developed countries during the twentieth century it has averaged around 5%. The equity market real capital gain return has been about the same as annual real GDP growth. The capital gains on the Dow Jones Industrial Average have been 1.6% per year over the period 1910-2005. The dividends have increased the total "real" return on average equity to the double, about 3.2%.

The sensitivity to market risk (β) is unique for each firm and depends on everything from management to its business and capital structure. This value cannot be known "ex ante" (beforehand), but can be estimated from ex post (past) returns and past experience with similar firms.

Cost of Retained Earnings/Cost of Internal Equity

Note that retained earnings are a component of equity, and, therefore, the cost of retained earnings (internal equity) is equal to the cost of equity as explained above. Dividends (earnings that are paid to investors and not retained) are a component of the return on capital to equity holders, and influence the cost of capital through that mechanism.

Cost of internal equity = [(next year's dividend per share/(current market price per share - flotation costs)] + growth rate of dividends)]

Weighted Average Cost of Capital

The weighted cost of capital (WACC) is used in finance to measure a firm's cost of capital. WACC is not dictated by management. Rather, it represents the minimum return that a company must earn on an existing asset base to satisfy its creditors, owners, and other providers of capital, or they will invest elsewhere.

The total capital for a firm is the value of its equity (for a firm without outstanding warrants and options, this is the same as the company's market capitalization) plus the cost of its debt (the cost of debt should be continually updated as the cost of debt changes as a result of interest rate changes). Notice that the "equity" in the debt to equity ratio is the market value of all equity, not the shareholders' equity on the balance sheet. To calculate the firm's weighted cost of capital, we must first calculate the costs of the individual financing sources: Cost of Debt, Cost of Preference Capital, and Cost of Equity Cap.

Calculation of WACC is an iterative procedure which requires estimation of the fair market value of equity capital.

Capital Structure

Because of tax advantages on debt issuance, it will be cheaper to issue debt rather than new equity (this is only true for profitable firms, tax breaks are available only to profitable firms). At some point, however, the cost of issuing new debt will be greater than the cost of issuing new equity. This is because adding debt increases the default risk - and thus the interest rate that the company must pay in order to borrow money. By utilizing too much debt in its capital structure, this increased default risk can also drive up the costs for other sources (such as retained earnings and preferred stock) as well. Management must identify the "optimal mix" of financing – the capital structure where the cost of capital is minimized so that the firm's value can be maximized.

The Thomson Financial league tables show that global debt issuance exceeds equity issuance with a 90 to 10 margin.

The structure of capital should be determined considering the weighted average cost of capital.

Modigliani–Miller Theorem

If there were no tax advantages for issuing debt, and equity could be freely issued, Miller and Modigliani showed that, under certain assumptions, the value of a leveraged firm and the value of an unleveraged firm should be the same.

The Real Risk Free Rate (RFR): This is the return that has no risk the following features:

- Assumes no inflation.
- Assumes no uncertainty about future cash flows.
- Influenced by time preference for consumption of income and investment opportunities in the economy.

By adjusting for inflation, nominal risk free rate can be converted into real RFR.

$$\text{Real RFR} = \frac{1 + \text{Nominal RFR}}{1 + \text{Inflation rate}} - 1$$

Nominal Risk-Free Rate is dependent upon the conditions in the Capital Markets and expected rate of inflation

Risk Premium

For an individual, a risk premium is the minimum amount of money by which the expected return on a risky asset must exceed the known return on a risk-free asset in order to induce an individual to hold the risky asset rather than the risk-free asset. It is positive if the person is risk averse. Thus it is the minimum willingness to accept compensation for the risk.

The certainty equivalent, a related concept, is the guaranteed amount of money that an individual would view as equally desirable as a risky asset.

For market outcomes, a risk premium is the actual excess of the expected return on a risky asset over the known return on the risk-free asset.

Formal Definitions for an Individual

Let an individual's increasing, concave von Neumann-Morgenstern utility function be u, let r_f be the return on the risk-free asset, and let r be the random return on the risky asset. Write r as the sum of its expected return $r_f + \pi$, necessary for indifference between the risky and risk-free assets, and its zero-mean risky component x. Then the risk premium π is defined by

$$u(r_f) = Eu(r_f + \pi + x).$$

Here the left side is the degree of attractiveness of the risk-free asset—the known utility of its known return—and the right side is the degree of attractiveness of the risky asset—the expected utility of its risky return. Thus the risk premium is the amount by which the risky asset's expected return must in fact exceed the risk-free return in order to make the risky and risk-free assets equally attractive.

Further, the certainty equivalent C is defined by

$$u(C) = Eu(r);$$

thus the certainty equivalent is the certain value which is equally attractive as the risky asset; due to risk aversion the certainty equivalent will be less than the expected return on the risky asset.

Example of Observed Risk Premium

Suppose a game show participant may choose one of two doors, one that hides $1,000 and one that hides $0. Further suppose that the host also allows the contestant to take $500 instead of choosing a door. The two options (choosing between door 1 and door 2, or taking $500) have the same expected value of $500, so no risk premium is being offered for choosing the doors rather than the guaranteed $500.

A contestant unconcerned about risk is indifferent between these choices. A risk-averse contestant will choose no door and accept the guaranteed $500, while a risk-loving contestant will derive utility from the uncertainty and will therefore choose a door.

If too many contestants are risk averse, the game show may encourage selection of the riskier choice (gambling on one of the doors) by offering a positive risk premium. If the game show offers $1,600 behind the good door, increasing to $800 the expected value of choosing between doors 1 and 2, the risk premium becomes $300 (i.e., $800 expected value minus $500 guaranteed amount). Contestants requiring a minimum risk compensation of less than $300 will choose a door instead of accepting the guaranteed $500.

Finance

In finance, a common approach for measuring risk premia is to compare the risk-free return on T-bills and the risky return on other investments (using the *ex post* return as a proxy for the *ex ante* expected return). The difference between these two returns can be interpreted as a measure of the excess expected return on the risky asset. This excess expected return is known as the risk premium.

- Equity: In the stock market the risk premium is the expected return of a company stock, a group of company stocks, or a portfolio of all stock market company stocks, minus the risk-free rate. The return from equity is the sum of the dividend yield and capital gains. The risk premium for equities is also called the equity premium. Note that this is an unobservable quantity since no one knows for sure what the expected rate of return on equities is. Nonetheless, most people believe that there is a risk premium built into equities, and this is what encourages investors to place at least some of their money in equities.

- Debt: In the context of bonds, the term "risk premium" is often used to refer to the credit spread (the difference between the bond interest rate and the risk-free rate).

Facets of Fundamental Risk

Facets of Fundamental Risk: Risk is fundamentally inherent to investment. All types of investments do not fit to the pattern of 'no risk, hence risk free return'. Since the investors bear the risk i.e. the uncertainty in future cash flows, they will be demanding a premium for the risk borne. Although, mathematically risk can involve upward or downward swing in the return, practically it is the downside that bothers the investor. The different types of risk that can drive the risk premium are:

- Business risk
- Financial risk
- Liquidity risk
- Exchange rate risk
- Country risk

For more details about these risks one may refer session # 3. These risks are also non diversifiable or systematic in nature.

Thus, Risk premium:

f(Business Risk, Financial Risk, Liquidity Risk, Exchange Rate Risk, Country Risk); or

f(Systematic Market Risk)

Risk Premiumand Portfolio Theory: The relevant risk measure for an individual asset is its co- movement with the market portfolio.Systematic risk relates the variance of the investment to the variance of the market.Beta measures this systematic risk of an asset. Beta is the regression coefficient of returns of security on returns of market portfolio.

Fundamental Risk versus Systematic Risk: Fundamental risk comprises of business risk, financial risk, liquidity risk, exchange rate risk, and country risk.Systematic risk refers to the portion of an individual asset's total variance attributable to the variability of the total market portfolio.

Relationship Between Risk and Return: The following figure depicts the relationship between risk and return. The line that combines return and risk is known as Security Market Line (SML). As one perceives more risk, one raises the expected rate of return. The return over and above RFR is known as risk premium.

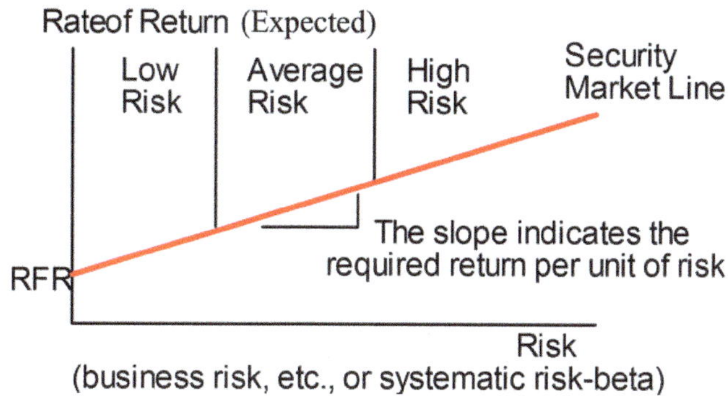

The required rate of return can change its position on SML based on the movement in the risk. Figure reflects that.

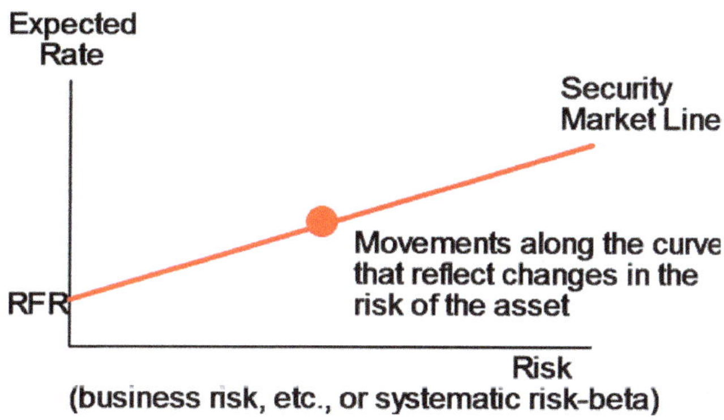

The risk premium can change because of change in the slope of the SML. Slope indicates the return per unit of risk premium.

$RP_i = E(R_i) - NRFR$

Where:

RP_i = risk premium for asset i

$E(R_i)$ = the expected return for asset i

NRFR = the nominal return on a risk-free asset

Similarly the market risk premium for the market portfolio (contains all the risky assets in the market) can be computed as below:

$RP_m = E(R_m) - NRFR$

Where:

RP_m = risk premium on the market portfolio

$E(R_m)$ = expected return on the market portfolio NRFR = expected return on a risk-free asset

Figure shows the new SML because of change in slope of SML.

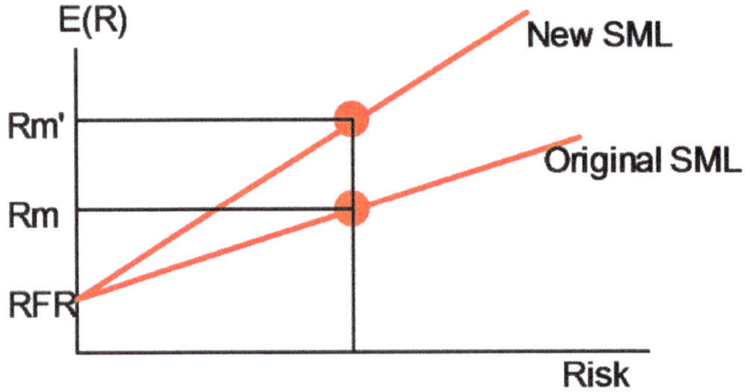

The security market line can shift because of change in macroeconomic conditions. For example if the inflation rate goes up, other things remaining constant, the SML will shift upward.

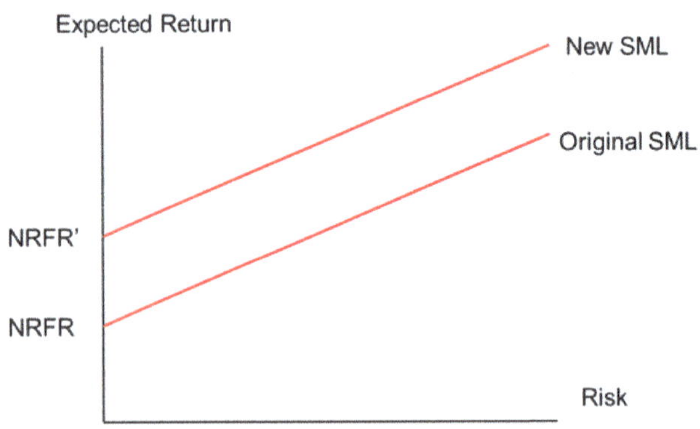

Measuring Portfolio Return and Risk

Portfolio return: This is the weighted average return of assets that are part of a portfolio and is measured as below:

$$R_p = w_1 \text{ x } R_1 + w_2 \text{ x } R_2 + \ldots\ldots w_n \text{ x } R_n$$

Otherwise

$$R_p = \sum_{j=1}^{n} w_j R_j$$

Where,

R_p = Expected return of portfolio;

R_j = Expected rate of return from j[th] asset and

W_j is the weight of investment in j[th] asset.

Example: the following table provides the proportion of investment and expected return on four different stocks.

Asset	A	B	C	D
Proportion in Portfolio (%)	20	30	40	10
Expected Return from Asset	.18	.16	.20	.24

Expected Return from Portfolio =

0.20 x .18 + 0.30 x 0.16 + 0.40 x 0.20 + 0.10 x 0.24

= 0.036 + 0.048 + 0.080 + 0.024

= 0.158 = 15.8%

Portfolio Risk

$$\sigma_p = \sqrt{Variance} = \sqrt{\sigma_p{}^2}$$

$$= \sqrt{\sum_{i=1}^{n} \left(R_{i-}\hat{R}\right)^2 p_i}$$

Where,

σ_p = Standard deviation of portfolio return

R_i = Expected return on portfolio in a given condition i

P_i = Probability of happening of condition i

n = number of conditions

Concept of Portfolio Risk: Risk of a portfolio depends on the risk of individual assets of portfolio and the covariance of returns of assets of the portfolio.Risk of portfolio is expected to be reduced with inclusion of more assets in the portfolio.In a two asset portfolio, if return on one asset is negatively correlated the portfolio risk will be lower than when the returns of assets are positively correlated.

- Alternate formula to measure of portfolio risk

$$\sigma_{port} = \sqrt{\sum_{i=1}^{n} w_i^2 \sigma_i^2 + \sum_{i=1}^{n} \sum_{\substack{j=1 \\ i \neq j}}^{n} w_i w_j Cov_{ij}}$$

Where,

σ_{port} = the standard deviation of the portfolio

W_i = the weights of an individual asset in the portfolio, where weights are determined by the proportion of value in the portfolio

The variance of rates of return for asset I

Cov_{ij} = the covariance between the rates of return for assets i and j where, $Cov_{ij} = \rho_{ij}\sigma_i\sigma_j$

Portfolio Risk: Example

Asset	$E(R_i)$	W_i	σ_i^2	σ_i
A	0.10	0.50	0.0049	0.07
B	0.20	0.50	0.0100	0.10

If correlation coefficient between returns of A and B is 0.6,

σ_{port} = (0.5 x 0.5 x 0.07 x 0.07 + 0.5 x 0.5 x 0.10 x 0.10 + 0.5 x 0.5 x 0.6 x 0.07 x 0.10 + 0.5 x 0.5 x 0.6 x 0.10 x 0.07)$^{1/2}$=(0.005825)$^{1/2}$=0.076322=7.632%

References

- Brown, Stephen and Jerold Warner, 1985, "Using daily stock returns: the case of event studies," Journal of Financial Economics 14, 3-31
- Strong, Robert (2009). Portfolio construction, management, and protection. Mason, Ohio: South-Western Cengage Learning. p. 527. ISBN 0-324-66510-5
- "Definition of Abnormal Returns". About.com - Economics. Archived from the original on 17 September 2008. Retrieved 2008-08-07
- Markowitz, Harry M. (1952). "Portfolio Selection". Journal of Finance. 7 (1): 77–91. JSTOR 2975974. doi:10.2307/2975974
- Samuelson, Paul, "General Proof that Diversification Pays,"Journal of Financial and Quantitative Analysis 2, March 1967, 1-13
- O'Sullivan, Arthur; Sheffrin, Steven M. (2003). Economics: Principles in Action. Upper Saddle River, New Jersey: Pearson Prentice Hall. p. 273. ISBN 0-13-063085-3
- "Property Yield – Calculating Property Yields & Return on Investment". Archived from the original on June 17, 2017. Retrieved June 17, 2017
- Eisenberg, L.; Noe, T.H. (2001). "Systemic Risk in Financial Systems". Management Science. 47 (2): 236–249. doi:10.1287/mnsc.47.2.236.9835
- Ross, Stephen, "Adding risks: Samuelson's fallacy of large numbers revisited," Journal of Financial and Quantitative Analysis 34, September 1999, 323-339
- Life Application Study Bible: New Living Translation. Wheaton, Illinois: Tyndale House Publishers, Inc. 1996. p. 1024. ISBN 0-8423-3267-7
- (English) "see Michael Prahl, "Asian Private Equity – Will it Deliver on its Promise?", INSEAD Global Private Equity Initiative (GPEI)" (PDF). Retrieved 2011-06-15

- Rabin, Matthew (2000). "Risk Aversion and Expected-Utility Theory: A Calibration Theorem". Econometrica. 68 (5): 1281–1292. doi:10.1111/1468-0262.00158
- Danielsson, J.; James, K.; Valenzuela, M.; Zer, I. (2016). "Model risk of risk models". Journal of Financial Stability. 23: 79–91. doi:10.1016/j.jfs.2016.02.002
- Mr Lev Virine; Mr Michael Trumper (28 October 2013). ProjectThink: Why Good Managers Make Poor Project Choices. Gower Publishing, Ltd. ISBN 978-1-4724-0403-9
- "What are the health risks associated with mobile phones and their base stations?". Online Q&A. World Health Organization. 2005-12-05. Retrieved 2008-01-19
- Barber, Brad; Odean, Terrance (2002). "Online Investors: Do the Slow Die First?". Review of Financial Studies. 15 (2): 455–488. doi:10.1093/rfs/15.2.455
- Merton, R.C. (1974). "On the pricing of corporate debt: the risk structure of interest rates". Journal of Finance. 29 (2): 449–470. doi:10.1111/j.1540-6261.1974.tb03058
- Levy, Haim (2006). Stochastic Dominance: Investment Decision Making under Uncertainty (Second ed.). New York: Springer. ISBN 0-387-29302-7

3

An Integrated Study of Market Efficiency

The efficiency of the market can be recognized on the basis of its informational efficiency. The different types of efficient market hypotheses are weak form of market efficiency, semi-strong form of market efficiency and strong form of market efficiency. This chapter provides a plethora of interdisciplinary topics for better comprehension of market efficiency.

Market Efficiency

In capital markets an investors' expectation of return is driven by the approach for making excess profit than to other potential investment options. This leads to the fundamental premise of an investment is expect higher return on higher risk. However when academic literature attempts to define market efficiency, it emphasises that is a market is efficient, then the market price is the true and unbiased estimate of the true value of investment. In other words a market can be categorised as efficient on the basis of its informational efficiency. If capital markets are efficient enough then all the relevant information is impounded into the stock price and the quoted stock prices always incorporate and reflect all relevant information. Under such conditions the investors are unable to beat the market with supernormal profit. Therefore, if a market is categorised as efficient with respect to information set it, then it is impossible for the market participants to make economic profits by trading on the basis of information set it. It can be also being considered as a zero profit competitive equilibrium condition with respect to the dynamic price behaviour of securities under conditions of uncertainty.

Conditions of Market Efficiency

The market in which the price for any security effectively represents the expected net present value of all future profits can be characterised as efficient market. To say market is efficient is access the speed at which new information filters into the price. However the scenario of efficient market and different degree of market efficiency depend upon the following conditions:

- a large number of competing profit-maximizing participants analyse and value securities, each independently of the others
- active participation in the market

- individuals can not affect the market prices
- information must be free
- free entry and exit by market players must be uninhibited

In the 1970s Eugene Fama defined an efficient financial market as "*one in which prices always fully reflect available information*".

A trait of an allocatively efficient financial market is that it channels funds from the ultimate lenders to the ultimate borrowers in a way that the funds are used in the most socially useful manner.

Market Efficiency Levels

Eugene Fama identified three levels of market efficiency:

1. Weak-form efficiency

Prices of the securities instantly and fully reflect all information of the past prices. This means future price movements cannot be predicted by using past prices. This simply means that past data on stock prices are of no use in predicting future stock price changes.

2. Semi-strong efficiency

Asset prices fully reflect all of the publicly available information. Therefore, only investors with additional inside information could have an advantage in the market. Any price anomalies are quickly found out and the stock market adjusts.

3. Strong-form efficiency

Asset prices fully reflect all of the public and inside information available. Therefore, no one can have an advantage in the market in predicting prices since there is no data that would provide any additional value to the investors.

Efficient-market Hypothesis (EMH)

Fama also created the efficient-market hypothesis (EMH) theory, which states that in any given time, the prices on the market already reflect all known information, and also change fast to reflect new information.

Therefore, no one could outperform the market by using the same information that is already available to all investors, except through luck.

Random Walk Theory

Another theory related to the efficient market hypothesis created by Louis Bachelier is the "random walk" theory, which states that prices in the financial markets evolve randomly.

Therefore, identifying trends or patterns of price changes in a market couldn't be used to predict the future value of financial instruments.

Evidence

Evidence of Financial Market Efficiency

- Predicting future asset prices is not always accurate (represents weak efficiency form)
- Asset prices always reflect all new available information quickly (represents semi-strong efficiency form)
- Investors can't outperform on the market often (represents strong efficiency form)

Evidence of Financial Market Inefficiency

- There is a vast literature in academic finance dealing with the momentum effect that was identified by Jegadeesh and Titman. Stocks that have performed relatively well (poorly) over the past 3 to 12 months continue to do well (poorly) over the next 3 to 12 months. The momentum strategy is long recent winners and shorts recent losers, and produces positive risk-adjusted average returns. Being simply based on past stock returns that are functions of past prices (dividends can be ignored), the momentum effect produces strong evidence against weak-form market efficiency,and has been observed in the stock returns of most countries, in industry returns, and in national equity market indices. Moreover, Fama has accepted that momentum is the premier anomaly.
- January effect (repeating and predictable price movements and patterns occur on the market)
- Stock market crashes, Asset Bubbles, and Credit Bubbles
- Investors that often outperform on the market such as Warren Buffett, institutional investors, and corporations trading in their own stock
- Certain consumer credit market prices don't adjust to legal changes that affect future losses

Market Efficiency Types

James Tobin identified four efficiency types that could be present in a financial market:

1. Information arbitrage efficiency

Asset prices fully reflect all of the privately available information (the least demanding requirement for efficient market, since arbitrage includes realizable, risk free transactions)

Arbitrage involves taking advantage of price similarities of financial instruments between 2 or more markets by trading to generate losses.

It involves only risk-free transactions and the information used for trading is obtained at no cost. Therefore, the profit opportunities are not fully exploited, and it can be said that arbitrage is a result of market inefficiency.

This reflects the semi-strong efficiency model.

2. Fundamental valuation efficiency

Asset prices reflect the expected past flows of payments associated with holding the assets (profit forecasts are correct, they attract investors)

Fundamental valuation involves lower risks and less profit opportunities. It refers to the accuracy of the predicted return on the investment.

Financial markets are characterized by predictability and inconsistent misalignments that force the prices to always deviate from their fundamental valuations.

This reflects the weak information efficiency model.

3. Full insurance efficiency

It ensures the continuous delivery of goods and services in all contingencies.

4. Functional/Operational efficiency

The products and services available at the financial markets are provided for the least cost and are directly useful to the participants.

Every financial market will contain a unique mixture of the identified efficiency types.

Financial market efficiency is an important topic in the world of finance. While most financiers believe the markets are neither 100% efficient, nor 100% inefficient, many disagree where on the efficiency line the world's markets fall.

It can be concluded that in reality a financial market can't be considered to be extremely efficient, or completely inefficient.

The financial markets are a mixture of both, sometimes the market will provide fair returns on the investment for everyone, while at other times certain investors will generate above average returns on their investment.

Efficient-market Hypothesis

Efficient-market hypothesis (EMH) is a theory in financial economics that states that an asset's prices fully reflect all available information. A direct implication is that it is impossible to "beat the market" consistently on a risk-adjusted basis since market prices should only react to new information or changes in discount rates (the latter may be predictable or unpredictable).

The EMH was developed by Professor Eugene Fama who argued that stocks always trade at their fair value, making it impossible for investors to either purchase undervalued stocks or sell stocks for inflated prices. As such, it should be impossible to outperform the overall market through expert stock selection or market timing, and that the only way an investor can possibly obtain higher returns is by chance or by purchasing riskier investments. His 2012 study with Kenneth French confirmed this view, showing that the distribution of abnormal returns of US mutual funds is very similar to what would be expected if no fund managers had any skill—a necessary condition for the EMH to hold.

There are three variants of the hypothesis: "weak", "semi-strong", and "strong" form. The weak form of the EMH claims that prices on traded assets (*e.g.*, stocks, bonds, or property) already reflect all past publicly available information. The semi-strong form of the EMH claims both that prices reflect all publicly available information and that prices instantly change to reflect new public information. The strong form of the EMH additionally claims that prices instantly reflect even hidden "insider" information.

Critics have blamed the belief in rational markets for much of the late-2000s financial crisis. In response, proponents of the hypothesis have stated that market efficiency does not mean not having any uncertainty about the future, that market efficiency is a simplification of the world which may not always hold true, and that the market is practically efficient for investment purposes for most individuals.

Historical Background

Historically, the EMH is preceded by Hayek's (1945) argument that markets are the most effective way of aggregating the pieces of information dispersed amongst individuals within a society. Given the ability to profit from private information, self-interested traders are motivated to acquire and act on their private information. In doing so, traders contribute to more and more efficient market prices. In the competitive limit, market prices reflect all available information and prices can only move in response to news. Thus there is a very close link between EMH and the random walk hypothesis which was discussed in 1863 by Jules Regnault, a French broker. Later another French mathematician, Louis Bachelier, applied probability theory in his 1900 PhD thesis, "The Theory of Speculation." His work was largely ignored until the 1950s when financial economists began making heavy use of probability theory and statistics to model asset prices (in particular, options prices).

Empirically, a number of studies indicated that US stock prices and related financial series followed a random walk model in the short-term. Whilst there is some predictability over the long-term, the extent to which this is due to rational time-varying risk premia as opposed to behavioral reasons is a subject of debate. Research by Alfred Cowles in the 1930s and 1940s suggested that professional investors were in general unable to outperform the market.

EMH Anomalies and Rejection of the CAPM

While event studies of stock splits is consistent with the EMH (Fama, Fisher, Jensen, and Roll, 1969), other empirical analyses have found problems with the efficient-market hypothesis. Early examples include the observation that small neglected stocks and stocks with low book-market ratios (value stocks) tended to achieve abnormally high returns relative to what could be explained by the CAPM. Further tests of portfolio efficiency by Gibbons, Ross and Shakens (1989) (GJR) led to rejections of the CAPM, although tests of efficiency inevitably run into the joint hypothesis problem.

Following GJR's results and mounting empirical evidence of EMH anomalies, academics began to move away from the CAPM towards risk factor models such as the Fama-French 3 factor model. It should be noted that these risk factor models are not properly founded on economic theory (whereas CAPM is founded on Modern Portfolio Theory), but rather, constructed with long-short portfolios in response to the observed empirical EMH anomalies. For instance, the "small-minus-big" (SMB) factor in the FF3 factor model is simply a portfolio that holds long positions on small stocks and short positions on large stocks to mimic the risks small stocks face. These risk factors are said to represent some aspect or dimension of undiversifiable systematic risk which should be compensated with higher expected returns. Additional popular risk factors include the "HML" value factor (Fama and French, 1993); "MOM" momentum factor (Carhart, 1997); "ILLIQ" liquidity factors (Amihud et al. 2002).

Joint Hypothesis Problem

When testing the EMH one inevitably finds that 1) either the market is inefficient, or 2) the asset pricing model used to test market efficiency is incorrect. Hence tests of market efficiency run into this joint hypothesis problem. For instance, early tests of market efficiency used the CAPM, which could be an incomplete model of asset prices; test results on market efficiency would thus be inconclusive.

Formally, the joint hypothesis problem says that it is never possible to test (sufficiently, to prove or disprove) market efficiency. A test of market efficiency must include some model for how prices may be set efficiently. Then actual prices can be examined to see whether this holds true. Usually this fails and then this supports the case that markets are not efficient. The joint hypothesis problem says that, when this happens, it shows that the model is not complete. There are some factors that are not accounted for.

Impacts

The efficient-market hypothesis emerged as a prominent theory in the mid-1960s. Paul Samuelson had begun to circulate Bachelier's work among economists. In 1964 Bachelier's dissertation along with the empirical studies mentioned above were published in an anthology edited by Paul Cootner. In 1965, Eugene Fama published his dissertation arguing for the random walk hypothesis. Also, Samuelson published a proof showing that if the market is efficient prices will show random-walk behavior. This is often cited in support of the efficient-market theory, by the method of affirming the consequent, however in that same paper, Samuelson warns against such backward reasoning, saying "From a nonempirical base of axioms you never get empirical results." In 1970, Fama published a review of both the theory and the evidence for the hypothesis. The paper extended and refined the theory, included the definitions for three forms of financial market efficiency: weak, semi-strong and strong.

It has been argued that the stock market is "micro efficient" but not "macro efficient". The main proponent of this view was Samuelson, who asserted that the EMH is much better suited for individual stocks than it is for the aggregate stock market. Research based on regression and scatter diagrams has strongly supported Samuelson's dictum. This result is also the theoretical justification for the forecasting of broad economic trends, which is provided by a variety of groups including non-profit groups as well as by for-profit private institutions (such as brokerage houses and consulting companies).

Further to this evidence that the UK stock market is weak-form efficient, other studies of capital markets have pointed toward their being semi-strong-form efficient. A study by Khan of the grain futures market indicated semi-strong form efficiency following the release of large trader position information (Khan, 1986). Studies by Firth (1976, 1979, and 1980) in the United Kingdom have compared the share prices existing after a takeover announcement with the bid offer. Firth found that the share prices were fully and instantaneously adjusted to their correct levels, thus concluding that the UK stock market was semi-strong-form efficient. However, the market's ability to efficiently respond to a short term, widely publicized event such as a takeover announcement does not necessarily prove market efficiency related to other more long term, amorphous factors. David Dreman has criticized the evidence provided by this instant "efficient" response, pointing out that an immediate response is not necessarily efficient, and that the long-term performance of the stock in response to certain movements are better indications.

Theoretical Background

Beyond the normal utility maximizing agents, the efficient-market hypothesis requires that agents have rational expectations; that on average the population is correct (even if no one person is) and whenever new relevant information appears, the agents update their expectations appropriately. Note that it is not required that the agents be rational. EMH allows that when faced with new information, some investors may overreact and some may underreact. All that is required by the EMH is that investors' reactions be random and follow a normal distribution pattern so that the net effect on market prices cannot be reliably exploited to make an abnormal profit, especially when considering transaction costs (including commissions and spreads). Thus, any one person can be wrong about the market—indeed, everyone can be—but the market as a whole is always right. There are three common forms in which the efficient-market hypothesis is commonly stated—weak-form efficiency, semi-strong-form efficiency and strong-form efficiency, each of which has different implications for how markets work.

Weak-form Efficiency

In weak-form efficiency, future prices cannot be predicted by analyzing prices from the past. Excess returns cannot be earned *in the long run* by using investment strategies based on historical share prices or other historical data. Technical analysis techniques will not be able to consistently produce excess returns, though some forms of fundamental analysis may still provide excess returns. Share prices exhibit no serial dependencies, meaning that there are no "patterns" to asset prices. This implies that future price movements are determined entirely by information not contained in the price series. Hence, prices must follow a random walk. This 'soft' EMH does not require that prices remain at or near equilibrium, but only that market participants not be able to *systematically* profit from market 'inefficiencies'. However, while EMH predicts that all price movement (in the absence of change in fundamental information) is random (i.e., non-trending), many studies have shown a marked tendency for the stock markets to trend over time periods of weeks or longer and that, moreover, there is a positive correlation between degree of trending and length of time period studied (but note that over long time periods, the trending is sinusoidal in appearance). Various explanations for such large and apparently non-random price movements have been promulgated.

There is a vast literature in academic finance dealing with the momentum effect identified by Jegadeesh and Titman. Stocks that have performed relatively well (poorly) over the past 3 to 12 months continue to do well (poorly) over the next 3 to 12 months. The momentum strategy is long recent winners and shorts recent losers, and produces positive risk-adjusted average returns. Being simply based on past stock returns, the momentum effect produces strong evidence against weak-form market efficiency, and has been observed in the stock returns of most countries, in industry returns, and in national equity market indices. Moreover, Fama has accepted that momentum is the premier anomaly

The problem of algorithmically constructing prices which reflect all available information has been studied extensively in the field of computer science.

A novel approach for testing the weak form of the Efficient Market Hypothesis is using quantifers derived from Information Theory. In this line, Zunino et al. found that informational efficiency is related to market size and the stage of development of the economy. Using a similar technique, Bariviera et al. uncover the impact of important economic events on informational efficiency. The methodology proposed by econophysicists Zunino, Bariviera and coauthors is new and alternative to usual econometric techniques, and is able to detect changes in the stochastic and or chaotic underlying dynamics of prices time series.

Semi-strong-form Efficiency

In semi-strong-form efficiency, it is implied that share prices adjust to publicly available new information very rapidly and in an unbiased fashion, such that no excess returns can be earned by trading on that information. Semi-strong-form efficiency implies that neither fundamental analysis nor technical analysis techniques will be able to reliably produce excess returns. To test for semi-strong-form efficiency, the adjustments to previously unknown news must be of a reasonable size and must be instantaneous. To test for this, consistent upward or downward adjustments after the initial change must be looked for. If there are any such adjustments it would suggest that investors had interpreted the information in a biased fashion and hence in an inefficient manner.

Strong-form Efficiency

In strong-form efficiency, share prices reflect all information, public and private, and no one can earn excess returns. If there are legal barriers to private information becoming public, as with insider trading laws, strong-form efficiency is impossible, except in the case where the laws are universally ignored. To test for strong-form efficiency, a market needs to exist where investors cannot consistently earn excess returns over a long period of time. Even if some money managers are consistently observed to beat the market, no refutation even of strong-form efficiency follows: with hundreds of thousands of fund managers worldwide, even a normal distribution of returns (as efficiency predicts) should be expected to produce a few dozen "star" performers.

Criticism and Behavioral Finance

Investors, including the likes of Warren Buffett, and researchers have disputed the efficient-market hypothesis both empirically and theoretically. Behavioral economists attribute the imperfections in financial markets to a combination of cognitive biases such as overconfidence, overreaction, representative bias, information bias, and various other predictable human errors in reasoning and information processing. These have been researched by psychologists such as Daniel Kahneman, Amos Tversky, Richard Thaler, and Paul Slovic. These errors in reasoning lead most investors to avoid value stocks and buy growth stocks at expensive prices, which allow those who reason correctly to profit from bargains in neglected value stocks and the overreacted selling of growth stocks. Investors prefer riskier funds in spring and safer funds in autumn.

Empirical evidence has been mixed, but has generally not supported strong forms of the efficient-market hypothesis According to Dreman and Berry, in a 1995 paper, low P/E stocks have greater returns. In an earlier paper Dreman also refuted the assertion by Ray Ball that these higher returns could be attributed to higher beta, whose research had been accepted by efficient market theorists as explaining the anomaly in neat accordance with modern portfolio theory.

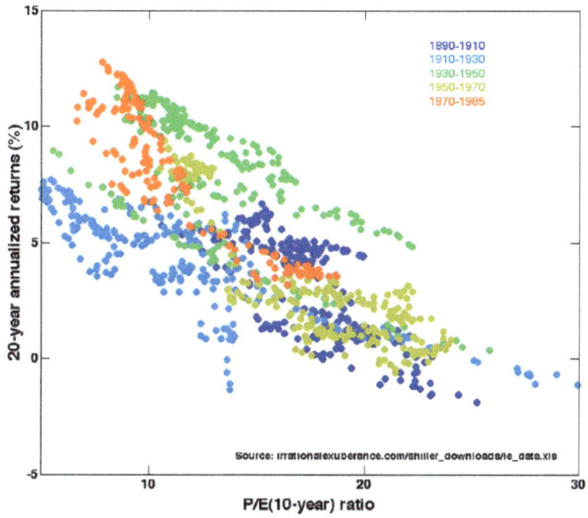

Price-Earnings ratios as a predictor of twenty-year returns based upon the plot by Robert Shiller.

The horizontal axis shows the real price-earnings ratio of the S&P Composite Stock Price Index as computed in *Irrational Exuberance* (inflation adjusted price divided by the prior ten-year mean of inflation-adjusted earnings). The vertical axis shows the geometric average real annual return on investing in the S&P Composite Stock Price Index, reinvesting dividends, and selling twenty years later. Data from different twenty-year periods is color-coded as shown in the key. Shiller states that this plot "confirms that long-term investors—investors who commit their money to an investment for ten full years—did do well when prices were low relative to earnings at the beginning of the ten years. Long-term investors would be well advised, individually, to lower their exposure to the stock market when it is high, as it has been recently, and get into the market when it is low." Burton Malkiel, a well-known proponent of the general validity of EMH, stated that this correlation may be consistent with an efficient market due to differences in interest rates.

One can identify "losers" as stocks that have had poor returns over some number of past years. "Winners" would be those stocks that had high returns over a similar period. The main result of one such study is that losers have much higher average returns than winners over the following period of the same number of years. A later study showed that beta (β) cannot account for this difference in average returns. This tendency of returns to reverse over long horizons (i.e., losers become winners) is yet another contradiction of EMH. Losers would have to have much higher betas than winners in order to justify the return difference. The study showed that the beta difference required to save the EMH is just not there. It is important to note, however, that these studies were compiled in the mid-1980s and may not be reflective of more modern trends of efficiency, which often rely around extensive internet and computer based information analytics.

Economic Bubbles and Irrational Exuberance

Speculative economic bubbles are an obvious anomaly, in that the market often appears to be driven by buyers operating on escalating market sentiment/ irrational exuberance, who take little notice of underlying value. These bubbles are typically followed by an overreaction of frantic selling, allowing shrewd investors to buy stocks at bargain prices. Rational investors have difficulty profiting by shorting irrational bubbles because, in the words of a famous saying attributed to John Maynard Keynes, "Markets can stay irrational longer than you can stay solvent." Sudden market crashes as happened on Black Monday in 1987 are mysterious from the perspective of efficient markets, but allowed as a rare statistical event under the weak-form of EMH. Benoit Mandelbrot has argued that market bubbles are not anomalous but rather characteristic of price dynamics described by power laws such as Pareto, Zipf or Tracy-Widom combined with persistence in price change trends.

Burton Malkiel has warned that certain emerging markets such as China are not empirically efficient; that the Shanghai and Shenzhen markets, unlike markets in United States, exhibit considerable serial correlation (price trends), non-random walk, and evidence of manipulation.

Behavioral Psychology

Daniel Kahneman

Behavioral psychology approaches to stock market trading are among some of the more promising alternatives to EMH (and some investment strategies seek to exploit exactly such inefficiencies). But Nobel Laureate co-founder of the programme Daniel Kahneman —announced his skepticism of investors beating the market: “They’re [investors] just not going to do it [beat the market]. It’s just not going to happen.” Indeed, defenders of EMH maintain that Behavioral Finance strengthens the case for EMH in that it highlights biases in individuals and committees and not competitive markets. For example, one prominent finding in Behaviorial Finance is that individuals employ hyperbolic discounting. It is demonstrably true that bonds, mortgages, annuities and other similar financial instruments subject to competitive market forces do not. Any manifestation of hyperbolic discounting in the pricing of these obligations would invite arbitrage thereby quickly eliminating any vestige of individual biases. Similarly, diversification, derivative securities and other hedging strategies assuage if not eliminate potential mispricings from the severe risk-intolerance (loss aversion) of individuals underscored by behavioral finance. On the other hand, economists, behaviorial psychologists and mutual fund managers are drawn from the human population and are therefore subject to the biases that behavioralists showcase. By contrast, the price signals in markets are far less subject to individual biases highlighted by the Behavioral Finance programme. Richard Thaler has started a fund based on his research on cognitive biases. In a 2008 report he identified complexity and herd behavior as central to the global financial crisis of 2008.

Further empirical work has highlighted the impact transaction costs have on the concept of market efficiency, with much evidence suggesting that any anomalies pertaining to market inefficiencies are the result of a cost benefit analysis made by those willing to incur the cost of acquiring the valuable information in order to trade on it. Additionally the concept of liquidity is a critical component to capturing “inefficiencies” in tests for abnormal returns. Any test of this proposition faces the joint hypothesis problem, where it is impossible to ever test for market efficiency, since to do so requires the use of a measuring stick against which abnormal returns are compared —one cannot know if the market is efficient if one does not know if a model correctly stipulates the required rate of return. Consequently, a situation arises where either the asset pricing model is incorrect or the market is inefficient, but one has no way of knowing which is the case.

The performance of stock markets is correlated with the amount of sunshine in the city where the main exchange is located.

A key work on random walk was done in the late 1980s by Profs. Andrew Lo and Craig MacKinlay; they effectively argue that a random walk does not exist, nor ever has. Their paper took almost two years to be accepted by academia and in 1999 they published “A Non-random Walk Down Wall St.” which collects their research papers on the topic up to that time.

View of Some Economists

Economists Matthew Bishop and Michael Green claim that full acceptance of the hypothesis goes against the thinking of Adam Smith and John Maynard Keynes, who both believed irrational behavior had a real impact on the markets.

Economist John Quiggin has claimed that "Bitcoin is perhaps the finest example of a pure bubble", and that it provides a conclusive refutation of EMH. While other assets used as currency (such as gold, tobacco) have value independent of people's willingness to accept them as payment, Quiggin argues that "in the case of Bitcoin there is no source of value whatsoever" and that:

Since Bitcoins do not generate any actual earnings, they must appreciate in value to ensure that people are willing to hold them. But an endless appreciation, with no flow of earnings or liquidation value, is precisely the kind of bubble the EMH says can't happen.

In 2013, Kim Man Lui pointed out that there is difference of performance between experienced and novice traders in a controlled experiment. If the market really walks randomly, there should be no difference between these two kinds of traders. However, traders who are more knowledgeable on technical analysis significantly outperform those who are less knowledgeable.

Tshilidzi Marwala surmised that artificial intelligence influences the applicability of the theory of the efficient market hypothesis in that the more artificial intelligence infused computer traders there are in the markets as traders the more efficient the markets become.

Warren Buffett has also argued against EMH, most notably in his 1984 presentation The Superinvestors of Graham-and-Doddsville, saying the preponderance of value investors among the world's best money managers rebuts the claim of EMH proponents that luck is the reason some investors appear more successful than others. As Malkiel has shown, over the 30 years (to 1996) more than two-thirds of professional portfolio managers have been outperformed by the S&P 500 Index.

Late 2000s Financial Crisis

The financial crisis of 2007–08 led to renewed scrutiny and criticism of the hypothesis. Market strategist Jeremy Grantham stated flatly that the EMH was responsible for the current financial crisis, claiming that belief in the hypothesis caused financial leaders to have a "chronic underestimation of the dangers of asset bubbles breaking". Noted financial journalist Roger Lowenstein blasted the theory, declaring "The upside of the current Great Recession is that it could drive a stake through the heart of the academic nostrum known as the efficient-market hypothesis." Former Federal Reserve chairman Paul Volcker chimed in, saying it's "clear that among the causes of the recent financial crisis was an unjustified faith in rational expectations [and] market efficiencies." "By 2007–2009, you had to be a fanatic to believe in the literal truth of the EMH", noted one financial analyst.

At the International Organization of Securities Commissions annual conference, held in June 2009, the hypothesis took center stage. Martin Wolf, the chief economics commentator for the *Financial Times*, dismissed the hypothesis as being a useless way to examine how markets function in reality. Paul McCulley, managing director of PIMCO, was less extreme in his criticism, saying that the hypothesis had not failed, but was "seriously flawed" in its neglect of human nature.

The financial crisis led Richard Posner, a prominent judge, University of Chicago law professor, and innovator in the field of Law and Economics, to back away from the hypothesis and express some degree of belief in Keynesian economics. Posner accused some of his Chicago School colleagues of being "asleep at the switch", saying that "the movement to deregulate the financial industry went too far by exaggerating the resilience—the self healing powers—of laissez-faire capitalism." Others, such as Fama, said that the hypothesis held up well during the crisis and that the markets were a casualty of the recession, not the cause of it. Despite this, Fama has conceded that "poorly informed investors could theoretically lead the market astray" and that stock prices could become "somewhat irrational" as a result.

Critics have suggested that financial institutions and corporations have been able to reduce the efficiency of financial markets by creating private information and reducing the accuracy of conventional disclosures, and by developing new and complex products which are challenging for most market participants to evaluate and correctly price.

Efficient Markets Applied in Securities Class Action Litigation

The theory of efficient markets has been practically applied in the field of Securities Class Action Litigation. Efficient market theory, in conjunction with "Fraud on the Market Theory," has been used in Securities Class Action Litigation to both justify and as mechanism for the calculation of damages. In the Supreme Court Case, Halliburton v. Erica P. John Fund, U.S. Supreme Court, No. 13-317, the use of efficient market theory in supporting securities class action litigation was affirmed. Supreme Court Justice Roberts wrote that "the court's ruling was consistent with the ruling in "Basic" because it allows "direct evidence when such evidence is available" instead of relying exclusively on the efficient markets theory."

Different Types of Efficient Market Hypotheses

Market efficiency is usually analyzed by addressing two questions: first can the market be predicted? and secondly are there strategies that "beat" the market? If the market can be predicted and there are strategies available to beat the market, then the basic tent of market efficiency hypothesis can never be accepted. Several versions of the Efficient Market Hypothesis have been widely discussed and tested in the literature. The differences revolve primarily around the definition of the information set used in those tests. In his original article, Fama (1970)[3] divided the overall efficient market hypothesis (EMH) and the empirical tests of the hypothesis into three sub hypotheses depending on the information set involved: (1) weak-form EMH, (2) semi strong-form EMH, and (3) strong-form EMH.

- Weak form of market efficiency: Prices reflect all information contained in past prices and returns (rules out technical analysis). Assumes that current stock prices fully reflect all security market information, including the historical sequence of prices, rates of return, trading volume data, and other market-generated information, such as odd-lot transactions, block trades, and transactions by exchange specialists. In other words, the information set *It* is taken to be solely the information contained in the past price history of the market as of time *t* and past rates of return and other historical market data should have no relationship with future rates of return.
- Semi-strong form of market efficiency: Prices reflect all public information (past prices, news papers contents, databases, etc.). It asserts that security prices adjust rapidly to the release of all public information; that is, current security prices fully reflect all public information. In this case *It* mistaken to be all information that is publicly available at time *t*. This also includes the past history of prices so the weak form is just a restricted version of this.
- Strong form of market efficiency: Prices reflect all available information, both public and private. This means that no group of investors has monopolistic access to information relevant to the formation of prices. Therefore, no group of investors should be able to consistently derive above-average risk-adjusted rates of return. In this case *It* is taken to be all information known to anyone at time *t*.

Implications of Efficient Market Hypothesis

- For professional money managers
    - Less time spent on individual securities
    - Passive investing favoured
    - Otherwise must believe in superior insight
- Tasks if markets informationally efficient
- Maintain correct diversification
- Achieve and maintain desired portfolio risk
- Manage tax burden
- Control transaction costs

Adaptive Market Hypothesis

The adaptive market hypothesis, as proposed by Andrew Lo, is an attempt to reconcile economic theories based on the efficient market hypothesis (which implies that markets are efficient) with behavioral economics, by applying the principles of evolution to financial interactions: competition, adaptation and natural selection.

Under this approach, the traditional models of modern financial economics can coexist with behavioral models. Lo argues that much of what behaviorists cite as counterexamples to economic rationality—loss aversion, overconfidence, overreaction, and other behavioral biases—are, in fact, consistent with an evolutionary model of individuals adapting to a changing environment using simple heuristics.

Details

According to Lo, the adaptive market hypothesis can be viewed as a new version of the efficient market hypothesis, derived from evolutionary principles:

Prices reflect as much information as dictated by the combination of environmental conditions and the number and nature of "species" in the economy.

By species, he means distinct groups of market participants, each behaving in a common manner—pension fund managers, retail investors, market makers, hedge fund managers, etc.

If multiple members of a single group are competing for rather scarce resources within a single market, then that market is likely to be highly efficient (for example, the market for 10-year U.S. Treasury notes, which reflects most relevant information very quickly indeed). On the other hand, if a small number of species are competing for rather abundant resources, then that market will be less efficient (for example, the market for oil paintings from the Italian Renaissance).

Market efficiency cannot be evaluated in a vacuum, but is highly context-dependent and dynamic. Shortly stated, the degree of market efficiency is related to environmental factors characterizing market ecology, such as the number of competitors in the market, the magnitude of profit opportunities available, and the adaptability of the market participants.

Implications

The adaptive market hypothesis has several implications that differentiate it from the efficient market hypothesis:

1. To the extent that a relation between risk and reward exists, it is unlikely to be stable over time.

2. There are opportunities for arbitrage.
3. Investment strategies—including quantitatively, fundamentally and technically based methods—will perform well in certain environments and poorly in others.
4. The primary objective is survival; profit and utility maximization are secondary.
5. The key to survival is innovation: as the risk/reward relation varies, the better way of achieving a consistent level of expected returns is to adapt to changing market conditions.

Noisy Market Hypothesis

In finance, the noisy market hypothesis contrasts the efficient-market hypothesis in that it claims that the prices of securities are not always the best estimate of the true underlying value of the firm. It argues that prices can be influenced by speculators and momentum traders, as well as by insiders and institutions that often buy and sell stocks for reasons unrelated to fundamental value, such as for diversification, liquidity and taxes. These temporary shocks referred to as "noise" can obscure the true value of securities and may result in mispricing of these securities, potentially for many years.

Testing Market Efficiency

Academicians and researchers have formulated two groups of tests of the weak form of EMH. The first category involves statistical tests of independence between rates of return and second entails a comparison of risk-return results from trading rules that make investment decisions based on the past market information relative to the results from buy and hold policy1. The Statistical Tests used to test the weak form EMH are (i) Autocorrelation test and (ii) Run Test.

(i) Autocorrelation test: Autocorrelation tests of independence measure the significance of positive or negative correlation in returns over time. Does the rate of return on day t correlate with the rate of return on day t – 1, t – 2, or t – 3? Those who believe that capital markets are efficient would expect insignificant correlations for all such combinations.

Example:

Consider the following closing prices of ABC Limited during the month of July 2004 and July 2007: Do they follow a random path? Check their independence employing auto-correlation test. It has been assumed that the investor you buy stock at the beginning of the test period and hold it to the end.

Trading Days July 2007	Closing price	Trading Days July 2004	Closing price
3	2016.85	2	785
4	2040.85	3	780
5	2058.00	6	770
6	2042.10	8	795
7	2026.50	9	770
10	2092.10	10	780
11	2170.00	13	775
12	2270	14	780
13	2327	15	780
14	2285	16	770
17	2240	17	761.75
18	2213	20	764.75
19	2207	21	764.25
20	2225.90	22	771.25
21	2254.75	23	774.75
24	2290	24	764
25	2330	27	768
26	2315.5	28	774
27	2284.75	30	775.75
28	2241	31	781.5
31	2295.8	---	---

Solution:

Price Change in (X)	Price Change in (Y)	X^2	Y^2	XY
-5	24	25	576	-120
-10	17.5	100	294.1225	-175.5
25	-15.9	625	252.81	-397.5
-25	50	625	2500	-1250
10	77.9	100	6068.41	779
-5	100	25	10000	-500
5	57	25	3249	285
0	-42	0	1764	0
-10	-45	100	2025	450
-5.25	-27	68.0625	729	222.75
3	-6	9	36	-18
-0.5	18.9	0.25	357.21	-9.45
7	28.85	49	832.32	201.95
3.5	35.25	12.25	1242.56	123.375

-10.75	40	115.56	1600	-430
4	-14.5	16	210.25	-58
6	-30.75	36	945.56	-184.5
1.75	-43.75	3.06	1914.06	-76.56
5. 75	54.8	33.06	3003.04	315.1
ΣX= -3.5	ΣY= 278.95	ΣX^2=1967.25	ΣY^2=37599.35	ΣXY=-838.33

Mean of X =(X bar) = -3.5/ 19 = -0.184, (X bar)^2 = 0.034, Y (bar) = 278.95/ 19 =14.68, (Y bar)^2 = 215.55

Using the formula given above:

$$b = \frac{-838.34 - 19\,(0.184)\,(14.68)}{1967.25 - 19\,(0.034)} = -787.02/1966.604 = -0.4002$$

$$a = 14.68 - (-0.4002)\,(-0.184) = 14.61$$

Putting the values of 'a' and 'b' we can calculate the r as follows: 14.61

$$r^2 = \frac{14.61(278.95) + (-0.04002)(-838.34) - 19(215.5)}{37599.35 - 19\,(215.55)} = 0.0094$$

r = 0.097

Since the correlation between the prices in two different periods is small we can conclude that the price move in a random fashion and the weak form of market efficiency is valid in this context.

(ii) Run Test: the runs test considers a series of price changes over a certain period of time (suppose from t_1-t_{10}) and each price change is either designated a plus (+) if it is an increase in price or a minus (–) if it is a decrease in price. For instance the result is a set of pluses and minuses as follows: $t_1+t_2+t_3+t_4+t_5+t_6+t_7+t_8+t_9+t_{10}$ A run exist when two consecutive changes are the same (i.e., ++ or --). When the price changes in a different direction, such as +- or -+ the run ends and a new run may begin. To test for independence, the number of runs for a given series of price changes compared with the number in a table of expected values for the number of runs that should occur in a random series.

To test the independence of the prices, we require:

Total Number of Runs: r

Number of Positive Price Changes from t_1-t_{10}: n_1

Number of Negative Price Changes from t_1-t_{10} : n_2

Once we have the data the mean and standard deviation of the mean are calculated by using the formula given below:

$$\mu_r = \frac{2n_1n_2}{n_1+n_2}+1, \qquad \sigma_r = \left[\frac{2n_1n_2(2n_1n_2-n_1-n_2)}{(n_1+n_2)^2(n_1+n_2-1)}\right]^{1/2}$$

At a given level of significance, we calculate the upper and lower limits and check whether the number of runs observed from the test falls within the limits or not. If it is between the limits we conclude that the prices are random or independent of each other, otherwise not.

Illustration: (all the data are continuous)

Trad-ing days April2007	Stock price	Trading days in May2007	Stock price	Trading days in June2007	Stock price	Trading days in July2007	Stock price
1	881.5	1	1458	3	1295.5	1	1520
2	856.5	2	1425	4	1292.25	2	1489.5
3	859.75	3	1350.75	5	1191.5	3	1397.75
4	918.5	6	1447.5	6	1179.5	4	1425
5	1010.25	7	1448.25	7	1279	5	1487
8	1072.25	8	1505.25	10	1280.25	8	1536.5
9	1074.5	9	1511.25	11	1247.5	9	1500.5
10	1123.5	10	1588.25	12	1186.5	10	1481.25
11	1203.5	13	1560	13	1207.75	11	1437.25
12	1256.25	14	1576	14	1323	12	1460.75
15	1341.5	15	1638.5	17	1366.75	15	1385.5
16	1469.75	16	1648.5	18	1312	16	1401.25
17	1450.25	17	1710.75	19	1412.75	17	1381.25
18	1306.5	20	1703	20	1420.5	18	1487.25
19	1258	21	1665	21	1375.5	19	1471.25
22	1332.75	22	1665.75	24	1377.5	22	1452.75
23	1315.75	23	1550.75	25	1304.5	23	1442.5
24	1351	24	1508	26	1395		
25	1407	27	1460	27	1498.75		
26	1547.75	28	1316.25	28	1549.75		
29	1521	29	1229				
30	1484.25	30	1324.75				
		31	1205.75				

Solution:

Days	Price	PC	Run	Days	Price	PC	Run	Days	Price	PC	Run	Days	Price	PC	Run
1	881.5			1	1458	-		3	1295.5	+	16	1	1520	-	
2	856.5	-	1	2	1425	-	7	4	1292.25	-		2	1489.5	-	27
3	859.75	+		3	1350.75	-		5	1191.5	-	17	3	1397.75	-	
4	918.5	+		6	1447.5	+		6	1179.5	-		4	1425	+	28
5	1010.25	+		7	1448.25	+		7	1279	+		5	1487	+	
8	1072.25	+		8	1505.25	+	8	10	1280.25	+	18	8	1536.5	+	
9	1074.5	+		9	1511.25	+		11	1247.5	-		9	1500.5	-	
10	1123.5	+	2	10	1588.25	+		12	1186.5	-	19	10	1481.25	-	29
11	1203.5	+		13	1560	-	9	13	1207.75	+		11	1437.25	-	
12	1256.25	+		14	1576	+		14	1323	+	20	12	1460.75	+	30
15	1341.5	+		15	1638.5	+		17	1366.75	+		15	1385.5	-	31
16	1469.75	+		16	1648.5	+	10	18	1312	-	21	16	1401.25	+	32
17	1450.25	-		17	1710.75	+		19	1412.75	+		17	1381.25	-	33
18	1306.5	-	3	20	1703	-		**20**	1420.5	+	22	**18**	1487.25	+	34
19	1258	-		21	1665	-	11 12	**21**	1375.5	-	23	**19**	1471.25	-	35
22	1332.75	+	4	22	1665.75	+		**24**	1377.5	+	24	**22**	1452.75	-	
23	1315.75	-	5	23	1550.75	-		**25**	1304.5	-	25	**23**	1442.5	-	
24	1351	+	6	24	1508	-	13 14	**26**	1395	+	26				
25	1407	+		27	1460	-	15	**27**	1498.75	+					
26	1547.75	+		28	1316.25	-		**28**	1549.75	+					
29	1521	- Cont.		29	1229	-									
30				30	1324.75	+									
				31	1205.75	-									

Note: PC= Price Change Total

Number of Runs (r) = 35

Number of Positive Price Changes (n_1) = 43

Number of Negative Price Changes (n_2) = 38

$$\mu_r = \frac{2n_1 n_2}{n_1 + n_2} + 1, \qquad = \frac{2(43)(38)}{43+38} = 41.34$$

$$\sigma_r = \left[\frac{2n_1 n_2 (2n_1 n_2 - n_1 - n_2)}{(n_1 + n_2)^2 (n_1 + n_2 - 1)}\right]^{1/2} = \left[\frac{2(43)(38)[2(43)(38) - 43 - 38]}{(43+38)^2 (43+38-1)}\right]^{1/2} = 4.45$$

Assuming that the distribution follows the normal distribution if we test at 5 percent significance level then Z = 1.96.

Lower Limit = 41.34 – 1.96 (4.45) = 32.62

Upper Limit = 41.34 + 1.96 (4.45) = 50.06

Since the observed number of runs (35) falls within the lower and upper limit, we can conclude that the prices are independent at 5 percent level of significance.

Tests of Trading Rules

Mechanical trading systems, such as filter rules and moving averages, provide a more sensitive test for randomness, because they do not depend on the pattern or cause of the price changes. Advocates of efficient market hypothesized that investors could not derive above normal profits above a buy-and hold policy using any trading rule that depend solely on past market information. More trading in a security should promote the market efficiency. Most popular trading technique is Filter Rule i.e. an investor trades a stock when the price change exceeds a filter value set for it (Buy-and-Hold Strategy). If the behaviour of the stock price changes is random, filter rules should not outperform a simple buy-and-hold strategy.

Tests of the Semi Strong Form of Market Efficiency

The two more popular methods in this regard are:

- Event studies: That examine how fast stock prices adjust to specific significant economic events.
- Portfolio Study or Return Prediction Study: That examines the possibility of earning superior risk-adjusted returns by trading on an observable characteristic of a firm like P/E ratio, dividend yield etc.

Event Study

An event study is a statistical method to assess the impact of an event on the value of a firm. For example, the announcement of a merger between two business entities can be analyzed to see whether investors believe the merger will create or destroy value.

The basic idea is to find the abnormal return attributable to the event being studied by adjusting for the return that stems from the price fluctuation of the market as a whole.

As the event methodology can be used to elicit the effects of any type of event on the direction and magnitude of stock price changes, it is very versatile. Event studies are thus common to various research areas, such as accounting and finance, management, economics, marketing, information technology, law, and political science.

One aspect often used to structure the overall body of event studies is the breadth of the studied event types. On the one hand, there is research investigating the stock market responses to economy-wide events (i.e., market shocks, such as regulatory changes, or catastrophic events). On the other hand, event studies are used to investigate the stock market responses to corporate events, such as mergers and acquisitions, earnings announcements, debt or equity issues, corporate reorganisations, investment decisions and corporate social responsibility (MacKinlay 1997; McWilliams & Siegel, 1997).

Methodology

The general event study methodology is explained in, for example, MacKinlay (1997) or Mitchell and Netter (1994). In MacKinlay (1997), this is done "using financial market data" to "measure the impact of a specific event on the value of a firm". He argues that "given rationality in the marketplace, the effects of an event will be reflected immediately in security prices. Thus a measure of the event's economic impact can be constructed using security prices observed over a relatively short time period". It is important to note that short-horizon event studies are more reliable than long-horizon event studies as the latter have many limitations. However, Kothari and Warner (2005) were able to refine long-horizon methodologies in order to improve the design and reliability of the studies over longer periods.

Empirical Methods

Methodologically, event studies imply the following: Based on an estimation window prior to the analyzed event, the method estimates what the normal stock returns of the affected firm(s) should be at the day of the event and several days prior and after the event (i.e., during the event window). Thereafter, the method deducts this 'normal returns' from the 'actual returns' to receive 'abnormal returns' attributed to the event.

Event studies, however, may differ with respect to their specification of normal returns. The most common model for normal returns is the 'market model' (MacKinlay 1997). Following this model, the analysis implies to use an estimation window (typically sized 120 days) prior to the event to derive the typical relationship between the firm's stock and a reference index through a regression analysis. Based on the regression coefficients, the normal returns are then projected and used to calculate the abnormal returns. Alternative models for the normal returns include the CAPM model, or more simplistic approaches such as mean returns.

Calculation of Abnormal Returns

Depending on the model chosen for the 'normal return', conducting event studies requires the researcher to implement a distinct sequence of steps. For the most common model, the 'market model', the steps are as follows:

1. Retrieve and match time series of financial returns of the focal firm's stock and its reference index.
2. For each event, identify the sequences of firm and market returns that need to be included in the estimation window.
3. Using regression analysis, calculate the alpha, beta and sigma coefficients that explicate the typical relationship between the stock and the reference index.
4. With these three parameters, predict the 'normal returns' for all days of the event window.
5. Deducting these 'normal returns' from the 'actual returns' gives you the 'abnormal returns' which are the metrics of interest.

Significance of Abnormal Returns

To specify if individual abnormal returns differ from zero with some statistical validity, test statistics need to be applied. Various test statistics at the different levels of analysis (i.e., AR-, CAR-, AAR- and CAAR-level) exist for this purpose. The most common test, the t-test, divides the abnormal returns through the root mean square error of the regression. Resulting t-values need then to be compared with the critical values of the Student's t-distribution. There is some evidence that during times of high volatility (e.g. financial crisis of 2007–2008), too many companies tend to show significantly abnormal returns using the t-test, which makes it more difficult to determine which returns are truly "abnormal".

Software for Conducting Event Studies

Event studies can be implemented with various different tools. Single event studies can easily be implemented with MS Excel, event studies covering multiple events need to be built using statistical software packages (e.g., STATA, Matlab). Besides of these multi-use tools, there are solutions tailored to conducting event study analyses (e.g., Eventus, Event Study Metrics, EventStudyTools).

Application to Merger Analysis

The logic behind the event study methodology (within the specific context of mergers) is explained in Warren-Boulton and Dalkir (2001):

> Investors in financial markets bet their dollars on whether a merger will raise or lower prices. A merger that raises market prices will benefit both the merging

parties and their rivals and thus raise the prices for all their shares. Conversely, the financial community may expect the efficiencies from the merger to be sufficiently large to drive down prices. In this case, the share values of the merging firms' rivals fall as the probability of the merger goes up. Thus, evidence from financial markets can be used to predict market price effects when significant merger-related events have taken place.

Warren-Boulton and Dalkir (2001) apply their event-probability methodology to the proposed merger between *Staples, Inc.* and *Office Depot* (1996), which was challenged by the Federal Trade Commission and eventually withdrawn.

Findings

Warren-Boulton and Dalkir (2001) find highly significant returns to the only rival firm in the relevant market. Based on these returns, they are able to estimate the price effect of the merger in the product market which is highly consistent with the estimates of the likely price increase from other independent sources.

Steps involved with this process:

- Identify the event to be studied and pin point the date on which the event was announced
- Collect returns data around the announcement date
- Calculate the excess returns by period around the announcement date for each firm in the sample
- Compute the average excess returns across all firms
- Assess whether the excess returns around the announcement date are different from zero

Results of Available Earlier Event Studies:

- Stock split studies show that splits do not result in abnormal gains after the split announcement, but before
- Initial public offerings seems to be under priced by almost 18%, but that varies over time, and the price is adjusted within one day after the offering
- Announcements of accounting changes are quickly adjusted for and do not seem to provide opportunities
- Stock prices rapidly adjust to corporate events such as mergers and offerings

Example:

Two companies, Cargo Mutas Ltd. and Telco Farma Ltd., have increased their level of cash dividends for the year 2010-2011. A financial analyst at a mutual fund wanted to test the consistency of the semi-strong form of market efficiency. He calculated the characteristic lines for a period of six years on a monthly basis up to four months before the announcement took place. The relationship between the returns on these four companies and the market are given by:

Cargo Mutas Ltd.		Telco Farma Ltd.	
$R_{C\arg o_t} = 1.70\% + 1.05\, R_{mt}$		$R_{Telco_t} = 1.53\% + 1.08 R_{mt}$	
Periods	Actual Return		Market Return
	$R_{C\arg o_t}$	R_{Telco_t}	R_{mt}
4	13.47	13.61	11.00
3	11.90	12.04	10.00
2	13.50	13.67	11.15
1	12.97	13.12	10.88
0	13.43	13.60	10.90
1	12.50	12.62	10.05
2	13.09	13.25	11.05
3	14.51	14.71	12.15
4	14.80	14.99	12.67

Solution:

Cargo Mutas Ltd.				
Periods	Actual Return	Market Return	Expected Return	Abnormal Return
4	13.47	11.00	13.25	0.22
3	11.90	10.00	12.20	-0.30
2	13.50	11.15	13.40	0.10
1	12.97	10.88	13.12	-0.15
0	13.43	10.90	13.15	0.28
1	12.50	10.05	12.25	0.25
2	13.09	11.05	13.30	-0.21
3	14.51	12.15	14.45	0.06
4	14.80	12.67	15.00	-0.20
Telco Farma Ltd.				
Periods	Actual Return	Market Return	Expected Return	Abnormal Return
4	13.61	11.00	13.41	0.20
3	12.04	10.00	12.33	-0.29
2	13.67	11.15	13.57	0.10
1	13.12	10.88	13.28	-0.16
0	13.60	10.90	13.30	0.30
1	12.62	10.05	12.38	0.24

2	13.25	11.05	13.46	-0.21
3	14.71	12.15	14.65	0.06
4	14.99	12.67	15.21	-0.22

Expected return is calculated by substituting market returns in the characteristic line equation. For the market return of 10.88%, the expected return is given by:

$$R_{Cargo_t} = 1.70\% + 1.05R_{mt} = 1.70\% + 1.05(10.88) = 13.12\%$$

The abnormal return is given by the difference between the actual return and the expected return. Now, we have to calculate the average abnormal returns (AAR) for each of the week before and after the dividend were announced:

Period	Calculation of Average Abnormal Returns (AAR)	AAR
4	(1/4) (0.22+0.20)	0.21
3	(1/2) (-0.30-0.29)	-0.295
2	(1/2)(0.10+0.10)	0.1
1	(1/2)(-0.15-0.16)	-0.155
0	(1/2)(0.28+0.30)	0.29
1	(1/2)(0.25+0.24)	0.245
2	(1/2)(-0.21-0.21)	-0.21
3	(1/2)(0.06+0.06)	0.06
4	(1/2)(-0.20-0.20)	-0.21

The cumulative average abnormal returns (CAAR)

= (0.21-0.295+0.1+-0.155+0.29+0.245-0.21+0.06-0.21) = 0.003889

Since as per our analysis the value of CAAR is close to zero, we can conclude that markets are efficient in the semi strong form.

Portfolio Study or Return Prediction Study

This method follows the following steps:

- Define the variable (characteristic) on which firms will be classified
- Classify firms into portfolios based upon the magnitude of the variable
- Compute the returns for each portfolio
- Calculate the excess returns for each portfolio
- Assess whether the average excess returns are different across the portfolios However there are two implications for the results of abnormal return in the

portfolio study: (i) abnormal returns could occur because either markets are inefficient, or (ii) market model is not properly specified and provides incorrect estimates of risk and expected returns. In other words it tests the joint hypothesis of market efficiency and the testing of equilibrium asset pricing models.

Results of prior Portfolio Study in the context of several developed and emerging markets:

- Low P/E stocks experienced superior risk-adjusted results relative to the market, whereas high P/E stocks had significantly inferior risk-adjusted results. Publicly available P/E ratios possess valuable information regarding future returns. This is inconsistent with semi strong efficiency.
- Studies have hypothesized an inverse relationship between the Price- Earnings/ Growth Rate (PEG) ratio and subsequent rates of return. This is inconsistent with the EMH.
- Several studies have examined the impact of size on the risk-adjusted rates of return. The studies indicate that risk-adjusted returns for extended periods indicate that the small firms consistently experienced significantly larger risk- adjusted returns than large firms. Firm size is a major efficient market anomaly and a serious challenge to the market efficiency hypothesis.
- Ratios of Book Value of a firm's Equity to Market Value of its equity (BV/MV) have shown a significant positive relationship with future stock returns. This results are also inconsistent with the EMH
- In total along with the findings of several market anomalies like sz, BV/ MV,PE,PEG studies on predicting rates of return for a cross-section of stocks indicates markets are not semi strong efficient.

Tests of the Strong-form Efficient Market Hypothesis

Strong-form EMH contends that stock prices fully reflect all information, both public and private. This implies that no group of investors has access to private information that will allow them to consistently earn above-average profits. The tests are based on the group of investors.

Testing Groups of Investors:

- Corporate insiders: Insiders include major corporate officers, directors, and owners of 10% or more of any equity class of securities.
- Stock exchange specialists: Specialists have monopolistic access to information about unfilled limit orders
- Security analysts: There is evidence in favour of existence of superior analysts who apparently possess private information

- Professional money managers: Trained professionals, working full time at investment management.

Evidences for Strong Form: Mixed results, but much support

- Tests for corporate insiders and stock exchange specialists do not support the hypothesis (Both groups seem to have monopolistic access to important information and use it to derive above-average returns)

Market Efficiency and Corporate Managers

Market efficiency has implications for corporate managers as well as for investors. This takes a lot of the "gamesmanship" out of corporate management. If a market is efficient, it is difficult to fool the public for long and by very much. for instance, only genuine "news" can move the stock price. It is hard to pump-up the stock price by claims that are not verifiable by investors. "Fake" news will not move the price -- or if it does, the price will quickly revert to the pre-announcement value when the news proves hollow. Publicly available information is probably impounded in the price already. This is hard for some managers to believe. Accounting tricks don't fool anybody. Don't worry about timing accounting charges and don't worry about whether information is revealed in the footnotes or in the statements. An efficient market will quickly figure out the meaning of the information, once it is made public.

References

- Jegadeesh, N; Titman, S (1993). "Returns to Buying winners and selling losers: Implications for stock market efficiency". Journal of Finance. 48 (1): 65–91. doi:10.1111/j.1540-6261.1993.tb04702
- Andrew Wen-Chuan Lo, Andrew W. Lo (1997). Market Efficiency: Stock Market Behaviour in Theory and Practice. Edward Elgar. ISBN 978-1858981611
- Fama, E; French, K (1996). "Multifactor explanation of asset pricing anomalies". Journal of Finance. 51 (1): 55–84. doi:10.1111/j.1540-6261.1996.tb05202
- Fama, E; French, K (2008). "Dissecting Anomalies". Journal of Finance. 63 (4): 1653–1678. doi: 10.1111/j.1540-6261.2008.01371
- Hebner, Mark T. (2007), Index Funds: The 12-Step Program for Active Investors, IFA Publishing, 2007, ISBN 0-9768023-0-9
- Cowles, Alfred; H. Jones (1937). "Some A Posteriori Probabilities in Stock Market Action". Econometrica. 5 (3): 280–294. JSTOR 1905515. doi:10.2307/1905515
- Khan, Arshad M. (1986). "Conformity with Large Speculators: A Test of Efficiency in the Grain Futures Market". Atlantic Economic Journal. 14 (3): 51–55. doi:10.1007/BF02304624
- Lo, Andrew (2004). "The Adaptive Market Hypothesis: Market Efficiency from an Evolutionary Perspective" (pdf). Journal of Portfolio Management. 5. 30: 15–29
- Bodie, Z., Kane, A. and Marcus, A. J. Essentials of Investments, McGraw Hill Irwin, 2013, Chapter 8. ISBN 0078034698

4

Concepts and Theories of Portfolio Management

Modern portfolio theory is a theory used for creating a portfolio of assets. This is done with the intention of increasing the expected returns. The aspects elucidated in this chapter are of vital importance, and provide a better understanding of portfolio management.

Modern Portfolio Theory

Modern portfolio theory (MPT), or mean-variance analysis, is a mathematical framework for assembling a portfolio of assets such that the expected return is maximized for a given level of risk, defined as variance. Its key insight is that an asset's risk and return should not be assessed by itself, but by how it contributes to a portfolio's overall risk and return.

Economist Harry Markowitz introduced MPT in a 1952 essay, for which he was later awarded a Nobel Prize in economics.

Mathematical Model

Risk and Expected Return

MPT assumes that investors are risk averse, meaning that given two portfolios that offer the same expected return, investors will prefer the less risky one. Thus, an investor will take on increased risk only if compensated by higher expected returns. Conversely, an investor who wants higher expected returns must accept more risk. The exact trade-off will be the same for all investors, but different investors will evaluate the trade-off differently based on individual risk aversion characteristics. The implication is that a rational investor will not invest in a portfolio if a second portfolio exists with a more favorable risk-expected return profile – i.e., if for that level of risk an alternative portfolio exists that has better expected returns.

Under the model:

- Portfolio return is the proportion-weighted combination of the constituent assets' returns.

- Portfolio volatility is a function of the correlations ρ_{ij} of the component assets, for all asset pairs (i, j).

In general:

- Expected return:

$$E(R_p) = \sum_i w_i E(R_i)$$

where R_p is the return on the portfolio, R_i is the return on asset i and w_i is the weighting of component asset i (that is, the proportion of asset "i" in the portfolio).

- Portfolio return variance:

$$\sigma_p^2 = \sum_i w_i^2 \sigma_i^2 + \sum_i \sum_{j \neq i} w_i w_j \sigma_i \sigma_j \rho_{ij},$$

where σ is the (sample) standard deviation of the periodic returns on an asset, and ρ_{ij} is the correlation coefficient between the returns on assets i and j. Alternatively the expression can be written as:

$$\sigma_p^2 = \sum_i \sum_j w_i w_j \sigma_i \sigma_j \rho_{ij},$$

where $\rho_{ij} = 1$ for $i = j$, or

$$\sigma_p^2 = \sum_i \sum_j w_i w_j \sigma_{ij},$$

where $\sigma_{ij} = \sigma_i \sigma_j \rho_{ij}$ is the (sample) covariance of the periodic returns on the two assets, or alternatively denoted as $\sigma(i, j)$, cov_{ij} or $cov(i, j)$.

- Portfolio return volatility (standard deviation):

$$\sigma_p = \sqrt{\sigma_p^2}$$

For a two asset portfolio:

- Portfolio return: $E(R_p) = w_A E(R_A) + w_B E(R_B) = w_A E(R_A) + (1 - w_A) E(R_B)$.
- Portfolio variance: $\sigma_p^2 = w_A^2 \sigma_A^2 + w_B^2 \sigma_B^2 + 2 w_A w_B \sigma_A \sigma_B \rho_{AB}$

For a three asset portfolio:

- Portfolio return: $E(R_p) = w_A E(R_A) + w_B E(R_B) + w_C E(R_C)$

- Portfolio variance:
  $$\sigma_p^2 = w_A^2\sigma_A^2 + w_B^2\sigma_B^2 + w_C^2\sigma_C^2 + 2w_Aw_B\sigma_A\sigma_B\rho_{AB} + 2w_Aw_C\sigma_A\sigma_C\rho_{AC} + 2w_Bw_C\sigma_B\sigma_C\rho_{BC}$$

Diversification

An investor can reduce portfolio risk simply by holding combinations of instruments that are not perfectly positively correlated (correlation coefficient $-1 \le \rho_{ij} < 1$). In other words, investors can reduce their exposure to individual asset risk by holding a diversified portfolio of assets. Diversification may allow for the same portfolio expected return with reduced risk. These ideas have been started with Markowitz and then reinforced by other economists and mathematicians such as Andrew Brennan who have expressed ideas in the limitation of variance through portfolio theory.

If all the asset pairs have correlations of 0—they are perfectly uncorrelated—the portfolio's return variance is the sum over all assets of the square of the fraction held in the asset times the asset's return variance (and the portfolio standard deviation is the square root of this sum).

If all the asset pairs have correlations of 1, i.e. they are perfectly positively correlated, then the portfolio's volatility is the sum of each asset's volatility weighted by its fraction held in the portfolio. This is the maximum volatility the portfolio of these assets would reach.

Efficient Frontier with No Risk-free Asset

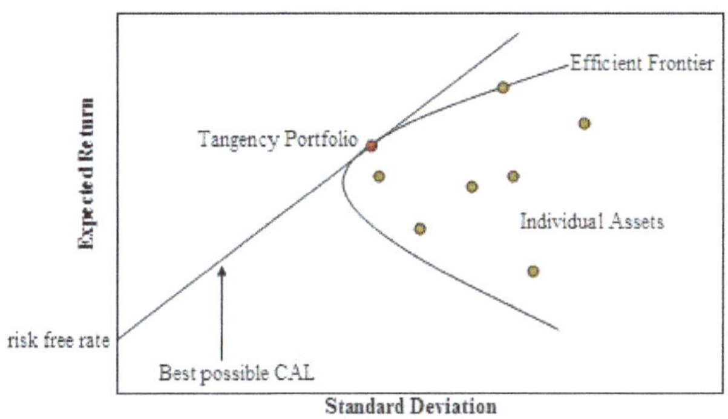

Efficient Frontier. The hyperbola is sometimes referred to as the 'Markowitz Bullet', and is the efficient frontier if no risk-free asset is available. With a risk-free asset, the straight line is the efficient frontier.

This graph shows expected return (vertical) versus standard deviation. This is called the 'risk-expected return space.' Every possible combination of risky assets, can be plotted in this risk-expected return space, and the collection of all such possible portfolios defines a region in this space. The left boundary of this region is a hyperbola, and the upper edge of this region is the *efficient frontier* in the absence of a risk-free asset (sometimes called "the Markowitz bullet"). Combinations along this upper edge represent portfolios (including no holdings of the risk-free asset) for which there is lowest risk for a given level of expected return. Equivalently, a portfolio lying on the efficient frontier represents the combination offering the best possible expected return for given risk level. The tangent to the hyperbola at the tangency point indicates the best possible capital allocation line (CAL).

Matrices are preferred for calculations of the efficient frontier.

In matrix form, for a given "risk tolerance" $q \in [0, \infty)$, the efficient frontier is found by minimizing the following expression:

$$w^T \Sigma w - q * R^T w$$

where

- w is a vector of portfolio weights and $\sum_i w_i = 1$. (The weights can be negative, which means investors can short a security.);
- Σ is the covariance matrix for the returns on the assets in the portfolio;
- $q \geq 0$ is a "risk tolerance" factor, where 0 results in the portfolio with minimal risk and ∞ results in the portfolio infinitely far out on the frontier with both expected return and risk unbounded; and
- R is a vector of expected returns.
- $w^T \Sigma w$ is the variance of portfolio return.
- $R^T w$ is the expected return on the portfolio.

The above optimization finds the point on the frontier at which the inverse of the slope of the frontier would be q if portfolio return variance instead of standard deviation were plotted horizontally. The frontier in its entirety is parametric on q.

Many software packages, including MATLAB, Microsoft Excel, Mathematica and R, provide optimization routines suitable for the above problem.

An alternative approach to specifying the efficient frontier is to do so parametrically on the expected portfolio return $R^T w$. This version of the problem requires that we minimize

$$w^T \Sigma w$$

subject to

$$R^T w = \mu$$

for parameter μ. This problem is easily solved using a Lagrange multiplier.

Two Mutual Fund Theorem

One key result of the above analysis is the two mutual fund theorem. This theorem states that any portfolio on the efficient frontier can be generated by holding a combination of any two given portfolios on the frontier; the latter two given portfolios are the "mutual funds" in the theorem's name. So in the absence of a risk-free asset, an investor can achieve any desired efficient portfolio even if all that is accessible is a pair of efficient mutual funds. If the location of the desired portfolio on the frontier is between the locations of the two mutual funds, both mutual funds will be held in positive quantities. If the desired portfolio is outside the range spanned by the two mutual funds, then one of the mutual funds must be sold short (held in negative quantity) while the size of the investment in the other mutual fund must be greater than the amount available for investment (the excess being funded by the borrowing from the other fund).

Risk-free Asset and the Capital Allocation line

The risk-free asset is the (hypothetical) asset that pays a risk-free rate. In practice, short-term government securities (such as US treasury bills) are used as a risk-free asset, because they pay a fixed rate of interest and have exceptionally low default risk. The risk-free asset has zero variance in returns (hence is risk-free); it is also uncorrelated with any other asset (by definition, since its variance is zero). As a result, when it is combined with any other asset or portfolio of assets, the change in return is linearly related to the change in risk as the proportions in the combination vary.

When a risk-free asset is introduced, the half-line shown in the figure is the new efficient frontier. It is tangent to the hyperbola at the pure risky portfolio with the highest Sharpe ratio. Its vertical intercept represents a portfolio with 100% of holdings in the risk-free asset; the tangency with the hyperbola represents a portfolio with no risk-free holdings and 100% of assets held in the portfolio occurring at the tangency point; points between those points are portfolios containing positive amounts of both the risky tangency portfolio and the risk-free asset; and points on the half-line beyond the tangency point are leveraged portfolios involving negative holdings of the risk-free asset (the latter has been sold short—in other words, the investor has borrowed at the risk-free rate) and an amount invested in the tangency portfolio equal to more than 100% of the investor's initial capital. This efficient half-line is called the capital allocation line (CAL), and its formula can be shown to be

$$E(R_C) = R_F + \sigma_C \frac{E(R_P) - R_F}{\sigma_P}.$$

In this formula *P* is the sub-portfolio of risky assets at the tangency with the Markowitz bullet, *F* is the risk-free asset, and *C* is a combination of portfolios *P* and *F*.

By the diagram, the introduction of the risk-free asset as a possible component of the portfolio has improved the range of risk-expected return combinations available, because everywhere except at the tangency portfolio the half-line gives a higher expected return than the hyperbola does at every possible risk level. The fact that all points on the linear efficient locus can be achieved by a combination of holdings of the risk-free asset and the tangency portfolio is known as the one mutual fund theorem, where the mutual fund referred to is the tangency portfolio.

Asset Pricing

The above analysis describes optimal behavior of an individual investor. Asset pricing theory builds on this analysis in the following way. Since everyone holds the risky assets in identical proportions to each other—namely in the proportions given by the tangency portfolio—in market equilibrium the risky assets' prices, and therefore their expected returns, will adjust so that the ratios in the tangency portfolio are the same as the ratios in which the risky assets are supplied to the market. Thus relative supplies will equal relative demands. MPT derives the required expected return for a correctly priced asset in this context.

Systematic Risk and Specific Risk

Specific risk is the risk associated with individual assets - within a portfolio these risks can be reduced through diversification (specific risks "cancel out"). Specific risk is also called diversifiable, unique, unsystematic, or idiosyncratic risk. Systematic risk (a.k.a. portfolio risk or market risk) refers to the risk common to all securities—except for selling short as noted below, systematic risk cannot be diversified away (within one market). Within the market portfolio, asset specific risk will be diversified away to the extent possible. Systematic risk is therefore equated with the risk (standard deviation) of the market portfolio.

Since a security will be purchased only if it improves the risk-expected return characteristics of the market portfolio, the relevant measure of the risk of a security is the risk it adds to the market portfolio, and not its risk in isolation. In this context, the volatility of the asset, and its correlation with the market portfolio, are historically observed and are therefore given. (There are several approaches to asset pricing that attempt to price assets by modelling the stochastic properties of the moments of assets' returns - these are broadly referred to as conditional asset pricing models.)

Systematic risks within one market can be managed through a strategy of using both long and short positions within one portfolio, creating a "market neutral" portfolio. Market neutral portfolios, therefore will have a correlations of zero.

Capital Asset Pricing Model

The asset return depends on the amount paid for the asset today. The price paid must ensure that the market portfolio's risk / return characteristics improve when the asset is added to it. The CAPM is a model that derives the theoretical required expected return (i.e., discount rate) for an asset in a market, given the risk-free rate available to investors and the risk of the market as a whole. The CAPM is usually expressed:

$$\mathrm{E}(R_i) = R_f + \beta_i(\mathrm{E}(R_m) - R_f)$$

- β, Beta, is the measure of asset sensitivity to a movement in the overall market; Beta is usually found via regression on historical data. Betas exceeding one signify more than average "riskiness" in the sense of the asset's contribution to overall portfolio risk; betas below one indicate a lower than average risk contribution.
- $(\mathrm{E}(R_m) - R_f)$ is the market premium, the expected excess return of the market portfolio's expected return over the risk-free rate.

The derivation is as follows:

(1) The incremental impact on risk and expected return when an additional risky asset, a, is added to the market portfolio, m, follows from the formulae for a two-asset portfolio. These results are used to derive the asset-appropriate discount rate.

- Market portfolio's risk = $(w_m^2\sigma_m^2 + [w_a^2\sigma_a^2 + 2w_m w_a \rho_{am}\sigma_a\sigma_m])$

  Hence, risk added to portfolio = $[w_a^2\sigma_a^2 + 2w_m w_a \rho_{am}\sigma_a\sigma_m]$

  but since the weight of the asset will be relatively low, $w_a^2 \approx 0$

  i.e. additional risk = $[2w_m w_a \rho_{am}\sigma_a\sigma_m]$
- Market portfolio's expected return = $(w_m\ \mathrm{E}(R_m) + [w_a\ \mathrm{E}(R_a)])$

  Hence additional expected return = $[w_a\ \mathrm{E}(R_a)]$

(2) If an asset, a, is correctly priced, the improvement in its risk-to-expected return ratio achieved by adding it to the market portfolio, m, will at least match the gains of spending that money on an increased stake in the market portfolio. The assumption is that the investor will purchase the asset with funds borrowed at the risk-free rate, R_f; this is rational if $\mathrm{E}(R_a) > R_f$.

Thus: $[w_a(\mathrm{E}(R_a) - R_f)]/[2w_m w_a \rho_{am}\sigma_a\sigma_m] = [w_a(\mathrm{E}(R_m) - R_f)]/[2w_m w_a \sigma_m\sigma_m]$

i.e. : $[\mathrm{E}(R_a)] = R_f + [\mathrm{E}(R_m) - R_f]*[\rho_{am}\sigma_a\sigma_m]/[\sigma_m\sigma_m]$

i.e. : $[\mathrm{E}(R_a)] = R_f + [\mathrm{E}(R_m) - R_f]*[\sigma_{am}]/[\sigma_{mm}]$

$[\sigma_{am}]/[\sigma_{mm}]$ is the "beta", β return— the covariance between the asset's return and the market's return divided by the variance of the market return— i.e. the sensitivity of the asset price to movement in the market portfolio's value.

This equation can be estimated statistically using the following regression equation:

$$\text{SCL}: R_{i,t} - R_f = \alpha_i + \beta_i(R_{M,t} - R_f) + \epsilon_{i,t}$$

where α_i is called the asset's alpha, β_i is the asset's beta coefficient and SCL is the security characteristic line.

Once an asset's expected return, $E(R_i)$, is calculated using CAPM, the future cash flows of the asset can be discounted to their present value using this rate to establish the correct price for the asset. A riskier stock will have a higher beta and will be discounted at a higher rate; less sensitive stocks will have lower betas and be discounted at a lower rate. In theory, an asset is correctly priced when its observed price is the same as its value calculated using the CAPM derived discount rate. If the observed price is higher than the valuation, then the asset is overvalued; it is undervalued for a too low price.

Criticisms

Despite its theoretical importance, critics of MPT question whether it is an ideal investment tool, because its model of financial markets does not match the real world in many ways.

The risk, return, and correlation measures used by MPT are based on expected values, which means that they are mathematical statements about the future (the expected value of returns is explicit in the above equations, and implicit in the definitions of variance and covariance). In practice, investors must substitute predictions based on historical measurements of asset return and volatility for these values in the equations. Very often such expected values fail to take account of new circumstances that did not exist when the historical data were generated.

More fundamentally, investors are stuck with estimating key parameters from past market data because MPT attempts to model risk in terms of the likelihood of losses, but says nothing about why those losses might occur. The risk measurements used are probabilistic in nature, not structural. This is a major difference as compared to many engineering approaches to risk management. As estimation errors are critical in MPT, appropriate modeling approaches must be applied. In an MPT or mean-variance optimization framework, accurate estimation of the variance–covariance matrix is paramount. Thus, forecasting with Monte-Carlo simulation with the Gaussian copula and well-specified marginal distributions are effective. Allowing the modeling process to allow for empirical characteristics in stock returns such as auto-regression, asymmetric volatility, skewness, and kurtosis is important. Not accounting for these attributes can lead to severe estimation error in the correlation and variance–covariance matrices that have negative biases (as much as 70% of the true values).

Options theory and MPT have at least one important conceptual difference from the probabilistic risk assessment done by nuclear power [plants]. A PRA is what economists would call a *structural model.* The components of a system and their relationships are modeled in Monte Carlo simulations. If valve X fails, it causes a loss of back pressure on pump Y, causing a drop in flow to vessel Z, and so on.

But in the Black–Scholes equation and MPT, there is no attempt to explain an underlying structure to price changes. Various outcomes are simply given probabilities. And, unlike the PRA, if there is no history of a particular system-level event like a liquidity crisis, there is no way to compute the odds of it. If nuclear engineers ran risk management this way, they would never be able to compute the odds of a meltdown at a particular plant until several similar events occurred in the same reactor design.

—Douglas W. Hubbard, 'The Failure of Risk Management', p. 67, John Wiley & Sons, 2009. ISBN 978-0-470-38795-5

Mathematical risk measurements are also useful only to the degree that they reflect investors' true concerns—there is no point minimizing a variable that nobody cares about in practice. MPT uses the mathematical concept of variance to quantify risk, and this might be justified under the assumption of elliptically distributed returns such as normally distributed returns, but for general return distributions other risk measures (like coherent risk measures) might better reflect investors' true preferences.

In particular, variance is a symmetric measure that counts abnormally high returns as just as risky as abnormally low returns. Some would argue that, in reality, investors are only concerned about losses, and do not care about the dispersion or tightness of above-average returns. According to this view, our intuitive concept of risk is fundamentally asymmetric in nature.

Modern portfolio theory has also been criticized because it assumes that returns follow a Gaussian distribution. Already in the 1960s, Benoit Mandelbrot and Eugene Fama showed the inadequacy of this assumption and proposed the use of stable distributions instead. Stefan Mittnik and Svetlozar Rachev presented strategies for deriving optimal portfolios in such settings. More recently, financial economist Nassim Nicholas Taleb has also criticized modern portfolio theory on this ground, writing:

After the stock market crash (in 1987), they rewarded two theoreticians, Harry Markowitz and William Sharpe, who built beautifully Platonic models on a Gaussian base, contributing to what is called Modern Portfolio Theory. Simply, if you remove their Gaussian assumptions and treat prices as scalable, you are left with hot air. The Nobel Committee could have tested the Sharpe and Markowitz models—they work like quack remedies sold on the Internet—but nobody in Stockholm seems to have thought about it.

Contrarian/Value investors don't buy into Modern Portfolio Theory as it depends on the Efficient Market Hypothesis and conflates fluctuations in shareprice with "risk". This risk is only an opportunity to buy or sell assets at attractive prices inasmuch as it suits one's book.

Extensions

Since MPT's introduction in 1952, many attempts have been made to improve the model, especially by using more realistic assumptions.

Post-modern portfolio theory extends MPT by adopting non-normally distributed, asymmetric measures of risk. This helps with some of these problems, but not others.

Black-Litterman model optimization is an extension of unconstrained Markowitz optimization that incorporates relative and absolute 'views' on inputs of risk and returns.

Other Applications

In the 1970s, concepts from MPT found their way into the field of regional science. In a series of seminal works, Michael Conroy modeled the labor force in the economy using portfolio-theoretic methods to examine growth and variability in the labor force. This was followed by a long literature on the relationship between economic growth and volatility.

More recently, modern portfolio theory has been used to model the self-concept in social psychology. When the self attributes comprising the self-concept constitute a well-diversified portfolio, then psychological outcomes at the level of the individual such as mood and self-esteem should be more stable than when the self-concept is undiversified. This prediction has been confirmed in studies involving human subjects.

Recently, modern portfolio theory has been applied to modelling the uncertainty and correlation between documents in information retrieval. Given a query, the aim is to maximize the overall relevance of a ranked list of documents and at the same time minimize the overall uncertainty of the ranked list.

Project Portfolios and Other "Non-financial" Assets

Some experts apply MPT to portfolios of projects and other assets besides financial instruments. When MPT is applied outside of traditional financial portfolios, some differences between the different types of portfolios must be considered.

1. The assets in financial portfolios are, for practical purposes, continuously divisible while portfolios of projects are "lumpy". For example, while we can compute that the optimal portfolio position for 3 stocks is, say, 44%, 35%, 21%, the optimal position for a project portfolio may not allow us to simply change the amount spent on a project. Projects might be all or nothing or, at least, have logical units that cannot be separated. A portfolio optimization method would have to take the discrete nature of projects into account.

2. The assets of financial portfolios are liquid; they can be assessed or re-assessed at any point in time. But opportunities for launching new projects may be limited and

may occur in limited windows of time. Projects that have already been initiated cannot be abandoned without the loss of the sunk costs (i.e., there is little or no recovery/salvage value of a half-complete project).

Neither of these necessarily eliminate the possibility of using MPT and such portfolios. They simply indicate the need to run the optimization with an additional set of mathematically expressed constraints that would not normally apply to financial portfolios.

Furthermore, some of the simplest elements of Modern Portfolio Theory are applicable to virtually any kind of portfolio. The concept of capturing the risk tolerance of an investor by documenting how much risk is acceptable for a given return may be applied to a variety of decision analysis problems. MPT uses historical variance as a measure of risk, but portfolios of assets like major projects don't have a well-defined "historical variance". In this case, the MPT investment boundary can be expressed in more general terms like "chance of an ROI less than cost of capital" or "chance of losing more than half of the investment". When risk is put in terms of uncertainty about forecasts and possible losses then the concept is transferable to various types of investment.

Post-modern Portfolio Theory

Post-modern portfolio theory (or PMPT) is an extension of the traditional modern portfolio theory ("MPT", which is an application of mean-variance analysis or "MVA"). Both theories propose how rational investors should use diversification to optimize their portfolios, and how a risky asset should be priced.

History

The term post-modern portfolio theory was created in 1991 by software entrepreneurs Brian M. Rom and Kathleen Ferguson to differentiate the portfolio-construction software developed by their company, Investment Technologies from those provided by the traditional Modern Portfolio Theory. It first appeared in the literature in 1993 in an article by Rom and Ferguson in The Journal of Performance Measurement. It combines the theoretical research of many authors and has expanded over several decades as academics at universities in many countries tested these theories to determine whether or not they had merit. The essential difference between PMPT and the modern portfolio theory of Markowitz and Sharpe (MPT) is that PMPT focuses on the return that must be earned on the assets in a portfolio in order to meet some future payout. This internal rate of return (IRR) is the link between assets and liabilities. PMPT measures risk and reward relative to this IRR while MPT ignores this IRR and measures risk as dispersion about the mean or average return. The result is substantially different portfolio constructions.

Empirical investigations began in 1981 at the Pension Research Institute (PRI) at San Francisco State University. Dr. Hal Forsey and Dr. Frank Sortino were trying to apply Peter Fishburn's theory published in 1977 to Pension Fund Management. The result was an asset allocation model that PRI licensed Brian Rom to market in 1988. Mr. Rom coined the term PMPT and began using it to market portfolio optimization and performance measurement software developed by his company. These systems were built on the PRI downside risk algorithms. Sortino and Steven Satchell at Cambridge University co-authored the first book on PMPT. This was intended as a graduate seminar text in portfolio management. A more recent book by Sortino was written for practitioners. The first publication in a major journal was co-authored by Sortino and Dr. Robert van der Meer, then at Shell Oil Netherlands.

Sortino claims the major contributors to the underlying theory are:

- Peter Fishburn at the University of Pennsylvania who developed the mathematical equations for calculating downside risk and provided proofs that the Markowitz model was a subset of a richer framework.
- Atchison & Brown at Cambridge University who developed the three parameter lognormal distribution which was a more robust model of the pattern of returns than the bell shaped distribution of MPT.
- Bradley Efron, Stanford University, who developed the bootstrap procedure for better describing the nature of uncertainty in financial markets.
- William Sharpe at Stanford University who developed returns-based style analysis that allowed more accurate estimates of risk and return.
- Daniel Kahneman at Princeton & Amos Tversky at Stanford who pioneered the field of behavioral finance which contests many of the findings of MPT.

Overview

Harry Markowitz laid the foundations of MPT, the greatest contribution of which is the establishment of a formal risk/return framework for investment decision-making. By defining investment risk in quantitative terms, Markowitz gave investors a mathematical approach to asset-selection and portfolio management. But there are important limitations to the original MPT formulation.

Two major limitations of MPT are its assumptions that

1. the variance of portfolio returns is the correct measure of investment risk, and
2. the investment returns of all securities and portfolios can be adequately represented by a joint elliptical distribution, such as the normal distribution.

Stated another way, MPT is limited by measures of risk and return that do not always represent the realities of the investment markets.

The assumption of a normal distribution is a major practical limitation, because it is symmetrical. Using the variance (or its square root, the standard deviation) implies that uncertainty about better-than-expected returns is equally averred as uncertainty about returns that are worse than expected. Furthermore, using the normal distribution to model the pattern of investment returns makes investment results with more upside than downside returns appear more risky than they really are. The converse distortion applies to distributions with a predominance of downside returns. The result is that using traditional MPT techniques for measuring investment portfolio construction and evaluation frequently does not accurately model investment reality.

It has long been recognized that investors typically do not view as risky those returns *above* the minimum they must earn in order to achieve their investment objectives. They believe that risk has to do with the bad outcomes (i.e., returns below a required target), not the good outcomes (i.e., returns in excess of the target) and that losses weigh more heavily than gains. This view has been noted by researchers in finance, economics and psychology, including Sharpe (1964). "Under certain conditions the MVA can be shown to lead to unsatisfactory predictions of (investor) behavior. Markowitz suggests that a model based on the semivariance would be preferable; in light of the formidable computational problems, however, he bases his (MV) analysis on the mean and the standard deviation."

Recent advances in portfolio and financial theory, coupled with increased computing power, have overcome these limitations. The resulting expanded risk/return paradigm is known as Post-Modern Portfolio Theory, or PMPT. Thus, MPT becomes nothing more than a special (symmetrical) case of PMPT.

The Tools of PMPT

In 1987 The Pension Research Institute at San Francisco State University developed the practical mathematical algorithms of PMPT that are in use today. These methods provide a framework that recognizes investors' preferences for upside over downside volatility. At the same time, a more robust model for the pattern of investment returns, the three-parameter lognormal distribution, was introduced.

Downside Risk

Downside risk (DR) is measured by target semi-deviation (the square root of target semivariance) and is termed downside deviation. It is expressed in percentages and therefore allows for rankings in the same way as standard deviation.

An intuitive way to view downside risk is the annualized standard deviation of returns below the target. Another is the square root of the probability-weighted squared below-target returns. The squaring of the below-target returns has the effect of penalizing failures quadratically. This is consistent with observations made on the behavior of individual decision-making under

$$d = \sqrt{\int_{-\infty}^{t} (t-r)^2 f(r)dr}$$

where

d = downside deviation (commonly known in the financial community as 'downside risk'). Note: By extension, d^2 = downside variance.

t = the annual target return, originally termed the minimum acceptable return, or MAR.

r = the random variable representing the return for the distribution of annual returns $f(r)$,

$f(r)$ = the distribution for the annual returns, e.g. the three-parameter lognormal distribution

For the reasons provided below, this *continuous* formula is preferred over a simpler *discrete* version that determines the standard deviation of below-target periodic returns taken from the return series.

1. The continuous form permits all subsequent calculations to be made using annual returns which is the natural way for investors to specify their investment goals. The discrete form requires monthly returns for there to be sufficient data points to make a meaningful calculation, which in turn requires converting the annual target into a monthly target. This significantly affects the amount of risk that is identified. For example, a goal of earning 1% in every month of one year results in a greater risk than the seemingly equivalent goal of earning 12% in one year.
2. A second reason for strongly preferring the continuous form to the discrete form has been proposed by Sortino & Forsey (1996):

"Before we make an investment, we don't know what the outcome will be... After the investment is made, and we want to measure its performance, all we know is what the outcome was, not what it could have been. To cope with this uncertainty, we assume that a reasonable estimate of the range of possible returns, as well as the probabilities associated with estimation of those returns...In statistical terms, the shape of [this] uncertainty is called a probability distribution. In other words, looking at just the discrete monthly or annual values does not tell the whole story."

Using the observed points to create a distribution is a staple of conventional performance measurement. For example, monthly returns are used to calculate a fund's mean and standard deviation. Using these values and the properties of the normal distribution, we can make statements such as the likelihood of losing money (even though no negative returns may actually have been observed), or the range within which two-thirds of all returns lies (even though the specific returns identifying this range have not necessarily occurred). Our ability to make these statements comes from the process of assuming the continuous form of the normal distribution and certain of its well-known properties.

In PMPT an analogous process is followed:

1. Observe the monthly returns,
2. Fit a distribution that permits asymmetry to the observations,
3. Annualize the monthly returns, making sure the shape characteristics of the distribution are retained,
4. Apply integral calculus to the resultant distribution to calculate the appropriate statistics.

Sortino Ratio

The Sortino ratio, developed by Rom's company, Investment Technologies, was the first new element in the PMPT rubric. It was designed to replace MPT's Sharpe ratio as a measure of risk-adjusted return. It is defined as:

$$\frac{r-t}{d}$$

where

r = the annualized rate of return,

t = the target return,

d = downside risk.

The following table shows that this ratio is demonstrably superior to the traditional Sharpe ratio as a means for ranking investment results. The table shows risk-adjusted ratios for several major indexes using both Sortino and Sharpe ratios. The data cover the five years 1992-1996 and are based on monthly total returns. The Sortino ratio is calculated against a 9.0% target.

Index	Sortino ratio	Sharpe ratio
90-day T-bill	-1.00	0.00
Lehman Aggregate	-0.29	0.63
MSCI EAFE	-0.05	0.30
Russell 2000	0.55	0.93
S&P 500	0.84	1.25

As an example of the different conclusions that can be drawn using these two ratios, notice how the Lehman Aggregate and MSCI EAFE compare - the Lehman ranks higher using the Sharpe ratio whereas EAFE ranks higher using the Sortino ratio. In many cases, manager or index rankings will be different, depending on the risk-adjusted measure used. These patterns will change again for different values of t. For example, when t is close to the risk-free rate, the Sortino Ratio for T-Bill's will be higher than that for the S&P 500, while the Sharpe ratio remains unchanged.

In March 2008, researchers at the Queensland Investment Corporation and Queensland University of Technology showed that for skewed return distributions, the Sortino ratio is superior to the Sharpe ratio as a measure of portfolio risk.

Volatility Skewness

Volatility skewness is the second portfolio-analysis statistic introduced by Rom and Ferguson under the PMPT rubric. It measures the ratio of a distribution's percentage of total variance from returns above the mean, to the percentage of the distribution's total variance from returns below the mean. Thus, if a distribution is symmetrical (as in the normal case, as is assumed under MPT), it has a volatility skewness of 1.00. Values greater than 1.00 indicate positive skewness; values less than 1.00 indicate negative skewness. While closely correlated with the traditional statistical measure of skewness (viz., the third moment of a distribution), the authors of PMPT argue that their volatility skewness measure has the advantage of being intuitively more understandable to non-statisticians who are the primary practical users of these tools.

The importance of skewness lies in the fact that the more non-normal (i.e., skewed) a return series is, the more its true risk will be distorted by traditional MPT measures such as the Sharpe ratio. Thus, with the recent advent of hedging and derivative strategies, which are asymmetrical by design, MPT measures are essentially useless, while PMPT is able to capture significantly more of the true information contained in the returns under consideration. Many of the common market indices and the returns of stock and bond mutual funds cannot themselves always be assumed to be accurately represented by the normal distribution.

Index	Upside Volatility(%)	Downside Volatility(%)	Volatility skewness
Lehman Aggregate	32.35	67.65	0.48
Russell 2000	37.19	62.81	0.59
S&P 500	38.63	61.37	0.63
90-day T-Bill	48.26	51.74	0.93
MSCI EAFE	54.67	45.33	1.21

Calculation of the Expected Rate of Return

The expected rate of return for an individual investment or portfolio can be computed as follows:

$$E\left(R_{por\,i}\right)=\sum_{i=1}^{n} W_i R_i$$

where:

W_i = the percent of the portfolio in asset i

$E(R_i)$= the expected rate of return for asset i

Expected rate of return for an individual investment based on an assumption of equal probabilities can be shown with the following example:

Possible Rate of Return (%)	Probability	Expected Return (%)
.60	0.25	0.15
.12	0.25	0.03
.09	0.25	0.02
·35	0.25	0.09
	E(*R*)	0.29

Following the above specification the expected rate of return for a portfolio of investments is simply the weighted average of the expected rates of return for the individual investments in the portfolio. The weights are the proportion of total value for the investment. The weights can be of equal weighted or value weighted. (price weighted portfolio).

Expected Security Return (%)	Market Capitalisation	Weight i.e., % of portfolio (value weighted)	Expected Return (%)
.60	Rs. 2,00,000	0.10	0.06
.12	Rs. 4,00,000	0.20	0.02
.09	Rs. 11,00,000	0.55	0.05
·35	Rs. 3,00,000	0.15	0.05
		E(*R*port)	0.19

Expected Security Return (%)	Market Capitalisation	Weight i.e., % of portfolio (Equal weighted)	Expected Return (%)
.60	Rs. 2,00,000	0.25	0.15
.12	Rs. 4,00,000	0.25	0.03
.09	Rs. 11,00,000	0.25	0.02
.35	Rs. 3,00,000	0.25	0.09
		E(*R*port)	0.29

In case of an equal weighted portfolio all securities in the portfolio gets the equal weight (1/number of stocks) irrespective of their size or market capitalisation (number of shares x share price). In case of a value weighted portfolio stocks/securities in the portfolio get the weight (market capitalisation of a stock/total market capitalisation of the portfolio) as per their market capitalisation. In the following example it can be observed that equal weighted portfolio out perform the value weighted portfolio. Market cap weighted or price weighted portfolio suffer from a systematic flaw i.e., they increase the amount they own of a particular company as that company's stock price increases. An equally-weighted portfolio will own too much of overpriced stocks and too little of low priced stocks. It has been found by many researchers that the equal-weighted portfolio with monthly rebalancing strategy outperforms the value or price-weighted portfolios in terms of total mean return even though the equal-weighted portfolio has greater portfolio risk and high transaction costs. The higher return of the equal-weighted portfolio arises from its higher exposure to the market, size, and value factors.

Variance (Standard Deviation) of Returns for an Individual Investment

In this section we will discuss upon the standard deviation of return (square root of the variance) as the measure of risk for an individual investment. The variance, or standard deviation, is a measure of the variation of possible rates of return (σ^2), R_i, from the expected rate of return [$E(R_i)$] as follows:

$$(\sigma^2) = \sum_{i=1}^{n} \left[R_i - E(R_i)\right]^2 P_i$$

Where, P_i is the probability of the possible rate of return, R_i. The standard deviation (σ)

in this regard will be:

$$\sigma = \sqrt{\sum_{i=1}^{n} \left[R_i - E(R_i)\right]^2 P_i}$$

Computation of the variance of the expected rate of return of an individual investment: Suppose the individual investment is having the following details:

Possible Rate of Return (%)	Probability	Expected Return (%)
.60	0.25	0.15
.12	0.25	0.03
.09	0.25	0.02
.35	0.25	0.09
	$E(R)$	0.29

Possible Rate of Return (%) R_i	Expected Return (%) $E(R_i)$	$R_i - E(R_i)$	$[R_i - E(R_i)]^2$	P_i	$[R_i - E(R_i)]^2 P_i$
.60	0.29	0.31	0.0961	.25	0.024025
.12	0.29	-0.17	0.0289	.25	0.007225
.09	0.29	-0.20	0.04	.25	0.01
.35	0.29	0.06	0.0036	.25	0.0009
				Variance (σ^2)	0.04215

So the standard deviation of this individual investment can be calculated as follows: Standard Deviation $\sigma = 0.18$.

Covariance of Returns

Covariance of returns measures the degree to which two variables (in this case return of two assets) "move together" relative to their individual mean values over time. Covariance can be positive or negative. A positive covariance means that the rates of return for two investments tend to move in the same direction relative to their individual means during the same time period. On the other hand a negative covariance indicates that the rates of return for two investments tend to move in different directions relative to their means during specified time intervals over time. For two assets, j and k, the covariance of rates of return can be defined as:

$$Cov_{jk} = E\{[R_j - E(R_j)][R_k - E(R_k)]\}$$

The monthly covariance between the rates of return for these two assets is:

$$\frac{1}{12}\sum_{j=1}^{n}[R_j - E(R_j)][R_k - E(R_k)]$$

If the rates of return for one asset/stock are above (below) its mean rate of return during a given period and the returns for the other asset are likewise above (below) its mean rate of return during this same period, then the product of these deviations or the covariance is positive. Similarly, if the rate of return for one of the asset is above its mean return while the return on the other asset is below its mean return, the product will be negative. If this contrary movement happened consistently, the covariance between the rates of return for the two assets would be a large negative value.

Covariance and Correlation Coefficient

The correlation between the two assets is calculated by considering the variability of the two return series of different assets or by standardising their covariance measure. The purpose for looking in to the correlation coefficient is to get the single point of reference as to whether the two assets have any kind of correlation in their movement or not. Usually the covariance figure between the two assets gives a broad idea about the variability of returns, whereas the correlation coefficient gives a microscopic view as to whether there is a positive or negative correlation between the two assets movement.

Usually if the stocks or securities belong to the same industry then the correlation is generally high as compared to the stock selected from different industries. A correlation of +1.0 would indicate perfect positive correlation, and a value of –1.0 would mean that the returns moved in a completely opposite direction. A value of zero would mean that the returns had no linear relationship, that is, they were uncorrelated statistically. That does not mean that they are independent. The correlation coefficient for the above mentioned two assets can be measures as follows:

$$r_{jk} = \frac{Cov_{jk}}{\sigma_j \sigma_k}$$

i.e., $$r_{jk} \frac{\frac{1}{12}\sum_{j=1}^{n}\left[R_j - E(R_j)\right]\left[R_k - E(R_k)\right]}{\sigma_j \sigma_k}$$

Standard Deviation of a Portfolio

The measure of risk for a portfolio is given as the standard deviation of returns for a portfolio of assets. Following the Markowitz the standard deviation of a portfolio of assets can be computed as follows:

$$\sigma_{port} = \sqrt{\sum_{i=1}^{n} w_i^2 \sigma_i^2} + \sum_{i=1}^{n}\sum_{i=1}^{n} w_i w_j Cov_{ij}$$

Where

σ_{port} = the standard deviation of the portfolio

W_i = the weights of the individual assets in the portfolio, where weights are determined by the proportion of value in the portfolio

σ_i^2 = the variance of rates of return for asset i

Cov_{ij} = the covariance between the rates of return for assets i and j, where $Cov_{ij} = r_{ij}\sigma_i\sigma_j$

The above mentioned formula indicates that the standard deviation for a portfolio of assets is a function of the weighted average of the individual variances (where the weights are squared), plus the weighted covariances between all the assets in the portfolio. The standard deviation for a portfolio of assets encompasses not only the variances of the individual assets but also includes the covariances between pairs of individual assets in the portfolio.

Any asset of a portfolio may be described by two characteristics: (1) the expected rate of return; (2) The expected standard deviations of returns. Assets may differ in expected rates of return and individual standard deviations. The correlation, measured by covariance, affects the portfolio standard deviation. Low correlation reduces portfolio risk while not affecting the expected return. Negative correlation reduces portfolio risk and combining two assets with -1.0 correlations reduces the portfolio standard deviation to zero only when individual standard deviations are equal.

Two Special Cases

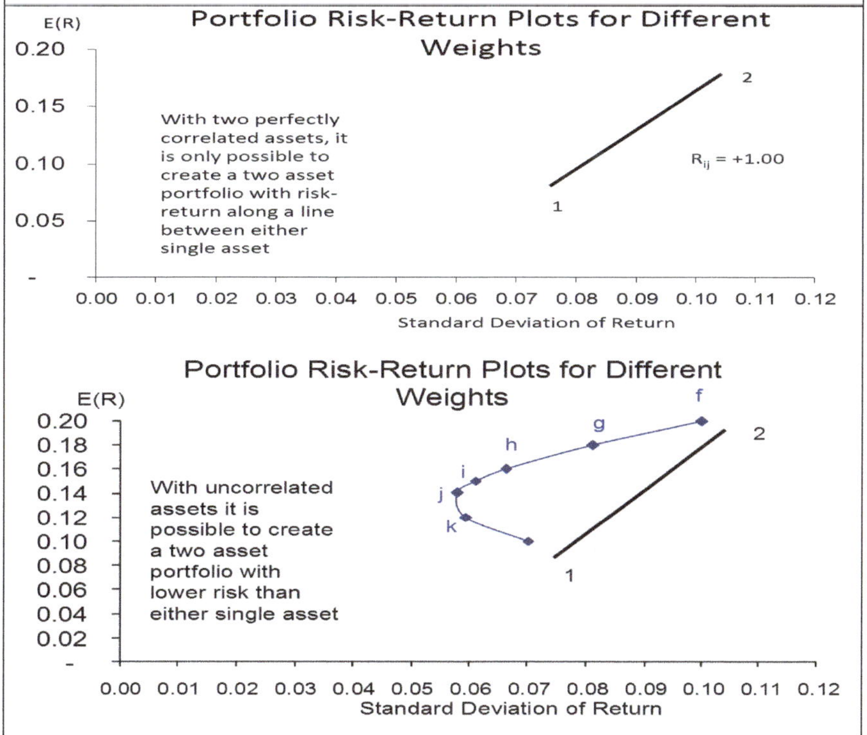

Capital Market Theory

Capital market theory extends portfolio theory and develops a model for pricing all risky assets. In this regard Capital asset pricing model (CAPM) allows us to determine the required rate of return for any risky asset.

Assumptions of Capital Market Theory

Capital market theory which builds on the Markowitz portfolio theory, is having the following assumptions:

- All investors are Markowitz efficient investors who want to target points on the efficient frontier.
- Investors can borrow or lend any amount of money at the risk-free rate of return (RFR).
- All investors have homogeneous expectations; that is, they estimate identical probability distributions for future rates of return.
- All investors have the same one-period time horizon such as one-month, six months, or one year.
- All investments are infinitely divisible, which means that it is possible to buy or sell fractional shares of any asset or portfolio.
- There are no taxes or transaction costs involved in buying or selling assets.
- There is no inflation or any change in interest rates, or inflation is fully anticipated.
- Capital markets are in equilibrium. This means that we begin with all investments properly priced in line with their risk levels.

The Capital Asset Pricing Model: Expected Return and Risk

CAPM indicates what should be the expected or required rates of return on risky assets. This helps to compare an estimated rate of return to the required rate of return implied by CAPM i.e., to know a certain stock is over/under valued. With the explanation of the existence of a risk-free asset resulted in deriving a capital market line (CML) that became the relevant frontier it explains that an asset's covariance with the market portfolio is the relevant risk measure. This can also be used to determine an appropriate expected rate of return on a risky asset by using the approach of CAPM and to value an asset by providing an appropriate discount rate to use in dividend valuation models.

The Concept of Risk-free Asset

Risk-free asset which provides the risk-free rate of return (RFR) is an asset with zero variance and have zero correlation with all other risky assets. Following the approach for the determination of covariance between assets i and risk free (RF) asset:

$$Cov_{RFi} = \sum_{i=1}^{n} \left[R_i - E(R_i)\right]\left[R_{RF} - E(R_{RF})\right] / n$$

Because the returns for the risk free asset are certain, i.e., the $\sigma_{RF} = 0$ and thus Thus R_i $= E(R_i)$, and $R_i - E(R_i) = 0$. Consequently, the covariance of the risk-free asset with any risky asset or portfolio will always equal zero. Similarly the correlation between any risky asset and the risk-free asset would be zero. Similarly the correlation between any risky asset i, and the risk-free asset (RF), would be zero because the $Cov_{RFi} = 0$.

$$r_{RF} = \frac{Cov_{RFi}}{\sigma_{RF}\sigma_i}$$

Combining a Risk-free Asset with a Risky Portfolio

The expected rate of return for a portfolio that includes a risk-free asset is the weighted average of the two returns:

$$E(R_{port}) = W_{RF}(RFR) + (1 - W_{RF})E(R_i)$$

Where, W_{RF} = the proportion of the portfolio invested in the risk-free asset, $E(R_i)$ = the expected rate of return on risky Portfolio i

Thus the expected variance for a two-asset portfolio is:

$$E(\sigma^2_{port}) = w_{RF}^2\sigma_{RF}^2 + (1 - w_{RF})^2 \sigma_i^2 + 2w_{RF}(1 - w_{RF}) r_{RF,i}\sigma_{RF}\sigma_i$$

Since we know that the variance of the risk-free asset is zero and the correlation between the risk-free asset and any risky asset i is zero we can adjust the formula

$$E(\sigma^2_{port}) = (1 - w_{RF})^2 \sigma_i^2$$

Given the variance formula the standard deviation is:

$$E(\sigma_{port}) = \sqrt{(1 - w_{RF})^2 \sigma_i^2} = (1 - w_{RF})\sigma_i$$

Therefore, the standard deviation of a portfolio that combines the risk-free asset with risky assets is the linear proportion of the standard deviation of the risky asset portfolio.

Since both the expected return and the standard deviation of return for such a portfolio are linear combinations, a graph of possible portfolio returns and risks looks like a straight line between the two assets. The efficient frontier which gives higher return is the point M where the line is tangent to the frontier. The set of portfolio possibilities along Line RFR-M dominates all portfolios below Point M. For example, an investor could attain a risk and return combination between the RFR and Point M (Point C) by investing one-half of the portfolio in the risk-free asset (that is, lending money at the RFR) and the other half in the risky portfolio at Point M.

Portfolio Possibilities Combining the Risk-Free Asset
and Risky Portfolios on the Efficient Frontier

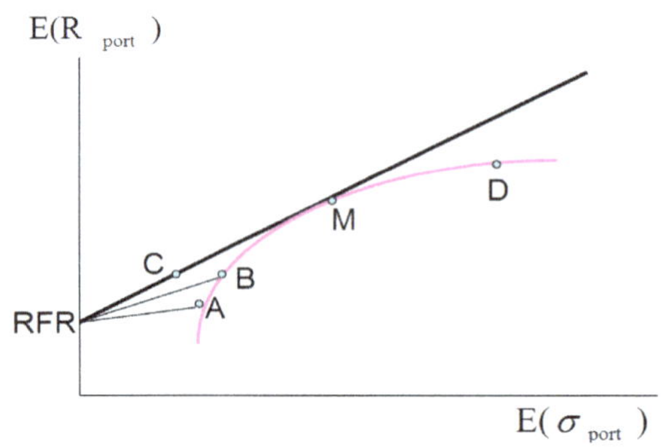

Risk-return Possibilities with Leverage

From the above discussion it is clear that to attain a higher expected return than is available at point M (in exchange for accepting higher risk). Either invest along the efficient frontier beyond point M, such as point D or, add leverage to the portfolio by borrowing money at the risk-free rate and investing in the risky portfolio at point M.

Portfolio Possibilities Combining the Risk-Free Asset
and Risky Portfolios on the Efficient Frontier

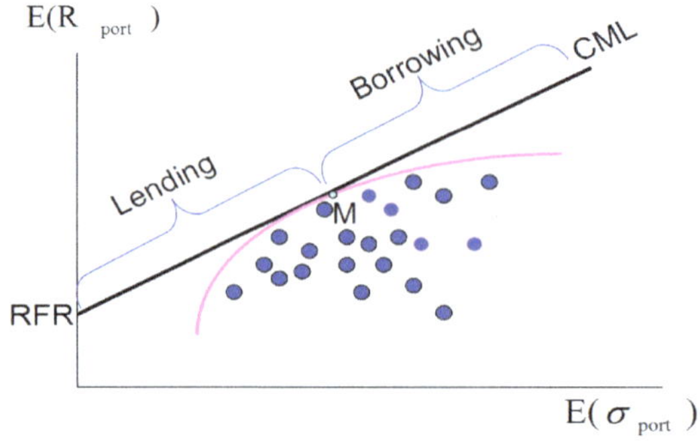

If an investor borrow an amount equal to 40 percent of the original wealth at the risk-free rate, w_{RF} will not be a positive fraction but, rather, a negative 60 percent $(w_{RF} = -0.60)$. The effect on the expected return for your portfolio is:

$$E(R_{Port}) = w_{RF}(RFR) + (1 - w_{RF})E(R_M)$$
$$= -.60(RFR) + (1 - (-.40)E(R_M)$$
$$= -.60RFR + 1.40E(R_M)$$

If for example the RFR=.04 and $E(R_M)$=.18, then

$$E(R_{Port}) = (-.60)(.04) + 1.40(.18) = 0.23$$

Thus return will increase in a linear fashion along the Line RFR-M because the gross return is increases with the high level of risk. Therefore, both return and risk increase in a linear fashion along the original Line RFR-M, and this extension dominates everything below the line on the original efficient frontier. Thus, we have a new efficient frontier: the straight line from the RFR tangent to Point M. This line is referred to as the capital market line (CML). Because the CML is a straight line, it implies that all the portfolios on the CML are perfectly positively correlated. The more conservative the investor the more is placed in risk-free lending and the less borrowing. The more aggressive the investor the less is placed in risk-free lending and the more borrowing. Most aggressive investors would use leverage to invest more in portfolio M.

Market Portfolio

Market portfolio is a portfolio consisting of a weighted sum of every asset in the market, with weights in the proportions that they exist in the market, with the necessary assumption that these assets are infinitely divisible.

Richard Roll's critique (1977) states that this is only a theoretical concept, as to create a market portfolio for investment purposes in practice would necessarily include every single possible available asset, including real estate, precious metals, stamp collections, jewelry, and anything with any worth, as the theoretical market being referred to would be the world market.

There is some question of whether what is used for the market portfolio really matters. Some authors say that it does not make a big difference; you can use any old index and get similar results. Roll gave an example where different indexes produce much different results, and that by choosing the index you can get any ranking you want. Brown and Brown examine this, using different indexes such as stocks only, stocks and bonds, and stocks plus bonds plus real estate. They find that using a market that includes real estate produces much different results. For example, with one measurement most mutual funds have alpha close to zero, while with another measurement most of them have significantly negative alpha.

Most index providers give indices for different components such as stocks only, bonds only, et cetera. As a result, proxies for the market (such as the FTSE 100 in the UK,

DAX in Germany or the S&P 500 in the US) are used in practice by investors. Roll's critique states that these proxies cannot provide an accurate representation of the entire market.

The concept of a market portfolio plays an important role in many financial theories and models, including the capital asset pricing model where it is the only fund in which investors need to invest, to be supplemented only by a risk-free asset, depending upon each investor's attitude towards risk.

Sharpe notes that many investors are at least targeted to a fixed ratio (e.g. 60% stocks, 40% bonds). He points out that this is sort of contrarian. The holdings of all investors combined must, by equation, be in the cap-weighted proportions. So many investors following this strategy implies some other investors must follow a buy-high, sell-low (trend following) strategy. He then says that he doesn't like it and people should use adjustments to the market proportions instead.

Doeswijk, Lam and Swinkels (2012) (2013) argue that the portfolio of the average investor contains important information for strategic asset allocation purposes. This portfolio shows the relative value of all assets according to the market crowd, which one could interpret as a benchmark or the optimal portfolio for the average investor. The authors determine the market values of equities, private equity, real estate, high yield bonds, emerging debt, non-government bonds, government bonds, inflation linked bonds, commodities, and hedge funds. For this range of assets, they estimate the invested global market portfolio for the period 1990-2012. For the main asset categories equities, real estate, non-government bonds and government bonds they extend the period to 1959-2012.

In the above example because Portfolio M lies at the point of tangency, it has the highest portfolio possibility line, and everybody will want to invest in Portfolio M and borrow or lend to be somewhere on the CML. This portfolio must, therefore, include all risky assets. If a risky asset were not in this portfolio in which everyone wants to invest, there would be no demand for it and therefore it would have no value. This portfolio that includes all risky assets is referred to as the market portfolio. Because the market portfolio contains all risky assets, it is a completely diversified portfolio, which means that all the risk unique to individual assets in the portfolio is diversified away. This unique (diversifiable) risk is also referred to as unsystematic risk. The optimal portfolio is at the highest point of tangency between Capital Market Line (CML) and the efficient frontier. The CML leads all investors to invest in the same risky asset portfolio, the M portfolio. Individual investors should only differ regarding their position on the CML, which depends on their risk preferences. The risk preference of individual investors can be regarded as their choice or preferable position along the CML line with respect to their financing decision. In other words when an investor decides to invest in the market Portfolio M nad wants to be on the CML is because of the investment decision. But the decision either to borrow or to lend to attain the preferred risk position on the CML is known as the financing decision.

This division of the investment decision from the financing decision is known as the separation theorem. The major points of separation theorem are as follows:

- The CML leads all investors to invest in the M portfolio
- Individual investors should differ in position on the CML depending on risk preferences
- How an investor gets to a point on the CML is based on financing decisions
- Risk averse investors will lend part of the portfolio at the risk-free rate and invest the remainder in the market portfolio
- Investors preferring more risk might borrow funds at the RFR and invest everything in the market portfolio
- The decision of both investors is to invest in portfolio M along the CML (the investment decision)
- The decision to borrow or lend to obtain a point on the CML is a separate decision based on risk preferences (financing decision)
- Tobin refers to this separation of the investment decision from the financing decision, the separation theorem

Capital Market Line

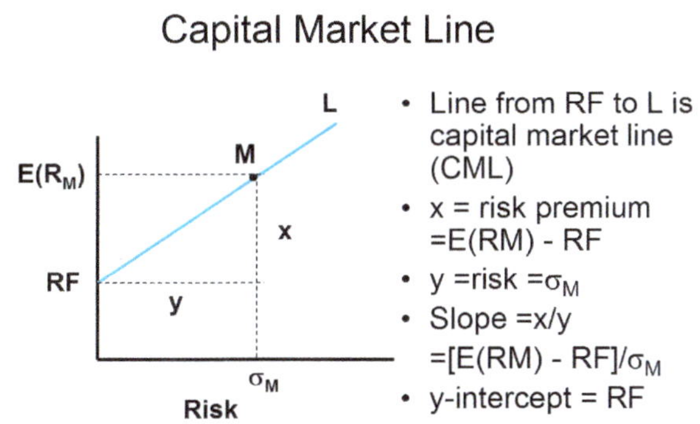

Slope of the CML is the market price of risk for efficient portfolios, or the equilibrium price of risk in the market.

The concept of capital Market Line (CML) states that the relevant risk measure for risky assets is their covariance with the Market portfolio (M), which is referred to as their systematic risk. Since all individual risky assets are a part of the M portfolio, the rates of return in relation to the returns for the M portfolio using the following linear model:

$$R_{it} = \alpha_i = \beta_i + R_{M_t} + \varepsilon$$

Where, R*i, t* is return for asset i during period *t, ai* is constant term for asset *i*, βi is the slope coefficient for asset *i*, R_{M_t} is the return for the M portfolio during period t, ε is the random error term.

The Security Market Line

The security market line (SML) visually represents the relationship between risk and the expected or the required rate of return on an asset. The equation of SML, together with estimates for the return on a risk-free asset and on the market portfolio, can generate expected or required rates of return for any asset based on its systematic risk. Given this standardized measure of systematic risk, the SML graph can be expressed as follows: The relevant risk measure for an individual risky asset is its covariance with the market portfolio (Covi,m). The equation for the risk-return line is:

Security Market Line

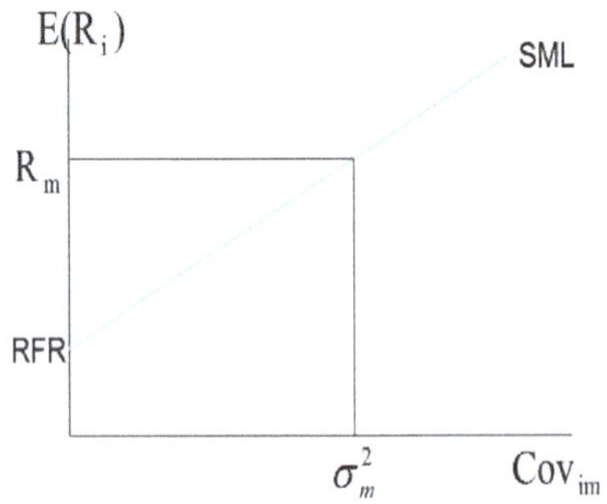

$$E(R_i) = RFR + \frac{R_M - RFR}{\sigma_M^2}(Cov_{i,M})$$

$$= RFR + \frac{Cov_{i,M}}{\sigma_M^2}(R_M - RFR)$$

$$We\,than\,define \frac{Cov_{i,M}}{\sigma_M^2}$$

$$as\ beta(\beta_i).$$

Thus the equation becomes:

$$E(R_i) = RFR + \beta_i(R_M - RFR)$$

Here the Beta can be viewed as a standardized measure of systematic risk.

Determining the Expected Rate of Return for a Risky Asset

The expected rate of return of a risk asset is determined by the RFR plus a risk premium for the individual asset. The risk premium for a security i is determined by the systematic risk of the asset (beta) and the prevailing market risk premium (R_M-RFR).

$$E(R_i) = RFR + \beta_i (R_M - RFR)$$

Following points are important to remember with respect to the determination of expected rate of return for risky assets:

- In equilibrium, all assets and all portfolios of assets should plot on the SML
- Any security with an estimated return that plots above the SML is under priced
- Any security with an estimated return that plots below the SML is overpriced
- A superior investor must derive value estimates for assets that are consistently superior to the consensus market evaluation to earn better risk-adjusted rates of return than the average investor
- Compare the required rate of return to the expected rate of return for a specific risky asset using the SML over a specific investment horizon to determine if it is an appropriate investment

Inputs Required for Applying CAPM

In this section we will briefly discuss the three major inputs that are required for the application of CAPM such as:

- Risk-Free Rate
- Market Risk Premium
- Beta

Risk-Free Asset

Risk-free asset which provides the risk-free rate of return (RFR) is an asset with zero variance and have zero correlation with all other risky assets. Following the approach for the determination of covariance between assets i and risk free (RF) asset:

$$Cov_{RFi} = \sum_{i=1}^{n} \left[R_i - E(R_i) \right] \left[R_{RF} - E(R_{RF}) \right] / n$$

Because the returns for the risk free asset are certain, i.e., the $\sigma_{RF} = 0$ and thus Thus R_i = $E(R_i)$, and R_i - $E(R_i)$ = 0. Consequently, the covariance of the risk-free asset with any risky asset or portfolio will always equal zero. Similarly the correlation between any risky asset i and the risk-free asset would be zero. Similarly the correlation between any risky asset i, and the risk-free asset (RF), would be zero because the $Cov_{RFi} = 0$.

$$r_{RF} = \frac{Cov_{RFi}}{\sigma_{RF}\sigma_i}$$

As per the empirical literature the standard practice for considering the proxy for the risk free asset is the yield on 91 days Treasury bill return.

Market Risk Premium

It is calculated as the difference between the average return on stocks and the average risk free rate $(R_M - R_F)$.In other words Risk premium is defined as the additional compensation required by investors for holding a risky security. For a successful investment decision an important element in interpreting financial market prices is the identification of the risk premia they contain. Consequently, it makes a difference in both how investors allocate wealth across different asset classes and which specific assets or securities investors chose to invest within each asset class. However, the risk premium may vary over time according to the investors' perception of the underlying risk of the asset and their attitude towards risk. The major determinants are variance in the underlying economy, political risk and market structure. Other determinants of the equity risk premium are: investor aversion to risk; macroeconomic risk, quantity and quality of investment information, investment liquidity, risk of catastrophe, and investor irrationality. However there are two fundamental questions that need to be addressed while measuring the market risk premium: How long should be the measurement period? And should geometric mean or arithmetic mean is the appropriate measure? Following table presents estimates of the equity risk premium for major international markets in the period from January 1995 to October 2008.

	1995-2008		1995-2008
Australia	5.1	Ireland	8.4
Austria	3.2	Italy	3.5
Belgium	4.4	Netherlands	4.6
Canada	3.9	Portugal	4.3
China	11.3	Singapore	5.7
Finland	3.3	Spain	5.2
France	5.2	Sweden	3.5
Germany	3.5	Switzerland	3.3
Hong Kong	6.0	United Kingdom	4.8
India	5.9	USA	3.1

Beta: The Systematic Risk

The systematic risk input of an individual asset is derived from a regression model, referred to as the asset's characteristic line with the model portfolio:

$$R_{i,t} = \alpha_i + \beta_i R_{M,t} + \varepsilon$$

Where $R_{i,t}$ is the rate of return for asset i during period t, and RM_t is the rate of return for the market portfolio M during t. $\alpha_i = R_i - \beta_i R_M$

$\beta i = Cov_{i,M/\sigma_M^2}$ and ε = the random error term

Issues related to the estimation of beta:

- Return Interval
- Market Index
- Adjusting Historical Beta: Measurement of past relationship can not be used as an estimate of future risk. The historical alignment may have been significantly influenced by chance of factors. Company's beta may change over time.
- Stability of Beta: betas for individual stocks are not stable, but portfolio betas are reasonably stable. Further, the larger the portfolio of stocks and longer the period, the more stable the beta of the portfolio

Other Approaches to Beta Estimation:

- Betas based on Fundamental Information: Industry Affiliation, Corporate Growth, Financial Leverage, Size
- Betas based on Accounting Earnings: Regressing the changes in company earnings against changes in the earnings for the market.
- Betas from Cross Sectional regressions: Coefficient of Variation of operating income, Debt to equity ratio, Earnings growth, Total assets

Relaxing the Assumptions of CAPM

- Differential Borrowing and Lending Rates: Heterogeneous Expectations and Planning Periods
- Zero Beta Model: does not require a risk-free asset
- Transaction Costs: with transactions costs, the SML will be a band of securities, rather than a straight line
- Heterogeneous Expectations and Planning Periods: will have an impact on the CML and SML
- Taxes: could cause major differences in the CML and SML among investors

Relationship between Systematic Risk and Return

- Effect of Skewness on Relationship: investors prefer stocks with high positive Skewness that provide an opportunity for very large returns
- Effect of Size, P/E, and Leverage: size, and P/E have an inverse impact on returns after considering the CAPM. Financial Leverage also helps explain cross-section of returns
- Effect of Book-to-Market Value: Fama and French (1992) questioned the relationship between returns and beta in their seminal 1992 study. They found the BV/MV ratio to be a key determinant of returns
- Summary of CAPM Risk-Return Empirical Results: the relationship between beta and rates of return is a moot point

The Market Portfolio: Theory versus Practice

- There is a controversy over the market portfolio. Hence, proxies are used
- There is no unanimity about which proxy to use
- An incorrect market proxy will affect both the beta risk measures and the position and slope of the SML that is used to evaluate portfolio performance
- CAPM is criticized because of the difficulties in selecting a proxy for the market portfolio as a benchmark

Arbitrage Pricing Theory

In finance, arbitrage pricing theory (APT) is a general theory of asset pricing that holds that the expected return of a financial asset can be modeled as a linear function of various macro-economic factors or theoretical market indices, where sensitivity to changes in each factor is represented by a factor-specific beta coefficient. The model-derived rate of return will then be used to price the asset correctly—the asset price should equal the expected end of period price discounted at the rate implied by the model. If the price diverges, arbitrage should bring it back into line.

The theory was proposed by the economist Stephen Ross in 1976.

Model

Risky asset returns are said to follow a *factor intensity structure* if they can be expressed as:

$$r_j = a_j + b_{j1}F_1 + b_{j2}F_2 + \cdots + b_{jn}F_n + \epsilon_j$$

where

- a_j is a constant for asset j
- F_k is a systematic factor
- b_{jk} is the sensitivity of the jth asset to factor k, also called factor loading,
- and ϵ_j is the risky asset's idiosyncratic random shock with mean zero.

Idiosyncratic shocks are assumed to be uncorrelated across assets and uncorrelated with the factors.

The APT states that if asset returns follow a factor structure then the following relation exists between expected returns and the factor sensitivities:

$$E(r_j) = r_f + b_{j1}RP_1 + b_{j2}RP_2 + \cdots + b_{jn}RP_n$$

where

- RP_k is the risk premium of the factor,
- r_f is the risk-free rate,

That is, the expected return of an asset j is a linear function of the asset's sensitivities to the n factors.

Note that there are some assumptions and requirements that have to be fulfilled for the latter to be correct: There must be perfect competition in the market, and the total number of factors may never surpass the total number of assets (in order to avoid the problem of matrix singularity).

Arbitrage

Arbitrage is the practice of taking positive expected return from overvalued or undervalued securities in the inefficient market without any incremental risk and zero additional investments.

Mechanics

In the APT context, arbitrage consists of trading in two assets – with at least one being mispriced. The arbitrageur sells the asset which is relatively too expensive and uses the proceeds to buy one which is relatively too cheap.

Under the APT, an asset is mispriced if its current price diverges from the price predicted by the model. The asset price today should equal the sum of all future cash flows discounted at the APT rate, where the expected return of the asset is a linear function of various factors, and sensitivity to changes in each factor is represented by a factor-specific beta coefficient.

A correctly priced asset here may be in fact a *synthetic* asset - a *portfolio* consisting of other correctly priced assets. This portfolio has the same exposure to each of the macroeconomic factors as the mispriced asset. The arbitrageur creates the portfolio by identifying x correctly priced assets (one per factor plus one) and then weighting the assets such that portfolio beta per factor is the same as for the mispriced asset.

When the investor is long the asset and short the portfolio (or vice versa) he has created a position which has a positive expected return (the difference between asset return and portfolio return) and which has a net-zero exposure to any macroeconomic factor and is therefore risk free (other than for firm specific risk). The arbitrageur is thus in a position to make a risk-free profit:

Where today's price is too low:

The implication is that at the end of the period the *portfolio* would have appreciated at the rate implied by the APT, whereas the mispriced asset would have appreciated at *more* than this rate. The arbitrageur could therefore:

Today:

1 short sell the *portfolio*

2 buy the mispriced asset with the proceeds.

At the end of the period:

1 sell the mispriced asset

2 use the proceeds to buy back the *portfolio*

3 pocket the difference.

Where today's price is too high:

The implication is that at the end of the period the *portfolio* would have appreciated at the rate implied by the APT, whereas the mispriced asset would have appreciated at *less* than this rate. The arbitrageur could therefore:

Today:

1 short sell the mispriced asset

2 buy the *portfolio* with the proceeds.

At the end of the period:

1 sell the *portfolio*

2 use the proceeds to buy back the mispriced asset

3 pocket the difference.

Relationship with the Capital Asset Pricing Model

The APT along with the capital asset pricing model (CAPM) is one of two influential theories on asset pricing. The APT differs from the CAPM in that it is less restrictive in its assumptions. It allows for an explanatory (as opposed to statistical) model of asset returns. It assumes that each investor will hold a unique portfolio with its own particular array of betas, as opposed to the identical "market portfolio". In some ways, the CAPM can be considered a "special case" of the APT in that the securities market line represents a single-factor model of the asset price, where beta is exposed to changes in value of the market.

Additionally, the APT can be seen as a "supply-side" model, since its beta coefficients reflect the sensitivity of the underlying asset to economic factors. Thus, factor shocks would cause structural changes in assets' expected returns, or in the case of stocks, in firms' profitabilities.

On the other side, the capital asset pricing model is considered a "demand side" model. Its results, although similar to those of the APT, arise from a maximization problem of each investor's utility function, and from the resulting market equilibrium (investors are considered to be the "consumers" of the assets).

Implementation

Factors

As with the CAPM, the factor-specific betas are found via a linear regression of historical security returns on the factor in question. Unlike the CAPM, the APT, however, does not itself reveal the identity of its priced factors - the number and nature of these factors is likely to change over time and between economies. As a result, this issue is essentially empirical in nature. Several *a priori* guidelines as to the characteristics required of potential factors are, however, suggested:

1. their impact on asset prices manifests in their *unexpected* movements
2. they should represent *undiversifiable* influences (these are, clearly, more likely to be macroeconomic rather than firm-specific in nature)
3. timely and accurate information on these variables is required
4. the relationship should be theoretically justifiable on economic grounds

Chen, Roll and Ross (1986) identified the following macro-economic factors as significant in explaining security returns:

- surprises in inflation;
- surprises in GNP as indicated by an industrial production index;
- surprises in investor confidence due to changes in default premium in corporate bonds;
- surprise shifts in the yield curve.

As a practical matter, indices or spot or futures market prices may be used in place of macro-economic factors, which are reported at low frequency (e.g. monthly) and often with significant estimation errors. Market indices are sometimes derived by means of factor analysis. More direct "indices" that might be used are:

- short-term interest rates;
- the difference in long-term and short-term interest rates;
- a diversified stock index such as the S&P 500 or NYSE Composite;
- oil prices
- gold or other precious metal prices
- Currency exchange rates

Asset Management

The linear factor model structure of the APT is used as the basis for many of the commercial risk systems employed by asset managers.

The fundamental principle of finance suggests that higher the risk, higher will be the return. This generalisation of risk return trade-off challenges the practitioners as well as academic literature to know what is the appropriate measure of risk. The failure of the conventional mean variance capital asset pricing model (CAPM) to adequately explain cross-sectional variation of risky asset return has spurred alternative explanations of asset pricing. The The Arbitrage Pricing Theory (APT) of Ross (1976)1, is one such alternative. Unlike Sharpe (1963) single-index model, according to APT there are multiple factors that represent the fundamental risks in the economy. Each measure of systematic risk relative to fundamental risk factors captures the sensitivity of the asset to the corresponding economic factor. The key difference between these two models lies in the way systematic investment risk is defined: CAPM -a single, market-wide risk factor and a few (or several) factors in the APT that capture the of that market-wide risk.

The traditional equilibrium model, the CAPM assumes that stock returns are generated by a one-factor model, where the factor represents the market portfolio of all risky assets. However the empirical tests of the CAPM across several markets have produced mixed results and more reasonably the finds conclude that the market factor as the sole determinant of systematic risk is not appropriate one. The critical point in the estimation of the CAPM is the difficulty of measuring the true market portfolio. As observed by Shanken (1985, p. 1190) "in the absence of what are essentially measurement problems, the central implication of the CAPM, that the market portfolio is efficient, may be tested. However, limited observability of the universe of assets and the consequent substitution of proxies for the true market portfolio make it difficult to reach In this regard APT, developed by Ross (1976) proposes that there are several sources of risk in the economy such as these risk factors arise from changes in some fundamental economic and financial variables such as interest rates, inflation, real business activity, a market index, investor confidence etc. that cannot be eliminated. The arbitrage pricing theory assumes that a security return is a linear function; not only of one, but also a set of common factors and the risk premium for an asset is related to the risk premium for each factor. The APT predicted that prices of all risky assets in the economy conformed to the condition of no arbitrage. No arbitrage mean that an individual holding a well diversified portfolio could not earn any additional return merely by changing the weights of the assets included in the portfolio, holding both systematic and unsystematic risk constant. In this regard APT has two basic postulates: returns are generated by a Linear Factor Model (postulate-1), assume pure arbitrage profits are impossible (postulate -2).

Other Assumptions

1. Capital markets are perfectly competitive.
2. Investors always prefer more wealth to less wealth with certainty.
3. The stochastic process generating asset returns can be expressed as a linear function of a set of K factors or indexes.
4. APT assumes that, in equilibrium, the return on a zero-investment, zero-systematic- risk portfolio is zero when the unique effects are diversified away.

Return Generating Process Under Equilibrium

The APT assumes that the return on any stock is linearly related to a set of factors also referred to as systematic factors or risk factors with following specifications:

$$R_{it} = a_i + \beta_{i1}k_1 + \beta_{i1}k_1 + \beta_{i2}k_2 + \beta_{i3}k_3 \dots\dots\dots\dots\dots\dots + \beta_{iJ}k_J + \varepsilon_i \; for \; i = 1 \dots N$$

Where R_{it} is the return on stock $i = a_i$ expected return on stock I if all factors have a value of zero. k_j is value of Jth factor which influences the return on stock $i\,(j = 1, \dots J)$. β_{iJ} is the sensitivity of stock *i's* return to the Jth factor. ε_i mean of zero and variance of σ_{ei}^2 .

Similar to the CAPM model, the APT assumes that the unique effects (εi) are independent and will be diversified away in a large portfolio. Further more, the error term is expected to have a mean value of zero, i.e., $E(\varepsilon)=0$ and is uncorrelated across securities, i.e., $E(\varepsilon_i\varepsilon_j)=0$ for all i and j where $i \neq j$. The assumption of uncorrelated error term or unique risk component of the security with each other as with all risk factors is essential as it is expected that all covariance relationships between securities can be captured through their relationships with J risk factors. Given the above mentioned return generating process the APT establishes an equilibrium risk return relationship which guides the basic idea that, two identical portfolios that have the same risk can not offer different expected returns. If it happens the arbitrageurs will step in and their actions will ensure that the law of one price holds good. The equilibrium relationship according to the APT is as follows:

$$E(R_i)=\lambda_0+\beta_{i1}\lambda_1+\beta_{i2}\lambda_2+\beta_{i3}\lambda_3\ldots\ldots\ldots\ldots\ldots\ldots+\beta_{ij}\lambda_j$$

Where, $E(R_i)$ is the expected return on stock i, λ_0 is the return on the risk-free asset, β_{iJ} is the sensitivity if stock i to risk factor $j. \lambda_J$ is the risk premium for the type of risk associated with factor *J*.

The factors that have been suggested by the APT literature with respected to their influence on security returns are: the growth rate in industrial production (business cycle risk), changes in expected inflation, changes in market risk premium as measured by the yield differential between long term corporate bond and government bonds, changes in oil prices, investor confidence risk (similar to market risk premium) measured as 20-year corporate bond return minus 25-year government bond return. In this regard a positive factor realization (J > 0) implies the yield spread between risky corporate bonds and safe government bonds has decreased indicates increased investor confidence or positive confidence risk. Market timing risk measured as that part of the S&P 500 return not explained by the first four factors. This captures the impacts of earthquakes, politics, and pure bull or bear markets. In this case if exposure would equal CAPM beta if the first four factor exposures were all zero.

APT : A Graphical Illustration

Let us consider a one factor APT model given as:

$$\bar{r}_i=\lambda_0+\lambda_1\beta_i$$

Where, λ_0 and λ_1 are constants and returns are generated by one factor. It is the equation of a straight line (APT asset pricing line) meaning that in equilibrium there will be a linear relationship between expected returns and sensitivities.

Suppose there are two assets A and B with expected return and risk characteristics as shown in Figure. Following the above specification of APT any security that has factor sensitivity and expected return that will be appear off the line and will be mispriced.

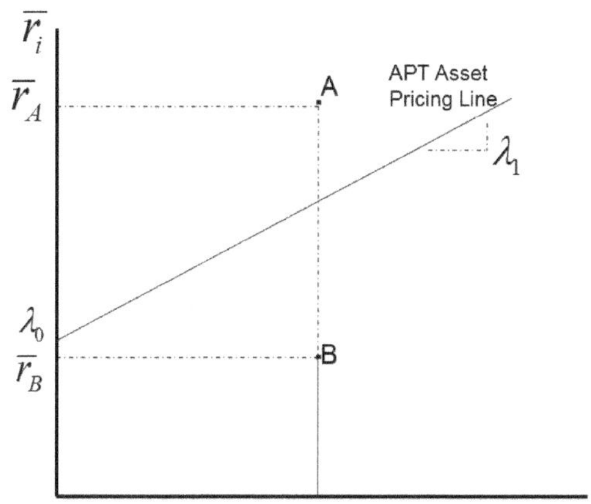

According to APT theoretical argument such security will present investors an opportunity of forming arbitrage portfolios. Here security A and B are the concerned securities that give a similar framework for analysis. Here both A and B violate the "law of one price' since two assets with same level of risk trading at different prices and offer different expected return. Security B is relatively over priced (lower expected return) and security A is relatively under priced (high expected return) with equal magnitude of risk. This offers an arbitrage opportunity or a chance to make risk less profit.

As per the APT framework the basic premise is that when two or more securities or portfolios that provide the same pay-off to the investors (i.e., same level of risk) are same and must therefore sell at the same price. This premise is also consistent with the law of one price. In other words, if there are two securities or portfolios that have same risk but different expected returns, investors will arbitrage by buying security with higher expected return (low price), and will sell the security with lower expected return (high price). This process of buying and selling will eliminate the price difference until the two securities will have same expected returns. The buying and selling activity of investors will cause the price of the security of the higher expected return to rise relatively to the one with the lower expected return. APT considers all assets like A and B, that are in the same risk class to be perfect substitutes and should be traded at the same equilibrium price level.

In figure the investor following APT approach will go short on security B and long on security A. This approach will not involve any additional commitment of funds. The investor will pay for security A by using the sales proceedings of the security B. Furthermore, since security B and security A have the same sensitivity to the factor, the selling of security B and buying of security A will constitute an arbitrage portfolio with no sensitivity to the factor. Finally, the new arbitrage portfolio will have a positive expected return because the expected return of security A is greater than expected return of security A. The above process will raise security A's price and its expected return will fall until it is located on the APT asset pricing line.

Example

Let us consider a situation where returns are generated by two factors given by the following specifications: $E(r_i) = 5 + 7\beta_{i1} + 4\beta_{i2}$ Let us also assume that there are three portfolios with the following risk return characteristics:

Portfolio	Expected Return	Risk (β_{i1})	Risk (β_{i2})
L	15.4	0.80	1.20
M	16.6	1.20	0.80
N	14.0	1.00	1.00

Here we can see that portfolio L and M are correctly priced whereas portfolio N is overpriced. Put it differently, expected return on portfolio N is not compatible with the underlying risk measured by β_{i1} and β_{i2} This offers a scope for arbitrage. Here it is worth to mention that arbitrage is the process of earning risk less profits by taking advantage of differential pricing for the same financial asset or security.

Here we can construct an arbitrage portfolio S, which has the same risk characteristics as that in portfolio N. This new portfolio S can be constructed by combining portfolios L and M in equal weights. Thus the risk return characteristics of portfolio S will be:

Expected Return or $E(r_s)$	Risk (β_{S1})	Risk (β_{S2})
(0.50 x 15.4)+(0.50 x 16.6)	(0.50 x 0.80)+(0.50 x 1.20)	(0.50 x 1.20)+(0.50 x 0.80)
16	1.00	1.00

Here we can see that portfolio S has the same systematic risk as portfolio N, but offers a higher return than portfolio N. Because of this arbitrage opportunity, the arbitrage portfolio can be constructed selling the relatively overpriced portfolio and buying the under priced portfolio. In other words the investor will try to take a short selling position for portfolio N and go for a long on portfolio S.

Following table illustrates how an arbitrage portfolio can be constructed to benefit from the differential return given by portfolio N and S. Suppose by the short selling portfolio N the investor can realise an inflow say Rs. 20,00. It can assumed that the sales proceed is realised immediately. This can also be treated as negative value for the investors investment. Investing the same proceedings in the arbitrage portfolio S will make the net investment in the arbitrage portfolio zero. Given the expected return of the portfolio N and S as 14 percent and 16 percent respectively, the return on portfolio N will be – Rs. 2,800 and on portfolio S will be +Rs.2,800. The net return in the arbitrage portfolio will be Rs. 400. Looking at the risk of arbitrage portfolio, since beta of both the portfolios N and S are equal in magnitude and opposite in sign, beta or net risk of the arbitrage portfolio will be zero. This is because beta of a portfolio is equivalent to the sum of weighted average of the betas of the individual assets.

Portfolio	Investment (Rs.)	Return (Rs.)	Risk (β_{i1})	Risk (β_{i2})
N	-20,000	-2,800	-1.0	-1.0
S	+20,000	+3,200	+1.0	+1.0
Arbitrage Profit	0	400	0	0

The arbitrage portfolio offers a profit potential without any net investment and risk. This risk less profit potential attracts investors who shot sell portfolio S and go long on portfolio N. This increases the price of portfolio N and decreases the price of portfolio S. This process of arbitrage goes on until the return differential for assets in the same risk class are eliminated. That is, both portfolios lie on the same arbitrage price line, ensuring equilibrium risk return relation for the securities.

Testability of the APT

The empirical testing of APT has itself not been without controversy. The common argument is that, APT is so imprecise that it makes it impossible ever to test whether the APT is true or false. The most notable findings of APT has been proposed by researchers (notably Roll and Ross, 1980) as a testable alternative and perhaps natural successor, to the CAPM. However, Roll and Ross (1984) acknowledged that the number of risk factors differ with 30 stocks versus 240 but contended that the important consideration is whether the resulting estimates are consistent because it is not feasible to consider all of the stocks together. Cho, Elton, and Gruber (1984) tested the APT by examining the number of factors in the return-generating process that were priced. An alternative set of tests of the APT considers anomalies like the small-firm effect and the January effect that are not explained by CAPM. In this regard, Reinganum (1981) found that APT can account for the differences in average returns between small firms and large firms. In another study Gultekin and Gultekin (1987) found that the APT model can adjust for the large returns in January as compared to any other month i.e., January effect. However, other researchers have claimed its applicability with caution as to the inconclusive evidence from the APT theory with respect to the choice of risk factors. For instance Shanken's challenge to the testability of APT can be outlined as follows:

- If returns are not explained by a model, it is not considered rejection of a model; however if the factors do explain returns, it is considered support
- APT has no advantage because the factors need not be observable, so equivalent sets may conform to different factor structures
- Empirical formulation of the APT may yield different implications regarding the expected returns for a given set of securities

- Thus, the theory cannot explain differential returns between securities because it cannot identify the relevant factor structure that explains the differential returns

Motivation for Multifactor Pricing Model

The goal of risk analysis is not only to minimize risk but also search for a methodology to properly weigh risk against return. The Multifactor Pricing Model captures the essence of the APT and relies on the direct specification of the form of the relationship to be estimated. The investor chooses the exact number and identifies the risk factors which affect the expected value of stock return. The basic motivation for the search of alternative multifactor models is from the limitations of the CAPM and APT. In case of CAPM the primary practical problem associated is to estimate the market portfolio accurately, a process that first requires identifying the relevant investment universe. On the other hand with the APT the identity and the exact number of the underlying risk factors are ambiguous. Other mainstream asset pricing models like Intertemporal Capital Asset Pricing Model (ICAPM) (Merton, 1973) which suggests that an asset's risk premium depends on the prospects of investing for the future with an adverse change in the future investment opportunity set, also fails to support adequate number of factors Similar is the case with the Consumption-based Capital Asset Pricing Model (CCAPM) (Breedin, 1979) which measures the risk of a security as the covariance of its return with consumption growth.

In the sideline of empirical evidences towards the failure of the conventional asset pricing models, literature also debate on the anomalous returns associated with several fundamental characteristics like size (SZ), book-to-market equity (BM) (Banz, 1981, Fama and French, 1992, Rosenberg et al., 1985), momentum (MOM) (Jegadeesh and Titman, 1993) and liquidity (LIQ) (Amihud, 2002). The risk premium associated with such firm specific characteristics (commonly called as market anomalies) that have shown cross sectional regularities with a predictable pattern. undermine the fact that risk factors defined by mainstream asset pricing models like CAPM, APT, ICAPM and CCAPM can never be the only relevant measure of risk.

Let suppose a security's excess return $\left(R_{ij}-r_j\right)$ can be estimated with the single index market model or CAPM give as:

$$R_{it}-r_f=\alpha_i+\left(R_m-r_f\right)+\varepsilon_{it}$$

Where r_f and R_m represent the risk free rate of return and market return respectively. In their critique of the CAPM, Fama and French (1992) noted that the linear relationship between the expected return of an asset and the market portfolio risk is not the sole determinant of a security's expected return. Several authors considered other firm specific characteristics such as the firm size, the Price-Earning Ratio (PE), the Book to Market Equity Ratio (BM) and the Cash Flow to Market Capitalization Ratio (CP) as other potential determinants for the stock return explanations. Following the specification given by Fama and French (1992) the above approach can be represented as:

$$R_{it} = \alpha + b_{1t}\beta_{it} + b_{2t}\ln(sz)_{it-1} + b_{3t}\ln(BM)_{it-1} + b_{4t}PE_{it-1} + b_{5t}CP_{it-1} + \varepsilon_{it}$$

Fama and French (1992) observes that " what ever the underlying economic causes, our main results are straight forward.Two easily measured variables, size (SZ) and book to market equity (BM or BE/ME), provide a simple and powerful characterisation of the cross section of average stock returns for the 1993-1990 period. There are also substantial evidences to suggest that the premiums earned by these fundamental risk characteristics are indeed pervasive across developed and emerging markets. As a whole the gamut of related literature on the validation of fundamental risk characteristics that can explain cross section of stock return found that across wide range of markets the magnitude of the risk premium associated with such characteristics may not be identical but their importance pertinent to statistical and economic explanations remain intact. Most arguably the source of deviation from the zero intercept hypothesis in case of mainstream asset pricing models and subsequent identification of characteristic based risk pricing have given rise to the advancement of multifactor explanations for cross section of stock return. However the basic source of theoretical motivation for the development of multifactor pricing models is attributed to the theoretical argument of APT.

Multiple Factor Models

In mathematical finance, multiple factor models are asset pricing models that can be used to estimate the discount rate for the valuation of financial assets. They are generally extensions of the single-factor capital asset pricing model (CAPM).

Model of Rosenberg and Marathe

The multifactor equity risk model was first developed by Barr Rosenberg and Vinay Marathe. Initially they proposed a linear model of beta

```
r(i,t)-r(0,t)=b(i,t)[m(t)-r(0,t)+g(i,t)
b(i,t)=sum_j X(i,j,t) f(j,t) + e(i,t)
```

where r(i,t) is the return to equity asset I in the period [t,t+1], r(0,t) is the risk free return, m(t) is the market index return, e(i,t) is a market residual return and b(i,t) is a parameter fit by a time series regression over history prior to time t. Then X(i,j,t) are risk exposure values calculated from fundamental and technical data, f(j,t) are factor returns determined by a cross-sectional regression for each time period and g(i,t) are the regression residuals. This model was reformulated by Rosenberg et al. into a direct model of asset return,

```
r(i,t)=sum_j X(i,j,t) f(i,j) + e(i,t)
```

Here the factor returns f(j,t) and specific returns e(i,t) are fit by a weighted regression over each time period t for a representative asset universe. For instance the model might be fit over the 3000 highest capitalization US common stocks. The primary application of the model is to estimate the asset by asset covariance matrix C of asset returns by the equation

```
C=XFX^t+D
```

where F is the covariance matrix of asset returns, and D is a block diagonal matrix of specific returns. The matrix C is then used for Markowitz portfolio construction which involves maximizing the quadratic utility function

```
u(h)=a^t h- k h^tCh
```

subject to linear constraints on the vector of asset holdings h. Here a is a vector of expected returns and k is a scalar parameter termed the risk aversion.

Modifications by Torre

Nicolo G. Torre made a number of improvements to this framework which importantly sharpened the risk control achievable by these means. In Rosenberg's model the risk indices X consisted of industry weights and risk indices. Each asset would be given an exposure to one or more industries, e. g. based on breakdowns of the firms balance sheet or earning statement into industry segments. These industry exposures would sum to 1 for each asset. Thus the model had no explicit market factor but rather the market return was projected on to the industry returns. Torre modified this scheme by introducing an explicit market factor (with unit exposure for each asset.) To keep the model identified by imposed the condition that the industry factor returns sum to zero in each time period. Thus the model is estimated as

```
f(i,t)=m(t)+sum_j X(i,j,t)f(j,t) + e(i,t)
```

subject to

```
sum_k f(k,t)=0 for all t
```

where the sum is over industry factors. Here m(t) is the market return. Explicitly identifying the market factor then permitted Torre to estimate the variance of this factor using a leveraged GARCH(1,1) model due to Robert Engle and Tim Bollerslev

```
s^2(t)=w+a s^2(t-1)+ b1 fp(m(t-1))^2 + b2 fm(m(t-1))^2
```

Here

```
fp(x)=x for x>0
      0 for x<=0
fm(x)=0 for x>=0
      x for x<0
```

and w, a, b1 and b2 are parameters fit from long time series estimations using maximum likelihood methods. This model provides a rapid update of market variance which is incorporated into the update of F, resulting in a more dynamic model of risk. In particular it accounts for the convergence of asset returns and consequent loss of diversification that occurs in portfolios during periods of market turbulence.

In the risk model industry factors carry about half the explanatory power after the market effect is accounted for. However, Rosenberg had left unsolved how the industry groupings should be defined – choosing to rely simply on a conventional set of industries. Defining industry sets is a problem in taxonomy. The basic difficulty is that the industry is defined by the members assigned to it, but which industry an individual equity should be assigned to is often unclear. Difficulties can be reduced by introducing a large number of narrowly defined industries, but this approach is in tension with the demands of risk estimation. For robust risk estimates we favor a moderate number of industries with each industry representing a few percentage points of market capitalization and not exclusively dominated by the largest company in the industry. Torre resolved this problem by introducing several hundred narrowly defined mini-industries and then applying guided clustering techniques to combine the mini-industries into industry groupings suitable for risk estimation.

In the initial Rosenberg approach factor and specific returns are assumed to be normally distributed. However experience turns up a number of outlying observations that are both too large and too frequent to be fit by a normal distribution Although introduction of a GARCH market factor partly reduces this difficulty, it does not eliminate it. Torre showed that return distributions can be modeled as a mixture of a normal distribution and a jump distribution. In the case of a single factor the mixing model is easily stated. Each time period t there is a binary mixing variable b(t). If b(t)=0 then the factor return in that period is drawn from the normal distribution and if b(t)=1 it drawn from the jump distribution. Torre found that simultaneous jumps occur in factors. Accordingly, in the multivariate case it is necessary to introduce a multivariate shock vector w(i,t) where w(i,t)=0 if the multivariate mixing variable b(i,t)=0 and w(i,t) is drawn from the ith jump distribution if b(i,t)=1. A transmission matrix T then maps w from the shock space into the factor space. Torre found that the market, factor and specific returns could all be described by a mixture of normal returns and power law distributed shocks occurring at a low frequency. This modeling refinement substantially improves the performance of the model with regard to extreme events. As such it makes possible construction of portfolios which behave in more expected manners during periods of market turbulence.

Extensions to other Market Types

Although originally developed for the US equity market, the multifactor risk model was rapidly extended to other equity markets and to other types of securities such as bonds and equity options. The problem of how to construct a multi-asset class risk model then arises. A first approach was made by Beckers, Rudd and Stefek for the global equity market. They estimated a model involving currency, country, global industries and global risk indices. This model worked well for portfolios constructed by the top down process of first selecting countries and then selecting assets within countries. It was less successful on portfolios constructed by a bottom up process in which portfolios within countries were first selected by country specialists and then a global overlay was applied. In addition the global model applied to a single country portfolio would often be at odds with the local market model. Torre resolved these difficulties by introducing a two-stage factor analysis. The first stage consists of fitting a series of local factor models of the familiar form resulting in a set of factor returns f(i,j,t) where f(i,j,t) is the return to factor i in the jth local model at t. The factor returns are then fit to a second stage model of the form

$$f(i,j,t)=\sum_k Y(i,j,k)\, g(k,t) + h(i,j,t)$$

Here Y gives the exposure of local factor (i,j) to the kth global factor whose return is g(k,t) and h(i,j,t) is the local specific factor return. The covariance matrix of factor returns is estimated as

$$F=YGY^t+H$$

where G is the covariance matrix of global factors and H is the block diagonal covariances of local specific factor returns. This modeling approach permits gluing any number of local models together to provide a comprehensive multi-asset class analysis. This is particularly relevant for global equity portfolios and for enterprise wide risk management.

The multifactor risk model with the refinements discussed above is the dominant method for controlling risk in professionally managed portfolios. It is estimated that more than half of world capital is managed using such models.

Academic Models

Many academics have attempted to construct factor models with a fairly small number of parameters. These include:

- Fama–French three-factor model
- Carhart four-factor model
- Arbitrage pricing theory

However, there is as yet no general agreement on how many factors there are. There are numerous commercial models available, including those from MSCI and the Goldman Sachs asset management factor model.

Advantages of Multiple-factor Models

A different approach to developing an empirical model that captures the essence of the APT relies on the direct specification of the form of the relationship to be estimated.

That is, in a multifactor model, the investor chooses the exact number and identity of risk factors. Following the APT multifactor specification suppose that returns of our test assets are generated by a k-factor linear asset-pricing model:

$$\mu_{pt} = \alpha_p + \sum_{j=1}^{k} \beta_{pj}\left(F_{jt}\right) + \varepsilon_{jt,}\ t = 1,....T, j = 1....N,$$

Where, μ_P is the excess return on portfolio over the risk free rate $\left(R_{pt} - r_{ft}\right)$, F_j is the excess return on the j_{th} factor portfolio β_{pj}, is portfolio P 's loading on factor j .In a more elaborative form it can be represented as:

$$R_{pt} = \alpha_i + \left[\beta_{i1}F_{1t} + \beta_{i2}F_{2t} + \beta_{i3}F_{3t} + ... + \beta_{ik}F_{kt}\right] + \varepsilon_{it}$$

Where, F_{kt} is the period t return to the kth designated risk factor and R_{pt} can be measured as either a nominal or excess return to security p or portfolio p.

The multiple factor models are formal statements about the relationships among asset returns in a portfolio. The basic premise is that similar assets display similar returns. Assets can be similar in terms of quantifiable attributes, such as market information (such as price changes and volume), fundamental company data (such as industry and capitalization), or exposure to other factors (such as interest rate changes and liquidity). Multiple-factor models have many advantages:

- It offers a more thorough breakdown of risk and, therefore, a more complete analysis of risk exposure than other methods, such as single-factor approaches.
- Because of the economic logic is used in their development, multi factor models are not limited by purely historical analysis.
- It can be built using methods that can withstand outliers in asset data.
- As the economy and characteristics of individual issuers change, multi factor models adapt to reflect changing asset characteristics.
- They can isolate the impact of individual factors, providing segmented analysis for better informed investment decisions.
- Lastly, multi factor models are realistic, tractable, and understandable to investors.

Nevertheless, multi factor models have their limitations. They predict much, but not all, of portfolio risk. In addition, they predict risk, not return; investors must choose the investment strategies themselves. The major limitation of a multifactor model is that it is developed with little theoretical guidance as to the true nature of the risk-return relationship and sometimes considered as an empirical exercise. In this sense, developing a useful factor model is as much an art form as it is a theoretical exercise. As already mentioned, the theory of multi-factor models does not define which factors and how many factors should be considered, therefore, this issue remains to be determined by the researcher. Factors in this model are selected based on the literature used in making this paper. Regarding the number of factors, recent studies show that it is sufficient to use between three and six factors in the model

Types of Factor Models

Multiple-factor models of security market returns can be divided into three types: macroeconomic, fundamental or micro economic, and statistical factor models.

(I) Macro Economic Factors: Macro economic factors are those exogenous factors that determine asset prices and identifiable within macroeconomic forces (e.g., inflation, growth rage of GDP, interest rate, unemployment etc). Macroeconomic factor models use observable economic time series, such as inflation and interest rates, as measures of the pervasive shocks to security returns. They are the simplest and most intuitive type and use observable economic time series as measures of the pervasive factors in security returns. The random return of each security is assumed to respond linearly to the macroeconomic shocks. A security's linear sensitivities to the factors are called the factor betas of the security. One of the limitations of macroeconomic factor models is related to the identification and measurement of all the pervasive shocks affecting security returns. Put it differently, a small number of pervasive sources of risk may exist, but without knowing exactly what they are, or lacking data to measure them, they are of little use.

One of the influential model in this regard was developed by Chen, Roll, and Ross (1986) who hypothesized that security returns are governed by a set of broad economic influences in the following fashion:

$$R_{it} = \alpha_i + [\beta_{i1} R_{mt} + \beta_2 MP_t + \beta_{i3} DEI_t + \beta_{i4} UI_t + \beta_{i5} UPR_t + \beta_{i6} UTS_t] + \varepsilon_{it}$$

Where: Rm is the return on a value-weighted index of NYSE-listed stocks, MP is monthly growth rate in U.S. industrial production, DEI is change in inflation, measured by the U.S. consumer price index, UI is the difference between actual and expected levels of inflation, UPR is the unanticipated change in the bond credit spread (Baa yield – RFR), and UTS is the unanticipated term structure shift (long-term less short-term RFR).

(II) Fundamental Factors: Fundamental factor models use the returns to portfolios associated with observed security attributes or characteristics such as size, book to market value, liquidity, momentum, liquidity, asset growth etc. The factors in a fundamental factor model are the realized returns to a set of mimicking portfolios designed to capture the marginal returns associated with a unit exposure to each attribute. A surprisingly powerful method for factor modelling of security returns is the characteristic-based factor model. Over the years several attempts has been made by researchers to identify and add more number of factors to form a better multifactor model. In the following lines we will discuss some of the major multi-factor models namely, three factor, four factor anf five factor.

Fama and French (1993) estimate a multi-factor model and show that it performs much better than CAPM. The three factors are: the market return $(R_m - R_f)$, the return on a portfolio of small stocks minus the return on a portfolio of big stocks (SMB), and the return on a portfolio with a high ratio of book value to market value minus the return on a portfolio with a low ratio (HML).Fama and French (1993) propose a two-stage method for estimating characteristic-based factor models. In the first stage they sort assets into fractile portfolios based on book-to-price and market value characteristics. They use the differences between returns on the top and bottom fractile portfolios as proxies for the factor returns. They also include a market factor proxied by the return on a capitalization-weighted market index. In the second stage, the factor betas of portfolios and/or assets are estimated by time-series regression of asset returns on the derived factors. The six value-weighted portfolios, S/L (small-low), S/M (small-medium), S/H (small-high), B/L (big-low), B/M (big-medium) and B/H (big- high) from the intersection of two ME and three BME groups. SMB (Small minus Big) is the average return on the three small portfolios minus the average return on the three big portfolios. HML (High minus Low) is the average return on the two value portfolios minus the average return on the two growth portfolios.

An Illustration of Fama and French Factors

Portfolio no.	Size (Sz)	Book to Market Equity (BM)	SMB and HML
1. S/L	Small-SZ	Low-BM (Growth)	**SMB** = 1/3 (Small Value + Small Neutral + Small Growth) - 1/3 (Big Value + Big Neutral + Big Growth).
2. S/M		Medium -BM	
3. S/H		High-BM (Value)	
4. B/L	Big-SZ	Low-BM (Growth)	
5. B/M		Medium -BM	**HML** = 1/2 (Small Value + Big Value) - 1/2 (Small Growth + Big Growth).
6. B/H		High-BM (Value)	

The Fama and French three factor model can be specified as:

$$R_{pt} - r_{ft} = \alpha_p + \beta_{mp}\left(r_{MKT_t}\right) + \beta_{SMB_p}\left(r_{SMB_t}\right) + \beta_{HML_P}\left(r_{HML_t}\right) + \varepsilon_{pt,} t = 1,\ldots,T, p = 1,\ldots,N,$$

Where r_{SMBt} and r_{HMLt} are the returns on SMB and HML portfolio at time t. β_{mp}, β_{SMBp}, and $\beta_{HML\,p}$ are the factor sensitivities of asset p to the returns on the MKT, SMB and HML portfolios respectively. Carhart (1997) and Jagadeesh and Titman (1993, 2001) show that the addition of a momentum factor (WML) adds explanatory power to the Fama-French three-factor model (1993), both in terms of explaining comovements and mean returns. The six value weighted portfolios used for this purpose are S/W (small-winner), S/N (small-neutral), S/L (small-looser), B/W (big-winner), B/N (big-neutral) and B/L (big-looser), as the intersection of two size and three return momentum groups. Their momentum factor WML is the equal-weight average of the returns on the winner stock portfolios minus the returns on the loser stock portfolios. The new four factor model can be specified as:

$$R_{pt} - r_{ft} = \alpha_p + \beta_{mp}\left(r_{MKT_t}\right) + \beta_{SMB_p}\left(r_{SMB_t}\right) + \beta_{HML_P}\left(r_{HML_t}\right) + \beta_{WMLp}\left(r_{WMLt}\right) + \varepsilon_{pt,}$$

Where $t = 1,...,T, p = 1,...,N$, r_{WMLt} and $\beta_{WML\,p}$ respectively represent the returns and factor sensitivities of test asset p to the WML portfolio

An Illustration of Momentum Factor

Portfolio no.	Size (Sz)	Momentum	SMB and HML
1. S/L	Small-SZ	Momentum-Looser (L)	WML= [(S/W+ B/W) – (S/L+ B/L)] / 2
2. S/N		Momentum-Neutral (N)	
3. S/W		Momentum-Winner (W)	
4. B/L	Big -SZ	Momentum-Looser (L)	
5. B/N		Momentum-Neutral (N)	
6. B/W		Momentum-Winner (W)	

Keene and Peterson (2007) and Lam and Tam (2011) advocated an additional liquidity factor in a five factor model which includes Fama and French factor, momentum factor and a liquidity Factor. The liquidity factor has been constructed by forming four portfolios from the intersection of two SZ-based and two LIQ-based portfolios i.e., S/HL (small-high liquid), S/LL (small-low liquid), B/HL (big-high liquid), B/LL (big-low liquid). The liquidity factor (LQF) is the difference between the simple average of returns from the two low liquid portfolios and the simple average of returns from the two high liquid portfolios.

The new five factor model can be specified as:

$$R_{pt} - r_{ft} = \alpha_p + \beta_{mp}\left(r_{MKT_t}\right) + \beta_{SMB_p}\left(r_{SMB_t}\right) + \beta_{HML_P}\left(r_{HML_t}\right) + \beta_{LQF_p}\left(r_{LQF_t}\right) + \varepsilon_{pt,}$$

Where $t = 1,\ldots\ldots, T, p = 1,\ldots\ldots, N, .r_{LQF_t}$ and β_{LQF_P} respectively represent the returns and factor sensitivities of test asset P to the LFP portfolio.

An Illustration of Liquidity Factors

Portfolio no.	Size (Sz)	Liquidity	SMB and HML
1. S/LL	Small-SZ	Low Liquidity (LL)	
2. S/HL		High Liquidity (HL)	LQF= [(S/LL + B/LL) – (S/HL + B/HL)] / 2
3. B/LL	Big -SZ	Low Liquidity (LL)	
5. B/HL		High Liquidity (HL)	

(III) Statistical Factor Model: Statistical factor models derive their pervasive factors from factor analysis of the panel dataset of security returns. These models use various maximum-likelihood and principal-components- based factor analysis procedures on the cross- sectional/time-series samples of security returns to identify the pervasive factors in returns. Statistical factor models do not allow the analyst to assign meaningful labels to the factors and betas; one can identify the k pervasive risks in the cross-section of returns, but not what these risks represent in terms of economic and financial theory.

Empirical Procedures for the Three Types of Factor Models

Types of Factor Model	**Inputs**	**Estimation Technique**	**Outputs**
Macroeconomic (inflation, the percentage change in industrial production, the excess return to long-term government bonds, and the realized return premium of low-grade corporate bonds relative to high-grade bonds, unemployment)	Security returns and macroeconomic variables	Time-series regression	Security factor betas
Statistical	Security returns	Time- series/Cross-sectional regression	Statistical factors and security factor betas
Fundamental (Size factor, value factor, liquidity factor, asset growth factor)	Security returns and security characteristics	Time- series/Cross-sectional regression	Fundamental factors

Financial researchers differentiate between macroeconomic, fundamental or characteristic-based, and statistical factor models. In macroeconomic factor models, the factors are linked to the innovations in observable economic time series such as inflation and unemployment. In a fundamental model the factor betas of asset are tied to observable characteristics of the securities, such as company size or the book-to-price ratio,liquidity,momentum,asset growth or the industry categories to which each security belongs. In a statistical factor model, neither factors nor betas are tied to any external data sources and the model is identified from the covariances of asset returns alone.

BARRA Characteristics Based Risk Factors

BARRA, a leading risk forecasting and investment consulting firm, provides a final example of the microeconomic approach to building a multifactor model. In its most expansive form, the BARRA model for analyzing U.S. equities includes as risk factors 13 characteristic-based variables and more than 50 industry indexes. The 13 characteristic based factors that form the heart of the BARRA approach to decomposing investment risk are as follows:

Volatility (VOL): captures both long-term and short-term dimensions of relative return Variability, Momentum (MOM): differentiates between stocks with positive and negative excess returns in the recent past, Size (SIZ): based on a firm's relative market capitalization, Size Nonlinearity (SNL): captures deviations from linearity in the relationship between returns and firm size, Trading Activity (TRA) : measures the relative trading in a stock, based on the premise that more actively traded stocks are more likely to be those with greater interest from institutional investors, Growth (GRO) : uses historical growth and profitability measures to predict future earnings growth, Earnings Yield (EYL) : combines current and historical earnings-to-price ratios with analyst forecasts under the assumption that stocks with similar earnings yields produce similar returns, Value (VAL): based on relative book-to-market ratios, Earnings Variability (EVR) : measures the variability in earnings and cash flows using both historical values and analyst forecasts, Leverage (LEV): measures the relative financial leverage of a company, Currency Sensitivity (CUR): based on the relative sensitivity of a company's stock return to movements in a basket of foreign currencies, Dividend Yield (YLD): computes a measure of the predicted dividend yield using a firm's past dividend and stock price history, Nonestimation Indicator (NEU): uses returns to firms outside the equity universe to account, for risk dimensions not captured by the other risk factors

Sharpe Single Index Model

The basic motivation is that the construction of the optimal portfolio would be greatly facilitated if the ability of the portfolio managers and security analysts ability to the construction of the optimal portfolios can be supported with a single number measure of the desirability of a stock to be (not to be) included in a portfolio. There are two elements of security returns-independent and dependent". The basic notion underlying the single index model is that the movements in stock market affect all stocks. Therefore, for the sake of simplicity, the return on security could be regarded as being linearly adapted to a single index like the market index. The Sharpe single index model is based up on the following assumptions:

(i) It summarizes all relevant economic factors by one macro-economic indicator and assumes that it moves the security market as a whole. This factor is called the Index, hence the name "Single Index Model" or "Market Model".

(ii) Beyond this common effect, all remaining uncertainty in stock return is firm specific; i.e. there is no other source of correlation between securities.

(iii) Stocks co vary together only because of their common relationship to the market index

Sharpe's single index model can be given as: $R_{it} = \alpha_i + \beta_i R_{M_t} + e_{it}$ Where, $i = 1,...,N; t = 1,......, T.R_{M_t}$ return on diversified market index portfolio and ε_{it} random error term. Random error term e_{it} captures firm specific newsunrelated to market wide news 9 or unsystematic risk). β_i measures sensitivity to "market-wide" news and is the sole systematic risk. It has been assumed that returns are correlated only through their exposures to common market wide news captured by β_i. It captures the contribution of asset i to the variance/risk of the market index and represented as:

$$\beta_i = \frac{Cov(R_{it} R_{M_t})}{Var(R_{M_t})} = \frac{\sigma_{iM}}{\sigma_M^2}$$

Implications: If $\beta i = 0$ then asset i do not respond to market news $(\sigma i = 0)$, if $\beta i > 0$, then asset i respond to market news in the same direction $(\sigma i > 0)$, and if $\beta i < 0$, then asset i respond to market news in opposite direction $(\sigma i > 0)$. In this context, if any person is willing to accept the standard for of the single-index model as describing the comovements between the securities, the justification of any stock in the optimal portfolio is directly related to its excess return-to-beta ration. Since the sole assumption is that beta is the non-diversifiable single number measure of risk, the excess return to beta ratio measures the additional return or excess return on a stock i i.e., $(R_i - R_f)$ per unit of non-diversiable risk i.e., β_i. This ratio gives a formal explanation for the relationship between potential reward and risk. Investors would only buy the securities (portfolios) with a higher reward-to-risk ratio.

The desirability of any stock in a portfolio as a function of the excess return to beta ratio can be given as:

$$\text{Excess Return to Beta Ratio} = \frac{(R_i - R_f)}{\beta_i}$$

If stocks are ranked by excess return to beta from highest to lowest, ranking represent the desirability of a security in the portfolio. The number of stocks selected depends on a unique cut-off rate such that all stocks with higher excess return to beta ratio will be included and all stocks with lower ratios can be eliminated. All securities whose excess return-to-risk ratios are above the cut-off rate (C^*) are selected and all whose ratios are below are rejected. The value of Ci is calculated when i securities are assumed to belong to the optimal portfolio by using the following formula:

For a portfolio of i stocks, Ci is given as $= C_i = \dfrac{\sigma^2{}_m \sum_{i=1}^{i} \dfrac{(R_i - R_f)\beta_i}{\sigma^2{}_{ei}}}{1 + \sigma^2{}_m \sum_{i=1}^{i} \dfrac{\beta_i^2}{\sigma^2{}_{ei}}}$

Where, σ^{2m} is the variance in the market index, $\sigma^2{}_{ei}$ is the variance of a stock's movement that is not associated with the movement of the market index: this is the stock's unsystematic risk. Remember that the value of C* is that optimum value of Ci for which all securities used in the calculation of Ci have excess return-to-beta ratio above Ci, and all securities not used to calculate Ci have excess return-to-beta ratio below Ci.

Once the cut-off rate is determined, we know which security will figure in the optimal portfolio. The next step is to calculate the proportion to be invested in each security. The proportion to be invested (weight) in each security is given as:

Percentage of fund to be invested

$$(Xi) = \frac{Z_i}{\sum_{j=1}^{N} Z_j}$$

Where , $Z_i = \dfrac{\beta_i}{\sigma_{e_i}^2}\left[\dfrac{R_i - R_f}{\beta_i} - C^*\right]$

While the first expression gives the weight on each security so they sum to one, and the second expression determines the relative investment in each security.

Example

(1) Construct an optimal portfolio based on the following information:

Security	Expected Return (%)	Residual Variance	Beta
ACC Ltd.	15	30	1.0
Reliance Ltd.	12	20	1.5
Bharati Ltd.	11	40	2.0
3i Micron Ltd.	8	10	0.8
Telco Ltd.	9	20	1.0
HDFC Bank	14	10	1.5
The risk free rate of return is 5% and variance of market return is 10%.			

Solution (1):

Given that $\sigma_m^2 = 10\%$ and $R_f = 5\%$

Calculation of Excess Return to Beta Ratio				
Security	R_i	$(R_i - R_f)$	$(R_i - R_f)/\beta_i$	Rank
ACC Ltd.	15	10	10.00	1
Reliance Ltd.	12	07	4.70	3
Bharati Ltd.	11	06	3.00	6
3i Micron Ltd.	08	03	3.75	5
Telco Ltd.	09	04	4.00	4
HDFC Bank	14	09	6.00	2

Calculation of Cut-off rate						
Security	$\frac{(R_i - R_f)}{\beta_i}$	$\frac{(R_i - R_f)\beta_i}{\sigma^{2ei}}$	$\frac{\beta_i^2}{\sigma^2_{ei}}$	$\sum_{i=1}^{i}\frac{(R_i - R_f)\beta_i}{\sigma^{2ei}}$	$\sum_{i=1}^{i}\frac{\beta_i^2}{\sigma^2_{ei}}$	Ci
ACC Ltd.	10.00	0.333	0.033	0.33	0.033	2.50
Reliance Ltd.	6.00	1.350	0.225	1.683	0.258	4.70
Bharati Ltd.	4.70	0.525	0.113	2.208	0.371	4.69
3i Micron Ltd.	4.00	0.200	0.050	2.408	0.421	4.62
Telco Ltd.	3.75	0.240	0.064	2.648	0.485	4.53
HDFC Bank	3.00	0.300	0.100	2.948	0.585	4.30
Total		2.948	0.585			

The cut of rate for each security has been calculated by: $\frac{\sigma^{2m}\sum_{i=1}^{i}\frac{(R_i-R_f)\beta_i}{\sigma^{2ei}}}{1+\sigma^{2m}\sum_{i=1}^{i}\frac{\beta_i^2}{\sigma^{2ei}}}$ The value of C* is 4.70 and is equal to C2. In this example two selected securities are ACC Ltd. (X1) and Reliance Ltd. (X2).

Calculation of Percent to be invested in each security $(Xi) = \frac{Z_i}{\sum_{j=1}^{N} z_j}$

Thus, $Z_i = \frac{\beta_i}{\sigma^2_{e_t}}\left[\frac{R_i - R_f}{\beta_i} - C^*\right]$

$$Z_1 = \frac{1}{30}(10-4.7) = 0.176$$

$$Z_2 = \frac{1.5}{10}(6-4.7) = 0.195$$

$$\sum_{i=1}^{2} Z_i = 0.371$$

$$X_1 = \frac{0.176}{0.371} = 0.4744 = 47.44\%$$

$$X_2 = \frac{0.195}{0.371} = 0.5256 = 52.56\%$$

Lagrangian Multiplier Methods

Basic Objective of this method is two fold: (i) Minimization of Risk, (ii) Maximization of Return. These two objectives are subject to the following constraints:

- The proportion of funds in different assets must add up to unity
- The weighted average of the returns on different assets must provide the targeted one period return from the selected portfolio
- There is no provision of short-selling

Differential calculus is used to maximise or minimise a function subject to given constraints. Let us assume that a function (x,y) is subject to a constraint g (x,y) = k (a constant). A new function F can be formed by following three steps:

1. Setting the constraint equal to zero

2. Multiplying the constraint by λ (the Lagrangian Multiplier)

3. Adding the product found in the second step with the original function f(x,y)

Therefore, setting the constraint equal to zero will give g(x, y) – k = 0 or k – g (x, y) = 0. Now, we will multiply this equation with the Lagrangian Multiplier λ and add this result to the original function (x,y) to get the required function F.

$$F(x, y, \lambda) = \{f(x, y) + \lambda[k - g(x, y)]\}$$

Example

(2) Mr. A Saha is trying to construct an optimal portfolio with at least possible risk. He would like to earn a return of 15 % p.a. from the three stocks under consideration. The other relevant data for thease stocks are given below:

Stock	Expected Return (%)	Variance Covariance Matrix		
		ACC Ltd.	HCL Ltd.	Emami Ltd.
ACC Ltd.	17	225	260	125

HCL Ltd.	20	260	625	425
Emami Ltd.	14	125	425	169

You are required to calculate the proportion of funds to be invested in each of the three securities by Mr. Saha so as to generate the required rate of return with least possible risk.

Solution(2)

Minimise (total risk of the portfolio)

$$Z = 225\times X_1^2 + 625\times X_2^2 + 169\times X_3^2 + 2\times 260X_1X_2 + 2\times 425X_2X_3 + 2X_1X_3 \text{.................}(i)$$

(Where X_1X_2 and X_3 are the proportion of fund to be invested in the stocks of ACC Ltd., HCL Ltd and Emami Ltd. respectively)

Subject to

$$17X_1 + 20X_2 + 14X_3 = 15 \text{.............................}(ii)$$
$$X_1 + \quad X_2 + \quad X_3 = 1.00 \text{...........................}(iii)$$

Now we have to incorporate return constraint (B) as part of the objective function

(i) using the lagrangian constraint λ. For this we will express X_3 in terms of X_1 and X_2 as $(1 - X_1 - X_2)$ in both the equations (ii) and (iii) into two variable equation. Thus,

$$\begin{aligned}
Z &= 225(X_1)^2 + 625(X_2)^2 + 169(1 - X_1 - X_2) + 2(260X_1X_2) \\
&\quad + 2\times 425X_2(1 - X_1 - X_2) + 2\times 125X_1(1 - X_1 - X_2) \\
&= 225(X_1)^2 + 625(X_2)^2 + 169 + 169(X_2)^2 + 169(X_2)^2 - 338(X_1) \\
&\quad - 338(X_2) + 338(X_1X_2) + 520(X_1X_2) + 850X_2 - 850(X_1X_2) - 850(X_2)^2 \\
&\quad + 250(X_1) - 250(X_1)^2 - 250(X_1X_2) \\
&= (X_1)^2(225 + 169 - 250) + (X_2)^2(625 + 169 - 850) + (X_1)(-338 + 250) \\
&\quad + (X_2)(-338 + 850) + (X_1X_2)(338 + 520 - 250 - 850) + 169 \\
&= 144(X_1)^2 - 56(X_2)^2 - 88(X_1) + 512(X_2) - 242(X_1X_2) + 169 \text{................}(iv)
\end{aligned}$$

Now we will transform the constraint of equation (ii) in two variables.

$$\begin{aligned}
&17X_1 + 20X_2 + 14(1 - X_1 - X_2) = 15 \\
&17X_1 + 20X_2 + 14 - 14X_1 - 14X_2) = 15 \\
&3X_1 + 6X_2 = 1 \\
&3X_1 + 6X_2 - 1 = 0 \text{...}(v)
\end{aligned}$$

Now we have to incorporate the equation (v) in the objective function using lagranjian multiplier λ. Thus,

$$144(X_1)2-56(X_2)^2-88(X_1)+512(X_2)-242(X_1X_2)+169+\lambda(3X_1+6X_2-1)=0$$

$$\frac{\delta Z}{\delta X_1}=288X_1-88-242X_2+3\lambda=0..............................(vi)$$

$$\frac{\delta Z}{\delta X_1}=112X_2+512-242X_1+6\lambda=0..............................(vii)$$

$$\frac{\delta Z}{\delta \lambda}=3X_1+6X_2-1=0..(viii)$$

2 x [(equation-vi) - (equation-vii)] we have,

$$576X_1-176-484X_2+6\lambda=0$$
$$-242X_1+512-112X_2+6\lambda=0$$
$$+ \quad - \quad + \quad -$$

$$812X_1-688-372X_2=0$$

Now putting $X_1=\frac{-6X_2+1}{3}$ in the above equation we get

$$812\left(\frac{-6X_2+1}{3}\right)-688-372X_2=0$$
$$-1624X_2+270.66-688-372X_2=0$$
$$-1996X_2+(-688.34)=0$$
$$X_2=\frac{418}{1996}=-.2094$$
$$X_1=\frac{-6X_2+1}{3}=\frac{-6(-0.2094)+1}{3}$$
$$X_1=0.752$$
$$X_3=1-0.752+0.2094=0.4574$$

Proportion for each stock:

ACC Ltd. =75.20%, HCL Ltd= 20.94% (short sold), Emami Ltd. =45.74%

References

- Markowitz, H.M. (March 1952). "Portfolio Selection". The Journal of Finance. 7 (1): 77–91. JSTOR 2975974. doi:10.2307/2975974
- Mahdavi Damghani B. (2013). "The Non-Misleading Value of Inferred Correlation: An Introduction to the Cointelation Model". Wilmott Magazine. doi:10.1002/wilm.10252
- Merton, Robert. "An analytic derivation of the efficient portfolio frontier," Journal of Financial and Quantitative Analysis 7, September 1972, 1851-1872

- Bawa, V. S. (1982). “Stochastic Dominance: A Research Bibliography”. Management Science. doi:10.1287/mnsc.28.6.698
- Taleb, Nassim Nicholas (2007), The Black Swan: The Impact of the Highly Improbable, Random House, ISBN 978-1-4000-6351-2
- Ross, Stephen (1976). “The arbitrage theory of capital asset pricing”. Journal of Economic Theory. 13 (3): 341–360. doi:10.1016/0022-0531(76)90046-6
- Portfolio Theory of Information Retrieval July 11th, 2009 (2009-07-11). “Portfolio Theory of Information Retrieval | Dr. Jun Wang’s Home Page”. Web4.cs.ucl.ac.uk. Retrieved 2012-09-05
- Grechuk, B., Molyboha, A., Zabarankin, M. (2012). Mean-deviation analysis in the theory of choice, Risk Analysis: An International Journal, 32(8), 1277-1292
- Hubbard, Douglas (2007). How to Measure Anything: Finding the Value of Intangibles in Business. Hoboken, NJ: John Wiley & Sons. ISBN 978-0-470-11012-6
- Sharpe, William F. (September 1964). “Capital Asset Prices: A Theory of Market Equilibrium under Consideration of Risk”. Journal of Finance. XIX. JSTOR 2977928. doi:10.2307/2977928
- Doganoglu, Toker; Hartz, Christoph; Mittnik, Stefan (2007). “Portfolio Optimization When Risk Factors Are Conditionally Varying and Heavy Tailed”. Computational Economics. 29: 333–354. doi:10.1007/s10614-006-9071-1
- Chandra, Siddharth (2003). “Regional Economy Size and the Growth-Instability Frontier: Evidence from Europe”. Journal of Regional Science. 43 (1): 95–122. doi:10.1111/1467-9787.00291

Permissions

All chapters in this book are published with permission under the Creative Commons Attribution Share Alike License or equivalent. Every chapter published in this book has been scrutinized by our experts. Their significance has been extensively debated. The topics covered herein carry significant information for a comprehensive understanding. They may even be implemented as practical applications or may be referred to as a beginning point for further studies.

We would like to thank the editorial team for lending their expertise to make the book truly unique. They have played a crucial role in the development of this book. Without their invaluable contributions this book wouldn't have been possible. They have made vital efforts to compile up to date information on the varied aspects of this subject to make this book a valuable addition to the collection of many professionals and students.

This book was conceptualized with the vision of imparting up-to-date and integrated information in this field. To ensure the same, a matchless editorial board was set up. Every individual on the board went through rigorous rounds of assessment to prove their worth. After which they invested a large part of their time researching and compiling the most relevant data for our readers.

The editorial board has been involved in producing this book since its inception. They have spent rigorous hours researching and exploring the diverse topics which have resulted in the successful publishing of this book. They have passed on their knowledge of decades through this book. To expedite this challenging task, the publisher supported the team at every step. A small team of assistant editors was also appointed to further simplify the editing procedure and attain best results for the readers.

Apart from the editorial board, the designing team has also invested a significant amount of their time in understanding the subject and creating the most relevant covers. They scrutinized every image to scout for the most suitable representation of the subject and create an appropriate cover for the book.

The publishing team has been an ardent support to the editorial, designing and production team. Their endless efforts to recruit the best for this project, has resulted in the accomplishment of this book. They are a veteran in the field of academics and their pool of knowledge is as vast as their experience in printing. Their expertise and guidance has proved useful at every step. Their uncompromising quality standards have made this book an exceptional effort. Their encouragement from time to time has been an inspiration for everyone.

The publisher and the editorial board hope that this book will prove to be a valuable piece of knowledge for students, practitioners and scholars across the globe.

Index

SI $150